ERNESTINE FRIEDL
Duke University

Women and Men
An Anthropologist's View

Waveland Press, Inc.
Prospect Heights, Illinois

For information about this book, please write or call:
Waveland Press, Inc.
P.O. Box 400
Prospect Heights, Illinois 60070
(312) 634-0081

Copyright © 1975 by Holt, Rinehart and Winston, Inc.
1984 reissued by Waveland Press, Inc., second printing

ISBN 0-88133-040-X

Printed in the United States of America.

Foreword

THE AUTHOR

Ernestine Friedl is Professor and Chairman of the Department of Anthropology at Duke University. She is Professor Emeritus of Queens College, City University of New York, where she served as Chairman of the Department of Anthropology. She holds the Queens College Alumni Distinguished Teacher Award. She also served as Executive Officer of the City University's Ph.D. Program in Anthropology. Holding her B.A. from Hunter College and her Ph.D. from Columbia University, Dr. Friedl has done field work among the Pomo and the Chippewa Indians, among the villagers of rural Greece, and among the migrants to Athens from a Greek village. She is President of the American Anthropological Association, and previously served as President of the American Ethnological Society and of the Northeastern Anthropological Association. She is the author of *Vasilika: A Village in Modern Greece* (Holt, Rinehart and Winston, 1962) and of numerous articles and reviews reflecting her field studies and her interest in the social roles of women and men.

ABOUT THIS BOOK

The topic of sex roles is important and controversial today. This Basic Unit by Ernestine Friedl is especially appropriate for the thoughtful student who desires an unbiased treatment of this complex matter. Women are rarely the cynosure of a culture and almost never occupy the most prestigeful, public statuses. And yet, the variation in types of roles played by women in all cultures and the effect these roles have upon their status, and the influence women have in decision making makes generalization hazardous.

According to Dr. Friedl, "At the time of this writing, an intellectual and political controversy is going on in the United States over the question of sex roles." The controversy is between those who claim that biological factors and those who claim that social and cultural conditions are the prime determinants of sex roles. Those arguing for biological determinants describe the situation as it has been for "man the hunter" for millions of years and infer that it cannot be suddenly changed. Those supporting the social and cultural determinants argument, the environmentalists, argue that there is a wide range of variation possible in the relationships and activities of men and women and that this range should be exploited. Dr. Friedl is in sympathy with the Women's Liberation Movement as it aims to develop for women an equality with men, as well as to increase the options available to both.

The author offers a series of hypotheses and inferences concerning the determinants and expressions of sex roles (among hunters and gatherers, and horticulturalists), based on extensive cross-cultural data of her own and that of others.

These hypotheses related to sex roles deal with factors such as subsistence techniques, child-rearing methods, the rights to distribute valued goods, and women's relationship to rituals and symbols.

An example of one of the specific relationships posited is that prevalence of male dominance is a consequence of the frequency with which men have greater rights than women to distribute goods outside the domestic group. Another is that from the standpoint of domestic authority and control, egalitarian, politically unstratified societies with patrilineal descent groups and virilocal residence have the greatest potentiality for strong, overt dominance of husband over wife or wives. Another interesting finding is that controls over the sexual activities of the young are most frequent in societies with substantial bride price payments.

Dr. Friedl attempts to relate some of her conclusions to contemporary industrial society. For example, she finds tensions suffered by husbands and wives to be related to conflict in loyalties—loyalty to the family versus loyalty to a career. This book is important for students because it presents them with complex types of data and analyses concerning the interrelatedness of factors influencing the status accorded women in a wide variety of cultures without prejudice or a covert political agenda.

George and Louise Spindler

Preface

This book began as an exploration of ways in which technological levels of society might constrain the roles of the sexes. It was originally intended to include an analysis of hunters and gatherers, horticulturalists, pastoralists, plow-agriculture peasants, and people living in industrial societies. As the work progressed, it became evident that if readers were to gain any real understanding of patterns of variation in sex roles in the first two levels of technology, relatively lengthy treatment of these two types of society was necessary. This treatment reached and indeed overshot the limits set by the editors for books of this series.

The decision to present relatively long descriptions of illustrative cultures for the horticulturalists instead of a series of short essays that would cover all the possible patterns of sexual division of labor was dictated by the conviction that the generalizations made about sex roles among horticulturalists could come alive for the reader only through an extended treatment of particular cultures. Space limitations precluded such treatment for more than two societies.

The professional reader will be aware that the theoretical approach of the book is essentially ecological and structural-functional. Considerations of history and change are for the most part missing. I believe that such a position is justified at what is, after all, an early stage in our attempts at studying sex roles. It is worth discovering how far ecological and structural-functional analysis can take us, so that we may eventually be able to ask more useful questions of the historical record.

At the time I started writing, increased anthropological interest in the subject of sex roles was near its beginnings. I am especially grateful for the help of scholars who generously sent me copies of papers which they read at the sessions on sex roles at the meetings of the American Anthropological Association in 1972 and 1973, and to other scholars who helped in similar ways. A number of friends and colleagues read and commented on various portions of the manuscript at different stages of its preparation, and I thank them all: Richard Fox, Mervyn Meggitt, William O'Barr, Naomi Quinn, Joyce Riegelhaupt, Sydel Silverman, Eric Wolf, Shirley Lindenbaum, and Jane Schneider. I am particularly grateful to the last two, who gave me the benefit of especially detailed and thoughtful discussions of the work as it progressed.

My thanks are also due to those who provided photographs, acknowledgments of which appear at the appropriate places, and to Roman Stankus, who devised and drew the illustrative map.

Finally, a special word of appreciation is due my husband, Harry L. Levy, who encouraged me to undertake the book, suffered with me through the usual agonies of composition, and gave me invaluable editorial assistance.

Ernestine Friedl

Durham, N.C.
January 1975

Contents

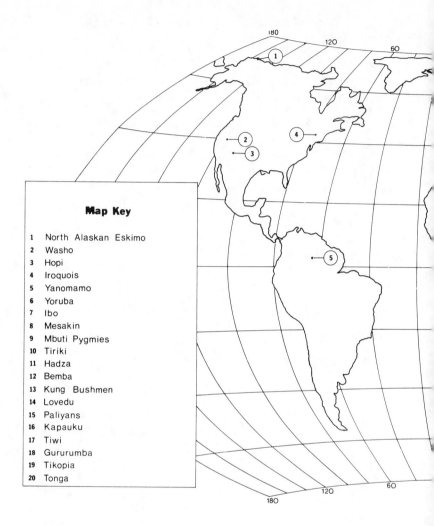

Map Key

1 North Alaskan Eskimo
2 Washo
3 Hopi
4 Iroquois
5 Yanomamo
6 Yoruba
7 Ibo
8 Mesakin
9 Mbuti Pygmies
10 Tiriki
11 Hadza
12 Bemba
13 Kung Bushmen
14 Lovedu
15 Paliyans
16 Kapauku
17 Tiwi
18 Gururumba
19 Tikopia
20 Tonga

Introduction

CONTROVERSY OVER DETERMINANTS OF SEX ROLES

Biological versus Social and Cultural Conditions as Determinants

At the time of this writing, an intellectual and political controversy is going on in the United States over the question of sex roles. Those on one side of the argument maintain that the innate biological and psychological differences between the sexes are the necessary and effective causes for the rights and duties assigned to men and women in all societies. Still on the same side, a rather more sophisticated argument is that the model for the social roles of the sexes in human society is one originally adapted for savannah-dwelling primates, modified by the development of hunting among early humans. The contention is that because human beings have depended on hunting, always a masculine specialty, as a basis for subsistence for millions of years of their evolutionary history, and on other means of subsistence for only about 10,000 years, there have been too few generations for the physical qualities of the human body and its behavioral concomitants to have changed appreciably (Tiger and Fox 1971).[1]

The political stance of this entire group of antagonists is frequently, but not always, that because sex roles as they exist are essentially·"natural," they *should* stay about what they are: major change would be unsuccessful, or would exact too high a price in emotional strain and consequent illness. Indeed, according to this view, the deviations in sex roles from those originally adapted to hunting societies have already caused much damage. At the opposite extreme is the position that sex roles are a function, not of biological heredity, but of social and cultural conditions. Those who take this view hold that the inherent physical and emotional characteristics of both men and women permit a wide range of variation in relationships and activities. The political stance is that this range of possibilities must be exploited to its limits to remove unnecessary differentiation between the roles of men and women.

According to this second view, it is because contemporary societies have not deviated sufficiently from what are falsely thought to be the "natural" roles that there has been so much physical and psychological stress among both men and women. It is also argued on this side that women, in particular, have been subject to

---

[1] References are to be found on pp. 143–146.

1

real injustice and discrimination because they have not been permitted access to many valued positions and rewards of society, on the mistaken assumption that their sex disqualifies them. On the grounds, then, of social justice, this group argues that major change in contemporary society is necessary.

ANTHROPOLOGICAL EVIDENCE CITED BY BIOLOGICALLY–ORIENTED GROUPS

Each side uses different sets of established anthropological knowledge to support its contentions. The biologically oriented group argue that if certain cultural and social forms occur in all known societies, such universals must imply traits that can be ascribed to genetic factors. They then cite evidence, agreed upon by most anthropologists, showing that first, in all societies, a distinction is made between tasks usually performed by men and those usually performed by women (in other words, that a division of labor by sex is universal), and second, certain specific powers are almost everywhere assigned to men and others to women. They point out that men are always the warriors; they have the major responsibility for the physical protection of the group from both internal and external threats; men in all societies exercise control over the significant resources of a society, very often including its women; activities in each society to which the greatest value is assigned, and which confer the largest rewards, are those performed by men.

In general, they inform us, men operate in both public and domestic contexts; the range of variation of opportunities available to them is greater. In contrast women's tasks, the "nature" advocates continue, are remarkably similar the world over and lack the diversity characteristic of men's tasks. Women work in a domestic context, within the household, and are very frequently limited to that context. They remind us that women are almost everywhere responsible for the care of infants and young children, and for domestic routine cooking. Women, with few exceptions, they say, are barred from certain activities. They never have the main responsibility for hunting large wild animals, nor for butchering large domesticated ones.

The particular genetically ascribed constraint which the biologically oriented contestants believe underlies such a universal division of labor between men and women is sexual dimorphism in *Homo sapiens*. The physical differences between the sexes often cited are that men on the average are larger than women, and can muster greater spurts of muscular energy; that woman's pelvic anatomy, adapted for child-bearing, prevents them from running as fast as men; that male hormones appear to trigger aggressive behavior. Female hormonal changes during the menstrual cycle, they say, result in a rhythmic variation in acuteness of perception, muscular coordination, and even mental concentration in the course of each month. In addition to this, pregnancy, childbirth, and lactation, with the relatively long period of helplessness of human infants and the immaturity of human young, this group maintains, account for women's preoccupation with children and for their limited participation in public affairs, particularly in war and politics. Consequently, they conclude, women are effectively and automatically barred from public social power.

ANTHROPOLOGICAL EVIDENCE CITED BY
SOCIALLY AND CULTURALLY ORIENTED GROUPS

The opposing group, the environmentalists, on the other hand, cite not the similarities in roles assigned to men and women everywhere, as shown in anthropological data, but the equally obvious differences (Oakley 1972; Mead 1953). They stress that, in some societies, women have not only participated indirectly in politics, as, for example, when they served as electors of sachems among the Iroquois, but also have held direct political power in their own right, for example, as chiefs in some African societies. They write about women warriors in West Africa. On the contemporary scene, they point to women who have been prime ministers in the states of India, Sri Lanka (Ceylon), and Israel. They cite women's participation in and control of significant nondomestic economic activities, such as trade in West Africa. They list the crafts, such as weaving, pottery-making, and tailoring, which are thought "naturally" women's jobs in one society; "naturally" men's jobs in another. In some societies, they point out, men bring wood and water for cooking; in others the women do these things. Women carry bricks and other building materials in some societies; men in others. In some contemporary nations, they show, dentistry and medicine are almost exclusively a man's professions, while women form a substantial corps of dentists and physicians in others. Men and women are assigned different relationships to supernatural forces, these advocates of the environmental approach declare. Among some peoples, the argument runs, shamans, witches, and curers are exclusively men; among others, exclusively women; and among still others both men and women are thought to control supernatural forces for both good and evil.

The act of sexual intercourse itself, these contestants argue, varies from society to society from the standpoint of whether men or women take the initiative, of whether men or women are more vigorous during coitus, and of the position or positions employed. It is further argued that attitudes toward the sex act and toward secondary sexual characteristics vary. In some societies women are expected to take more pleasure in sexual intercourse than men; in others, the reverse. Menstrual blood and the blood of childbirth are thought dangerously polluting to men in some societies and not in others. In some societies, men and women consider themselves, overtly or covertly, in opposing camps, and there is considerable sexual antagonism; in others, the lines of cleavage and opposition are stronger between kin groups, or economically or politically differentiated groups, than they are between men and women.

The environmentalists, like their opponents, base their arguments on biological factors but they interpret them differently. They argue that variations in the activities and behavior culturally assigned to the sexes are made possible by the fact that anatomical and physiological differences between the sexes are not as great as the genetically oriented biologists hold. They cite the very similar musculature of men and women among the Southeast Asian populations, and the existence of large numbers of people whose production of male and female hormones (both sexes produce both varieties) is found in a mixture lying closer to the middle than to the extremes of the range. Moreover, they cite evidence that the functioning of hormones can be influenced by social situations: girls living together in dormitories often develop the same menstrual cycles. Experimentation on men and animals demonstrates that sex hormones can have different effects in different group situations. The production of the male hormone, testosterone, varies for the same individual in different circumstances. The environmentalists sum up by stating that psychobiological qualities cannot adequately explain the differences which we have listed, and that therefore social conditions, not human biology, must be regarded as the significant determinants of sex roles.

The environmentalists do not deny the existence of male dominance in all known societies. Their argument is that it is not inevitable and need not remain a permanent state of affairs.

IS MALE DOMINANCE INEVITABLE?

Controversy over Matriarchy as a Stage in Human Evolution

Indeed, a group of those who stress the importance of social and cultural conditions as determinants of sex roles has recently revived an old question: Has male dominance always been characteristic of human society? The existence of matriarchal systems, vaguely defined as mother-dominated or woman-dominated societies in the remote past as a concomitant of early stages in the evolution of subsistence technologies, was postulated by nineteenth-century evolutionists, including Marx and Engels.

Since the 1930s there has been general agreement among anthropologists that evidence for matriarchy, past or present, is lacking. We now know that even in societies with matrilineal descent-reckoning, that is, those in which eligibility for marriage, the holding of property, inheritance, and succession to office all depend on a person's kin relationships through females (extended discussion of this system appears later, pp. 70–73), it is the men who hold the most prized offices and exercise basic control over resources. This is true in spite of the fact that, as we shall see, women do have some advantages in matrilineal systems.

Nevertheless, the Women's Movement of the late 1960s and early 1970s has encouraged a reexamination of the whole issue of matriarchy, or at least of the possibility of the existence of considerable power for women in some societies (Webster and Newton 1972). One line of argument has been that although male dominance is recorded everywhere in anthropological reports, these reports are based on incomplete data as to the relative power of men and women. The disputants who advance this point of view argue that even such data as have been collected are suspect because they are gathered primarily by male field workers who talk mostly to men. Male ethnographers, they say, have had little access to data on women and women's activities, and so are forced to underplay the role of women and its importance. Furthermore, it is argued, even women anthropologists and other observers who are participants in Euro-American culture expect and assume male dominance, so that their data and interpretations are likely to be biased (Ardener 1972).[2]

---

[2] Ardener also argues that women in all cultures generalize about their activities less often than men and are therefore not helpful as informants.

A second approach to the power issue has been the position that the evidence for male dominance is essentially accurate, but that the low social status of women constitutes a form of oppression of women by men, in which women have been more or less willing victims. The contemporary Marxist version of this position is that the oppression of women is one aspect of the power relationships engendered in all class societies, with women's oppressed status resulting particularly from the development of private property and the economic isolation of the nuclear family.

Although they do not postulate an early matriarchy, the Marxists maintain that preclass societies had relatively egalitarian relationships between the sexes, and that wherever male dominance now exists in societies of this type it is a consequence of colonial conquest (Leacock 1972). Evidence from egalitarian hunting and gathering societies, as we shall see, in part contradicts this view.

Universal Social and Cultural Conditions Which Contribute to the Belief in Male Superiority

Another question asked about male dominance has been not whether or why women are subordinate to men in the material world, but rather why the *belief* that women are inferior to men is so prevalent a trait of human culture. Why is there a universal cultural devaluation of women and their activities?

One provocative discussion of this issue is based on the assumption that all peoples, consciously or unconsciously, place a higher value on objects, activities, and events which are under human control (culture) than they do on phenomena unregulated by human intervention (nature). Women's bodies and women's activities, it is argued, tend to be construed in all societies as closer to nature than to culture and are therefore devalued (Ortner 1974).

The argument runs that certain universal (1) biological, (2) social, and (3) psychological conditions place women in situations which can be interpreted as less controlled, less artificial, and symbolically less cultural than the activities of men. Stated simply, these conditions include (1) biological: the dedication of women's bodies to the perpetuation of the species (the breasts, the uterus, and menstruation are features of women's anatomy and physiology devoted solely to preparation for pregnancy, childbirth, and child nurture); (2) social: (a) the forced association of women with children during the period of lactation and breast feeding (we must add that this is very widespread, but not absolutely universal) leading to a general assignment of child care to women, and (b) the more frequent location of women's activities, such as cooking, in a domestic setting; and (3) psychological: the identification of girls with the particular women whose activities, largely domestic, they can watch from their earliest infancy and continually throughout their childhood; in contrast with boys, who must ultimately identify with men whose extradomestic activities they first learn about as mere abstractions and which they do not actually experience until much later (Chodorow 1974).

The conditions listed under "biological" are obviously natural rather than cultural; the inclusion under the rubric "nature" rather than "culture" of the aspects of women's activities listed under "social" and "psychological" seems to represent an identification of the domestic with the natural, of the extradomestic with the cultural.

This brief and partial summary, which is all that space allows, falls far short of doing justice to the subtle and ingenious arguments presented in the references cited above. From the standpoint of our major interest in the determinants of sex roles, however, the conclusion of Ortner (1974:87) is relevant, and is closely akin to the viewpoint of the other environmentalists already discussed: The biological, social, and psychological conditions listed, however universal they may be, are not inevitable or permanent. As women gain greater control over their own bodies, involve men in the care of children, and move out of the domestic circle, the symbolic classification of women as closer to nature than to culture, and their consequent devaluation, may become obsolete.

THE POSITION OF THIS STUDY

I have sketched significant public and scholarly issues concerning sex roles in order to define the situation in which this book was written and by which it has inevitably been influenced.

My personal convictions are in harmony with the efforts of the Women's Movement of the 1960s and 1970s to develop for women an equality of opportunity with men, as well as to increase the options available to both men and women.

My scholarly training and preoccupations lead me to an interest in examining the social and cultural conditions under which sex roles vary, and to view the biological nature of men and women not as a narrow enclosure limiting the human organism, but rather as a broad base upon which a variety of structures can be built.

I am convinced that the best tactic for understanding what flexibility exists as well as what has been constant throughout our known history in the role of the sexes is to be found rather in an examination of diversity than in a concentration upon similarities. But merely to list the variety that exists in the role of the sexes in different world societies, even if it succeeds in destroying the myth that human biology permits only a very narrow range of masculine and feminine behavior, will not in and of itself free men and women in contemporary societies from either the obligation or the desire to pursue roles historically expected of them. Both the scholar and the activist need to know under what social, cultural, and physical environmental conditions variations in sex roles exist and what limits there are on diversity.

I agree with those who argue that our knowledge about sex roles is limited by the paucity of data collected from women. Most of our information does come from men, and is interpreted from a man's point of view, even by the small corps of women who write anthropological studies. This book is in all likelihood not a significant exception, but some effort has been made to give priority and emphasis to women's activities and political interests, and to the consequences for women of the customary roles of men.

This book is concerned with (1) describing the variety of roles available to men and women among hunters and gatherers and among horticulturalists; (2) suggesting hypotheses for the determinants of these roles; and (3) examining the degrees of dominance exercised by either sex over the other in a variety of contexts.

The criteria used as gross measures of overt power include: (a) the control of the production and, even more importantly, of the domestic and extradomestic distribution of strategic economic resources; (b) rights to participation in political, ritual, and religious activities and to leadership in them; and (c) the degree of autonomy enjoyed in decisions concerning sex relations, marriage, residence, divorce, and the lives of children. The description of the roles and the use of the criteria just listed require the assembling of evidence from the standpoint of an observer who looks at society and culture as an outsider (the "etic" view). The ideas of the participants in a society and culture about their own behavior, and their own evaluation of the relative position of the sexes (the "emic" view) contribute to our analysis, but are not basic to the main point of view from which we approach the subject.

We begin with the evidence that a degree of male dominance exists in all known societies, if we define male dominance as a situation in which men have highly preferential access, although not always exclusive rights, to those activities to which the society accords the greatest value, and the exercise of which permits a measure of control over others. I shall make some suggestions as to the basis for this dominance among hunters and gathers and among horticulturalists, and shall try also to show that the degree and kind of dominance varies significantly from society to society. In the concluding chapter I shall show how, in my belief, what we thus learn about the wide range of variation in sex roles and degrees of dominance can provide useful perspectives for understanding the roles of women and of men in industrial society, and for engaging in action based on this understanding.

BASIC PROPOSITIONS

There are five basic propositions which have influenced my descriptions and analyses of sex roles among the peoples discussed in this book. These propositions are hypotheses about the determinants and expressions of sex roles for which there is, in my judgment, substantial evidence, but which may still require further testing.

Subsistence Technology

The first is that the subsistence technology of a society and its social and political organization have crucial consequences for (1) the sexual division of labor, (2) the differential allocation of power and recognition to men and women, and (3) the quality of the relationships between the sexes. Therefore modes of subsistence, that is, the types of energy used by members of a society to procure its food, are used in this book as the base for the examination of sex roles. The two major modes which appear in the present volume are (1) hunting and gathering, or foraging as it is sometimes called, and (2) horticulture, a form of cultivation of the soil without the use of the plow.

Some of the reasoning behind the choice of the level of subsistence technology as a base for dealing with sex roles is as follows: Because the biological characteristics of men and women related to procreation have the same potentialities everywhere, the specific way, in any one society, in which the sexes are related to each other is a function of the allocation of their capability of working, a quality which men and women alike possess.

Women in all societies bear the children, and usually suckle them as well. The important question is, What else do they do? And what do the men do? In every society, the overwhelming majority of men and women do some work. The occupational choices open both to men and to women, of which household maintenance or housework is one, depend on the degree of occupational differentiation or specialization which characterizes the society. The range of choice is influenced by the level of subsistence technology: for example, more human energy is expended on warfare, politics, and specialized crafts among horticulturalists than among hunters and gatherers.

Child-Rearing

A second important proposition is that the spacing of children and the patterns of child-rearing are everywhere adjusted to whatever kind of work women customarily do.

Because no population can survive unless some women bear some children, and unless some of these children reach maturity, both lay men and women and anthropologists as well have concentrated their attention upon asking how the economic, political, or religious activities of women are compatible with their child-bearing and child-rearing tasks. Cross cultural studies based upon this phrasing of the question seem, at first blush, to demonstrate that where women contribute to subsistence, their tasks are adjusted to the needs of child care: their work is done near a home base, it is monotonous and does not require rapt attention, and it is not dangerous. Women's tasks, it is argued, can therefore be readily interrupted and resumed again without difficulty (Brown 1970b). Such a formulation of the issue does not take account of the large number of societies in which women regularly gather wild plants or cultivate crops or engage in trade in locations many miles from home base, and either walk back and forth each day or move out into distant locations for some seasons of the year taking children with them; nor does it take account of women who tend large cauldrons of boiling foods over open fires—a dangerous process—; nor, on the other hand, of the frequent practice of assigning baby-tending for long periods of a day either to children no more than five or six years old or to elderly people in the household or settlement; nor of the use of foods which supplement mother's milk even for young infants in many of the world's societies (Nerlove 1974). Mature, adult women as mothers are far from being the exclusive caretakers of children in many societies.

It is therefore more fruitful, I suggest, to look at the problem from the other end of the funnel, and to consider first how the energies of adult women are used for the acquisition of subsistence and for other economic tasks, and then, once these requirements have been established, to see how child-spacing and child-tending are accommodated to the requirements of the women's tasks.

Distribution

A third proposition is that it is the right to distribute and exchange valued goods and services to those not in a person's own domestic unit (extradomestic distribution) which confers power and prestige in all societies. It is indeed better to give than to receive. Those who work to produce goods have a greater chance to be assigned the control of distributing them, but do not automatically gain the right to do so. For the roles of men and women this argument leads to the particular hypothesis that the prevalence of male dominance is a consequence of the frequency with which, for reasons which we shall explain later, men have greater rights than women to distribute goods outside of the domestic group (see Rosaldo 1974; Sacks 1974; and Sanday 1974). Even if women contribute their labor to the acquisition of subsistence, the chances are better than if they do not that they will have distribution rights outside of their households, but there is no assurance that they will. If, on the other hand, they do not so contribute their labor, their chance of having such rights are negligible or nonexistent (see Sanday 1973, 1974).

Extraordinary Events

A fourth proposition is that because extradomestic exchanges occur most frequently in the course of special events, the total complex of roles associated with each sex in any society is influenced not only by the division of routine labor but by the principles and processes by which labor and materials are commandeered for extraordinary occasions.

In every society the routine tasks and activities with which the internal organization of the household is concerned, comprising the domestic life of the society, involve one set of roles and relationships, while its extradomestic activities—warfare, trade, feasts, and public rituals of all kinds—bring people into unusual juxtapositions as organizers, contributors, participants, or members of an audience. The roles which men and women play in these extradomestic, nonroutine affairs can influence the overall relationships between the sexes, especially in regard to the extent to which the persons involved can control the collection and distribution of valued goods and services.

Viewed in another way, this proposition can be stated as follows: Both the quality of the relationship between the sexes and the accepted cultural statements about the nature of males and females are consequences in large part of the structure of opportunities and constraints within which men and women are expected to manoeuver for position in any society (Meggitt 1964). In both domestic and extradomestic spheres, there is room for men and women to negotiate, to give and to receive, to help and to hinder, to be amiable or cantankerous. Whether men or women or both are thought to be the witches in a society, and do in actuality try to bewitch others, whether men or women or both are thought to be sexual aggressors in a society and behave as expected is a result not of innate qualities of males and females, but of the structural constraints within which they develop strategies for the acquisition of power and the maintenance of self-esteem.

Symbolism

The fifth and final proposition is that both attitudes toward sex and the actual social relations which exist between men and women receive significant expression in symbol and ritual.

The interpretation of ritual is extremely difficult; much thought has been expended on it in recent anthropological writings. The point of view which governs the discussion of rituals in this volume is that consciously or unconsciously the people of a society communicate to themselves and to each other information about their mental, physiological, and sociological states of being by the use of ritual (Rappaport 1971).[3]

The information that these people communicate is a symbolic reduplication and restatement of beliefs and social relationships. The communication of such information in ritual form appears to occur when an individual or a whole society is thought to be in a vulnerable state, either (1) because of an unusual personal or social crisis (illness, plague, famine), or (2) because of the start of a regularly recurring process vital to the society (the beginning of a group hunt or of planting), or (3) because an individual is going through a major change in social position (initiation, confirmation, marriage), or (4) because of the death of a member of the society. The actual performance of the ritual drama goes beyond restatement and reduplication; it has an efficacy in its own right. Its content reinforces the beliefs and social relations which are symbolically expressed, and, where a change of status is concerned, the ritual actually brings about the change which it celebrates.

For example, a wedding ceremony by its performance changes the status of a bride and groom from that of unmarried to married persons. In the United States, attempts in the 1960s to alter the content of the marriage ritual itself were the result of the unwillingness of some couples to restate and thus reinforce what they considered undesirable relationships symbolized by the traditional rites. They were unwilling for a father to escort his daughter to the altar to "give her away" to another man, the waiting groom, for they repudiated the view of marriage which represented it as a transaction between men.

Though most rituals have as part of their symbolic content the relationships between the sexes and ideas about maleness and femaleness, we shall stress in this volume those rituals which symbolize and bring about a change from one social status to another, the so-called "rites of passage." Among these, our main concern will be for puberty rites, female and male.

These rituals, whether public or private, like other rites of passage, have one basic symbolic structure in all cultures. There is (1) a period of separation of the candidate from others under conditions which are frequently symbolic of the person's invisibility in the womb; (2) a period in which the candidate is in a transitional or liminal state, symbolically neither alive nor dead, neither male nor female, but on the threshold between possibilities; and (3) a period of incorporation or reaggregation into the social body, symbolically a rebirth into a new status (Van Gennep 1960). The second period, the intermediate state, frequently involves an effort by painful means, degrading to the candidates, often symbolically to turn them away from or destroy the structural role they previously had as a preparation for the new one.

We shall also be concerned with an idea which finds frequent expression in symbol and ritual: pollution, the belief that (or behavior implying that) substances

---

[3] The view of ritual here presented differs from the positions held by many anthropologists. For example, some scholars hold that ritual, instead of recapitulating and restating the structures of a society, are intended to alleviate and compensate for the strains which these structures create for human beings.

or persons in certain states are unclean and mystically powerful, potentially dangerous to those who come into contact with them through any of the senses or through
mere proximity. (The power may sometimes be beneficial, or may be changed into
being so.)

Uncleanness and the power to pollute are frequently assigned to things, animate
or inanimate, which are considered ambiguous because they cannot easily be assigned to a category recognized by the culture (Douglas 1966). This feeling is akin
to the outrage caused by the unisex movement in certain segments of our population. For another example, is a corpse still a person, or is it an inanimate thing? The
polluting quality frequently assigned to corpses is, in this interpretation, concomitant with its ambiguousness. So with hair and bodily excretions. At what point do
they cease to be a part of the person? At all events, they blur the clear boundaries of
the body (Douglas 1970).

In Part I on hunters and gatherers (see section I/8), I try to show how menstrual
blood, one of the bodily excretions, can be construed as having additional ambiguous qualities, and how therefore it may come to be considered particularly polluting,
as it is in many cultures.

Regardless of what universal elements of the kind we have been discussing may
underly the symbolism of ritual in general, it should be emphasized that the understanding of the meanings of the information conveyed in the rituals of a particular
society depends for its validity upon a thorough analysis of the symbolic system of
that society itself.

The descriptive material in this volume is based on a variety of sources. Some are
reports on societies and cultures which were functioning as described when the
scholar visited the people. Others are reconstructions of earlier periods, and still
others fall somewhere in between. For simplicity, the "ethnographic present" tense
is used throughout, except for the description of the Washo, whose traditional
culture has almost completely vanished.

PART I

Hunting and Gathering Societies

Hunting and gathering societies have been particularly important for anthropologists because they represent a way of life which resembles, though it does not exactly duplicate, the technological adaptation of all *Homo sapiens* before the invention of plant and animal domestication about 10,000 years ago. Contemporary peoples for whom hunting and gathering still provide a major source of subsistence now constitute only about one one-hundredth of one percent of the world's population (some 300,000 human beings). They inhabit geographical environments such as the arctic tundras, the deserts of Australia, and the rain forests of the Congo, into which agricultural and industrial populations have not, for the most part, expanded as yet.

I/1 SUBSISTENCE

Techniques of Hunting and Gathering

How are hunting and gathering societies distinguished from those with other types of subsistence? Hunters and gatherers use one or more of three methods for obtaining the bulk of their food: (1) gathering—collecting wild plants, small land animals like mice, and small sea creatures like clams or mussels; (2) hunting—the pursuit of large land animals like deer or caribou, and of large sea mammals like whales or seal; (3) fishing—the catching of fish by angling, or by the use of nets, weirs, and the like. Which of these techniques are used and what proportion of the total subsistence of the society each provides varies with the nature of the environment and the technology of the local population (Lee 1968:41 f.).

Regional Variation

Only in very few societies (about 17 percent of one sample of foragers) does hunting provide the dominant source of food, that is, more than half the total food supply. Such societies are limited to the cold latitudes of northern Canada, Siberia, and the lands above the Arctic Circle. The Eskimo are the best known of these peoples. Fishing is a dominant food source for 33 percent of all foragers, found among groups like the Dogrib of Canada, who live slightly south of the northern hunters. Gathering is the dominant source of subsistence for the remaining 50 percent of foragers, such as the Australian aborigines, the Bushmen of the Kalahari Desert in Africa, and others who inhabit the band of latitudes between 40° north and 40° south. Some of the people for whom gathering is the major source of food appear not to suffer from food shortages, and their men and women spend only a few hours a day on the food quest (Lee 1968:42 f.).

Meat as a Valued Resource

Although some hunting goes on in all of these societies, the meat such hunting produces, except for the northern hunters, constitutes only 20 percent of the total diet. In all these societies, however, no matter what proportion of the diet it may represent, meat is always the favored food. It is the food that is believed to taste best, to be the most satisfying. The giving of the meat from big game animals always confers prestige on the giver. This situation has important consequences for sex roles among hunters and gatherers, and is a subject to which we shall return.

I/2 MOBILITY AND ORGANIZATION OF POPULATION

Nomadism: Low Population Density

The movements of animal populations, the distribution of roots, fruits and other vegetable foods according to soil conditions and seasonal variations in climate, and the spatial and seasonal variation in water resources impose on most hunters and gatherers some degree of nomadism and a relatively low density of population. For such peoples over the generations travel which might originally have arisen from necessity comes to be believed to be pleasurable as well.

Residential and Kinship Groups

A common pattern of movement is an alternation between large group congregations of 100 to 300 people for several months of the year—this has been called a public phase of life—and a longer period of separation into small local bands of some 25 to 50 people, a private phase for the rest of the year. The local bands typically consist of several nuclear families (each consisting of husband, wife, and their children), some of which have dependents like elderly parents or unmarried brothers and sisters of one of the spouses; about 10 bands constitute the population within which marriage takes place.

It should be stressed, first, that the conjugal unit itself (husband and wife) is loosely structured. The spouses, in many of these societies, can separate without seriously jeopardizing their own livelihood or that of their children. Secondly, band membership fluctuates everywhere, either from season to season or from year to year or both. Conjugal pairs, that is, a husband and wife and their dependents, are the detachable units. They join together or separate, or move alone or in groups as the exigencies of the quest for food require, or as they are impelled by their personal preferences, or their desire to move away from conflicts.

But conjugal pairs and their dependents are not equally welcome in all bands. A man or woman is sure to be welcome in a band in which he or she has a consanguineal (blood) relative like a brother or sister or a mother or a father, or an affinal relative (a relation by marriage) like a father-in-law or a mother-in-law. Kinship, then, both bilaterally consanguineal and affinal, is the most usual basis for residence within bands. A second basis can be the presence of an influential or respected man or woman whose band a person wishes to join, and who is receptive to the addition of new members to the band.

I/3   POSSIBLE BASES OF SEX DIFFERENTIATION IN ACQUISITION OF POWER

Control of Resources

TERRITORIES

What kind of rights to the territories they normally move about in do foragers (hunters and gatherers) establish? Do rights differ for men and women? In general, all members of a local band of foragers have relatively free access to the territory from which the group derives its nutrition. Among some hunters and gatherers, individual men or groups of men are recognized as "owners" of a water hole or a tract of land. But such "ownership" does not mean the right to exclusive use of the territory, or the right to give it away in exchange for other territories or goods. It means that the kin of such a man or group of men can always join bands in that territory, and that outsiders must ask permission if they wish to hunt or gather in the area. The ideology of generosity, always a highly prized cultural value among foragers, usually guarantees that permission will be freely granted. Control over territories holding strategic food resources is not, therefore, available as a means whereby either men or women can gain power or prominence.

WEALTH AND TRADE

The nomadism of foragers under conditions in which typically only human energy (except for dogs used as draught animals among the Eskimo) is available for burden bearing and movement sets limits on the amount of food or material property that can be accumulated and retained for periods longer than an annual cycle. Hunters and gatherers travel light. Trade with neighboring groups permits makers of objects such as spears or baskets to exchange these for other items they value.

Hunters may do the same with skins. Here the advantage gained is not through the accumulation of these goods, but through their availability for extradomestic distribution. Men can have an advantage over women where external trade is carried on if men have a monopoly on access to the goods traded, such as hides or honey. We shall return to this matter later.

INHERITANCE

With few commodities available for accumulation, inheritance is not significant; personal possessions like weapons and clothing are often destroyed at the death of their owner.

All these conditions preclude the development of great permanent differences in material wealth either among men or women in hunting and gathering societies, nor can there be major variations in economic or political power derived from such wealth.[1]

Warfare

Do warfare and defense provide significant roles for men in contrast to women among hunters and gatherers? Contests over territories between men of neighboring foraging groups are not unknown. Washo men will sometimes defend their fishing grounds; on the borders of a home region, north Alaskan Eskimo men will engage in group fights against men in a neighboring region. But on the whole, under aboriginal conditions, the amount of energy men devote to training for fighting or the time spent on war expeditions among hunters and gatherers is not very great. Hostilities break out more frequently between individuals or two sets of feuding kin than between groups of men engaged in warfare. Conflicts within bands, or within a group of intermarrying bands, are often settled simply by the departure, with his dependents, of one of the parties to the dispute. Another method is for the individual contestants in the dispute to engage in public ritualized contests, such as song competitions. Women join in decisions to move away from conflict; they also constitute part of the audience at contests, and express opinions as to which contestant is getting the better of the other.

Division of Labor in Food Acquisition and Distribution

If among hunters and gatherers control over band movements and strategic resources, the accumulation of wealth, and warfare do not give men and women significantly different bases for achieving esteem and power, are there any activities that do so? The answer is yes. First, the systems of food distribution and exchange create different opportunities for the sexes; and second, in some societies, men and women exercise different degrees of control over sexual rights.

---

[1] A well-known exception is made possible by the geographical conditions on the northwest coast of North America, where the quantity, types, and distribution of wild food sources permitted permanent settlements and relatively dense populations, as well as a class of chiefs who accumulated and then distributed large quantities of goods.

DIFFERENTIAL ACCESS TO FOOD RESOURCES

A difference in the access to esteem and power as between men and women depends first upon a division of labor between them which requires some form of food exchange. Why is food exchange a necessity? This comes from the fact that despite equality of access to resources in the sense that no ownership restrictions block the way, there is an actual differentiation of access, based on sex and age, to the various sources of foragers' subsistence.

Differences Inherent in Processes of Acquisition. The hunting of large game animals when it is done in groups of four or five is everywhere almost exclusively a man's occupation, as is dangerous seafishing. In some societies, women participate in communal hunts, and sometimes do some fishing. Under extraordinary circumstances, individual women have been known to go out hunting, and to bring back large game. But women never have the primary routine responsibility for supplying their households or their bands with meat from large animals. Women are the gatherers, the collectors of plant foods and small animals.

Why should this be so widespread a pattern for the division of labor between the sexes? Why are not women the hunters and men the gatherers? Or why cannot both men and women be responsible for both hunting and gathering? The answer lies, I suggest, in an interconnected set of conditions.

First, two different skills are involved: one in scanning the ground and the horizon for the traces of large animals; the other in recognizing the clues for the existence of roots and plant foods, and for the hiding places of small animals. But let us assume that both men and women could be trained to acquire both sets of skills (indeed in some societies gathering women report to men on animal traces they have seen). We can assume also that, while on a hunting foray for large game, either men or women or both could feed themselves on berries and small animals until such time as they make a major kill; hunters do in fact so provision themselves. But what no one, regardless of sex, can do while on a hunt is to gather and carry plant foods in sufficient quantities for feeding those left back in camp. Carrying burdens would interfere with a hunter's ability to run long distances while tracking animals. A pack of any kind would interfere with the body balance and coordination needed to throw a spear or to release an arrow. The effect of the limitations on simultaneous carrying and hunting is that if a surplus of food is to be brought back to camp, any particular foraging expedition must concentrate either on hunting or on gathering.

It would still be theoretically possible for both men and women to hunt and gather on alternate days, let us say. Such a system is unlikely to develop because of the short-range unreliability of the hunt. Meat is always supplied at irregular intervals. Any one hunting foray may be unsuccessful; days may go by without a kill and yet hunters must keep trying. In such circumstances, no orderly rotation of hunting and gathering would be feasible. While the hunters are meeting with ill success, the population still requires food. This is provided by the much more regularly available plant foods and small creatures, which in most areas can be relied on whenever food is needed.

Difference Based on Functions of Women as Child-Bearers and Child Trans-porters. But we have still not explained why hunting individually or in small groups has been a man's specialty and gathering a woman's. Here the function of women as child-bearers becomes significant. Women bear children in two senses: as carriers of the fetus during pregnancy, and as carriers of the infants and children for at least the first year or two of the young one's life. Nursing infants have to be accompanied, at least part of the time, by a lactating woman. Women, then, are barred from hunting during the later stages of pregnancy by the shifts which their condition produces in body balance; after childbirth, by the actual burden of transporting the child.

The importance of developing an adjustment to burden bearing among hunters and gatherers cannot be overestimated. In a study of the Dobe Bushmen of the Kalahari Desert in Africa, it has been calculated that women provide two-thirds of the food consumed in camp; that each adult woman goes out to gather about 2 or 3 days a week; on those days she walks from 2 to 12 miles, round trip, and on the way back carries loads of 15 to 33 pounds of vegetable foods. In addition to collecting expeditions, women walk to visit other camps and, along with men, move long distances to new camp sites. A woman walks about 1500 miles during the course of an annual round. For at least half the distance, she carries burdens of food, water, and goods. Most importantly, however, she also carries any of her children who are under 4 years old: those under 2 at all times, those between 2 and 4 part of the time. Breast feeding among the Bushmen continues into the fourth year. Births are usually spaced 4 years apart. A woman who gives birth more frequently is said by the people to have a permanent backache; she must carry 2 or more children at once as well as the food and objects normally entrusted to her (Lee 1972b).

If women are gatherers, therefore, a low fertility rate is an adaptive mechanism for the survival of the population (Sussman 1972). Gathering by women, then, does not mean that because they venture less far from homesites than the hunters their work is entirely compatible with the care of young children. In fact, it has been suggested that the spacing of children and the low fertility rates among some foragers accounts for the fact that their populations are below the number of people the food and water resources of the area could support.

But why, we can still ask, cannot adolescent girls and mature women who are not pregnant or lactating hunt, leaving the other women to do the gathering, to nurse their own infants, and to care for their own children and others who have been weaned? One can envision a system in which at any one time half, let us say, of the women in a group would be alternately hunting and gathering, and all the men would be doing the same. Under these circumstances, both boys and girls would have to be trained for both skills, but women would take time off from the hunting quest now and then to bear and suckle children, while men would hunt and gather alternately without interruption.

The difficulty with such a solution as a routine system lies in the demographic structure of hunting and gathering societies. As we have seen, local bands during most of the year consist of 25 to 50 people, including both adults and children. If we estimate an average of 7 to 10 women of child-bearing age, and postulate an infant mortality rate of 30 percent to 50 percent (which is not uncommon), then simply to maintain population size virtually all the women would need to be pregnant or nursing throughout their child-bearing years. It would simply not be feasible for any substantial segment of the mature women, even if possessed of sufficient mastery in hunting, to constitute a significant pool of potential hunters. Because young girls marry at just about the time they have achieved sufficient size and strength to become skilled hunters, they are not available for hunting either.

Alternative Explanation. The usual explanation of the exclusive allocation to men of the major role in hunting is their physical suitability for this activity: their size, running ability, muscular strength, lung capacity, and a hormone-based aggressiveness. But though such advantages undoubtedly make men in the top range of these physical characteristics the best potential hunters, it is hard to see why they should make the general run of men the only hunters. The overlap between the sexes in respect to the physical characteristics listed is considerable.

Summary. To sum up, men become hunters and women gatherers in nomadic foraging societies as a consequence of the combined effects and interrelationships of the following factors: the incompatibility of simultaneous burden bearing and hunting, the functions of women as child-bearers and child-carriers, and the limited population size of foraging groups for most of the year.

Although we have established that men are hunters among foragers, and women do most of the gathering, it is still possible for men on occasion to gather plants to feed themselves. Moreover, women can help men in large-scale communal hunts as net holders and beaters, while men can help women in large-scale communal gathering of fruits and vegetables that are abundant only during short periods of the year. The proportion of time and energy that men allocate to hunting and occasional gathering, and women to gathering, and the proportion of the total subsistence that each sex produces, vary as a result of the different geographical environments in the different regions of the world in which foragers live.

FOUR PATTERNS OF SEXUAL DIVISION OF LABOR

The variations have important consequences for sex roles. There are four major patterns of sexual division of labor among foragers.

First are the foragers among whom each man collects plants for the major part of his individual subsistence, and women do the same for themselves and their children. Only a minor part of male energies is devoted to hunting, and little meat is available for distribution. Both men and women spend most of their time gathering. The conjugal pair does not share jointly in the food that is gathered, but each fends for himself, with the mother assuming the major responsibility for the children, though the father contributes to some extent. The Hadza of Tanzania in Africa (Woodburn 1968, and pp. 33–34 below), and the Paliyans of Southwest India (Gardner 1972) are examples of hunters and gatherers with this pattern.

The *second* pattern is one in which task forces of both sexes representing several households are involved in communal hunts, in gathering, and in fishing. Hunting forays, under these conditions, are usually drives in which animals are forced either into a net or into some other central impounding-place by the joint efforts of men and women, although the men actually kill the animals. All households which constitute the task force share immediately in the proceeds. Men and women sometimes also simultaneously gather and transport foods like nuts when they are in season, and both sexes join in fishing during heavy fish runs. Under these conditions, if a husband and wife work as a team, the team keeps what it has collected. Otherwise the proceeds are shared out immediately to all who formed part of the task force. The Washo of the Great Basin of North America (Downs 1966, and pp. 34–36 below), and the Mbuti pigmies of the Congo rain forests in Africa (Turnbull 1961, 1968) are examples of the second pattern.

The *third* pattern among foragers is that in which men and women are almost always separated from each other in the course of the food quest, men hunting singly or in groups, sometimes at considerable distance from the camp, and women gathering foodstuffs within several miles of the camp site. These are societies in which women contribute more than half the food supply, but men's hunting activity accounts for at least 30 to 40 percent. Men must distribute meat not only to members of their own households but outside it as well. Household members, both men and women, may share their individual portions with outsiders. The Bushmen of the Kalahari Desert in Africa (Lee 1968, 1972a; Marshall 1965; and pp. 37–39 below), and the Tiwi of North Australia (Hart and Pilling 1960; Goodale 1971) are examples of this pattern.

Finally, the *fourth* pattern is one in which the provision of large game by men is virtually the only source of food for the society. Women's contribution is limited to the processing of meat and skins. Women stay close to camp or to the shelters which are used. It is important to note that here women are almost totally dependent on men for all the foodstuffs and for the raw materials, the carcasses, which they process. Men even manufacture the tools which women use in their work. Therefore a woman cannot initiate activities which independently provide her and her children with the staples of a livelihood. Men distribute meat not only to the members of their own households but to outsiders as well. The Eskimo in general exemplify this pattern (Chance 1966; Spencer 1959, 1972; Burch and Correll 1972, and pp. 39–45 below).

Such are the four patterns of division of labor among foragers. Although women provide half or more of the subsistence among those with the first three patterns, in all foraging societies it is exclusively men who hunt whatever large game animals can be taken either by a man hunting alone or by groups of four or five men (as contrasted with communal hunts). This fact has important ramifications for sex roles reaching far beyond the matter of division of labor. We shall turn, therefore, to a discussion of the consequences of the male monopoly of individual or small-group game hunts.

I/4   DIFFERENTIAL CONTROL OF MEN AND WOMEN OVER FOOD EXCHANGE

Where any of the first three patterns we have discussed prevails, there must be an exchange of foodstuffs between men and women. Because of the short-range uncertainties of the hunt, even in regions in which game is plentiful in the long run, men must receive vegetable food from women either when the hunt fails, or when they have not gone out to hunt, or when they are too young or too old to hunt. Women, in their turn, must receive meat from men when the hunt is successful if they and their children are to share in the benefits of a mixed protein-vegetable diet. We assume that those early foragers among whom protein was distributed to women and children had a better chance of survival, and that the extant hunting and gathering societies are derived from such populations.

In addition to direct exchanges of different nutrients between the sexes, food is also distributed by men to other men who have not hunted that day, and by women to other women, children, and the elderly. How are all these exchanges and distributions accomplished? How are these rights to receive and these duties to give determined?

Raw Food

KINSHIP AND MARRIAGE AS BASES FOR DOMESTIC AND EXTRADOMESTIC EXCHANGE

The obligation to give and the privilege of receiving are always expressed in these societies as cultural rules associated with social roles. Here kin roles are the most important. Which relatives?

First, the nuclear family (a married pair and their children) is a base for domestic exchange within each household; second, marriage adds affinals to those to whom food is distributed. A common pattern for an unmarried man is for him to be expected to give meat to his parents, brothers, and sisters in his role as son and brother. Within the nuclear family the obligations are reciprocal. Once married, a man adds his wife and often his mother-in-law and other affinal ("in-law") relatives to the list of those to whom he is obligated to give meat. Eventually his own children are added to the list. A woman's obligations as an unmarried girl are to parents, brothers, and sisters; as a wife and mother she adds to these her husband, his near kin, her children, and eventually her son- or sons-in-law. One function of marriage in these societies is thus to create for each partner additional role relationships within which food exchanges will occur. Affinal relatives of both sexes are added to one's own nuclear family of origin. Marriage enlarges the network of kin from whom food can be received and to whom it will be distributed. Marriage reduces the risk of starvation for any one individual. In this sense, marriage is a system of recruiting the labor of men and women outside the nuclear family in a society in which other forms of recruitment, such as slavery, serfdom, or wage labor, are not possible.

Marriage and residential mobility provide a basis for extradomestic food exchanges. In-laws are not necessarily resident in the same household as a husband and wife and their children, and adult spouses do not necessarily live in the same household as their own parents or brothers and sisters. But such relatives and their dependents can be in the same band temporarily or permanently, or meet each other during the public phases of life when several bands congregate. In practice, because of the high perishability of food, the extent and the times at which extradomestic exchanges take place depend on these kinds of physical proximity among the relatives concerned.

THEORETICAL ALTERNATIVE TO MARRIAGE

The importance of marriage for food exchange must be emphasized, because theoretically a sibling group of brothers and sisters could, with their parents, constitute the labor force for the collection of foods, and the exchange group for its distribution between men and women of different ages. Procreation could be accomplished by irregular sexual encounters with men and women of other sibling groups, with each set of brothers and sisters supporting the children of the sisters only. But this system would lack the advantage of the relatively long-term exchange between two or more nuclear families that marriage brings about; in other words, the exchange between affinals, who, by definition, without marriage do not exist. Probably the development of the cultural concept of the "in-law" is as important a human invention as is the incest rule.

TASKMATES AND FRIENDS

Food distribution also occurs as an aspect of the role of friend or taskmate. In societies in which a group of men cooperate in the hunt, even where the recruitment of members of such a group is not based solely on kinship, the kill or catch, as we have seen, is usually distributed immediately among the group's members. Large-scale communal hunts, in which women sometimes take part, involve immediate distribution to all participants.

CONSEQUENCES OF SEXUAL DIVISION OF LABOR FOR EXCHANGE

The most important consequence of the male monopoly on big-game hunting is connected with the fact that all foraging cultures have rules by which meat must be shared. The sharing usually involves an obligation to distribute meat to those not in one's own household. By contrast, among hunters and gatherers the bulk of vegetable foods and small animals which women collect is rarely shared extradomestically. It is difficult to get information from the accounts of anthropologist as to just how women manage vegetable food, while descriptions of the rules for distributing meat are common. I believe that this state of affairs reflects the actual situation: a narrower range of distribution for the regularly available and therefore less valued plant foods in contrast with a wider distribution of the scarce commodity meat.

If this is true, men have a larger circle of people with whom reciprocal relations exist. This is a major source of difference in the power of men and women.

Cooked Food

We have thus far concentrated our attention on the exchanges of raw food. The processing and cooking of food involve different social groups and result in different social units for the exchange. This stems from the fact that it is the women, the tenders of the fire at the camp site, rather than the far-ranging hunters, who are in charge of distributing cooked food at the hearth. In general, the grinding of seeds, the pounding of roots, and the cooking of vegetable foods are done by women. The origin of cooking as woman's work may lie in the fact that cooking is needed to make many roots and seeds digestible for human beings, and it was as collectors of these foodstuffs that women proceeded to cook them as well. Butchering at the site of the kill is normally a man's job. Men sometimes cook part of the meat at the site, but frequently they bring some back raw for the women to process. Cooked foods are routinely distributed by the women to the domestic unit, that is, to the household members who are sharing a fireside: the foods go from wife to husband, from mother to child, occasionally from sister to brother. Women also give cooked food to visitors who arrive at meal times. Except for ceremonial occasions, therefore, the distribution of cooked food usually takes place among smaller units than those involved in the distribution of food in the raw state. Interestingly enough, among some Kalahari Bushmen, a person's portion of raw meat is cooked individually by the recipient, male or female, so that it is not shared even within the household.

Ideology of Exhange

All the systems of food exchange which we have described are called "generalized reciprocity." Givers expect no immediate return, and do not consciously calculate the value of the products or services involved. The giving is viewed by the participants in the culture concerned rather as an expected duty associated with particular roles.

Those foraging societies survived in which ways were found to encourage the fulfillment of exchange obligations. This encouragement involves certain values or ideologies consciously expressed by most hunters and gatherers. First, as we have seen, meat as a scarce food is valued above all others; second, the hunter of meat animals is correspondingly valued, and third, honor and prestige are accorded the generous giver. Spontaneous, generous distributors of goods are not what we find among foragers, as the romantic view would have it. Descriptions of living hunters and gatherers demonstrate that sharing is considered a burden, the distastefulness of which is overcome by the expectation of the social rewards that are accorded those who give lavishly and with apparent cheerfulness.

Conclusion: Differential Opportunities for Men and Women

It is the men and not the women in hunting and gathering societies, as we have seen, who have the opportunity to achieve recognition and esteem by acting publicly as generous hosts, thus validating their skill as hunters.[2] Men who have made a kill and distributed it according to normal priorities automatically obligate others eventually to do the same in return. They not only gain immediate honor and prestige, but they bind others to repay them and thereby exercise a kind of superior power as creditors until the return transaction takes place. Obviously, the more skillful the hunter, the greater are his dividends in prestige and power, and the more frequent his public gifts of scarce resources.

Let us contrast the situation of women as gatherers and processors. There is no pattern of wide and generous distribution of unprocessed vegetable foods either to men or to other women. Each woman regularly obtains enough food for herself and

[2] The Dobe Bushmen of Africa differ from this pattern in minor ways; see the discussion below, pp. 37–39.

her household. She may work in the company of other women, but she need not coordinate her activities with those of her companions.

Nor is the cooked food usually distributed outside the circle of household residents, unless there are visitors. These exchanges involve foods that are not scarce, and the reciprocal obligations engendered by them are regular, nondramatic, and without marked expansion of the circle bound to the woman by reciprocity.

At best, an older woman who is a skilled gatherer and has a forceful personality may gain some repute, and may thus draw other families to the band so that their women may profit from her expertise. But even this falls far short of the recognition available to even a moderately successful hunter.

Significantly, women suffer from less disadvantage in comparison with men in the first two patterns of division of labor which we referred to earlier; the first, in which men do little hunting and spend most of their time gathering on a par with the women, and the second, in which communal hunts and communal gathering activities are important. Women are most severely handicapped from this point of view in societies with the fourth pattern, in which men provide almost all the food.

I/5   DIFFERENTIAL CONTROL OVER SEXUAL ACCESS AND OVER PROCREATION

We have so far been concerned with marriage primarily as a mechanism for the recruitment of labor and the distribution of food. We can now consider it as an institution for procreation and sexual gratification. We have already seen, in our discussion of the theoretical possibility of siblings as a basis for society, that marriage is not essential for food production and distribution, for procreation, or for sexual satisfaction; that its salient advantage for the first two purposes was the enlargement of the network of food givers and receivers by the establishment of a new category of relatives, the affinals. What are the advantages of marriage for the other two goals, procreation and sexual satisfaction, and how, if at all, does the division of labor affect the differential control of men and women over sexual access and procreation?

Premarital Intercourse; Marriage

At the outset it must be said that sex relations before marriage are usually permitted in hunting and gathering societies. After a period of shifting partners, men and women eventually marry. A man and a woman in a foraging society consider themselves and are considered married when they have entered into a transaction in which they agree to accord each other rights to priority in sexual access, to fulfill obligations to each other's kin, to have joint rights in the control of any children they may have while they live together, and, as we have seen, to exchange the fruits of their labor. Married couples also expect to have a common residence, that is, they travel in the same band. For first marriages the approval of both sets of parents is frequently required. Marriages need not last a lifetime, but after several unions of short duration it is common for men and women to find permanent spouses.

The advantage of marriage from the standpoint of sexual relations is that it provides both husband and wife with at least a minimal regularity of sexual access. Although adultery occurs sporadically, the frequency of promiscuous sex relations is diminished. In evolutionary terms, marriage may well have a biologically adaptive function if it is true, as experimental evidence from animal laboratories suggests, that promiscuity reduces the fertility of females.

Marriage Rules

Unlike the free access to game animals and plant foods, access to prospective spouses is controlled. It is regulated in two ways. The first is the incest rule, which in virtually all the world's societies prohibits sex relations and marriage with those who are in a relation to each other of parent and child or of brother and sister. The second is a positive rule and characterizes only some foraging societies. It is a cultural rule which designates "cross cousins" as preferred spouses. A pair of cross cousins is one whose cousinship is the result of the fact that the mother of one and the father of the other are sister and brother. A pair of cross cousins is not, that is, the offspring of two brothers or two sisters; these are called "parallel cousins."

Even if all marriages in societies following the cross-cousin rule do not actually take place between cross cousins, the rule of preference directs attention away from men and women who are the cross cousins of others, leaving mostly brothers and parallel cousins to compete with each other for wives, and similarly situated women to compete with each other for husbands. This situation is replicated for widows and widowers who wish to marry again by the cultural rules called the sororate— the prior right of a man to marry his dead wife's sister if she is still unmarried, and the levirate, the prior right of a woman to marry her dead husband's brother either as a first or a subsequent wife.

Apart from limiting competition between unrelated men and women an effect of cross-cousin marriage is that a brother and sister are likely to encourage the mating of their children to each other. In a sense, through cross-cousin marriage, sets of brothers and sisters insure that the exchange relationships and bases of band affiliation that they had with each other will be continued into a new generation, as those children who would have no special obligation to them as uncles and aunts acquire such obligations as sons- and daughters-in-law.

Australian aborigines have extensions of cross-cousin rules to the generations both above and below; these extensions further limit the range of eligible spouses for any one person.

Choice of Spouses and Sex Partners

In the differential control over the choice of spouses and sex-partners, the sexual division of labor among hunters and gatherers has some influence. Let us begin with the first two patterns of sexual division of labor described above, (1) that in which men and women both engage in gathering, and male distributions of meat are rare, and (2) that in which the male advantage in meat distribution is minimized by collective methods of hunting and gathering. In both of these the limited control of men over meat is paralleled by their limited control over women. Polygyny, the marriage of one man to more than one woman, is permitted, as among all foragers, but in these two groups is rare. Men and women are equally free to choose spouses, to take on lovers after marriage, and to separate when they wish. Occasionally, two men, brothers or friends, find it convenient to share a wife, or a married woman may not wish to give up a lover, and the husband agrees to let the lover join the household. Such polyandrous arrangements (the simultaneous marriage of one woman to more than one man) are usually not long lasting. Sexual jealousies are causes of conflict among men (and probably among women as well, although these are less frequently reported), but they usually remain the affair of the individuals concerned.

In the third pattern of the sexual division of labor, that in which men produce 30 to 40 percent of the food supply, men's monopoly on the distribution of meat, and often of trade goods as well, may give them an opportunity to gain access not only to a wide network of partners in food exchange but also to women. Among the men themselves, a skilled and diligent hunter is in a better position to find a wife than other men. Young women's parents are eager to have a daughter marry such a man, and adult women are eager to have such men as mates. In a sense, meat can be exchanged not only for meat but also for women.[3] Indeed, a form of "bride service," in which a man lives in the same band with, and hunts for, his bride's parents for a period of 5 to 10 or 15 years is not uncommon among these foragers.

The Australians, however, constitute a special case. Here men's monopoly of game is supplemented by male control over what is believed to be an important body of ritual knowledge; men conduct extradomestic ceremonies associated with that knowledge. Under these circumstances, men's control over women increases. A higher proportion of polygynous unions is made possible in these Australian societies by cultural rules which delay the marriage of men until their midtwenties. Men when they are old can still acquire new wives, while girls are betrothed or married at 5 to 10 years of age, and, in some societies, are promised as wives even before the girls are born. All this creates an artificial plurality of potential mates for men. Under these conditions, men negotiate and manoeuver to exchange women as wives. They increase the complexity of the obligations they have to each other. Marriage has clear political purposes as well as economic, sexual, and procreational ends. Mature and older women exert influence on their own marital careers, and on those of their sons and daughters, by suggesting possibilities to men. Such women can exercise some negative control by refusing to participate in proposed marital arrangements distasteful to them. Sex relations are not limited to married couples. Adultery, frequently occurring between young unmarried men and married women, results in conflicts among men, and in wife beating, with occasional physical retaliation on the part of the wife. In Australia such incidents can sometimes involve a whole camp, although matters can also be settled between individuals.

In other societies of the third pattern, the situation is different. Exclusive male ritual knowledge is not an important factor. Here, as in the first two patterns for the division of labor, women's contributions to subsistence make them valuable enough so that bride service alone, as among the Kalahari Bushmen, or simple reciprocity suffices as a significant basis for alliances with in-laws, without the development of elaborate negotiations over women.

[3] I am indebted to Shirley Lindenbaum for the development of this theme.

It is in our fourth pattern for the division of labor, the one in which game hunted by men furnishes close to 100 percent of the food supply, that male sexual aggression toward women is greatest. Among the Eskimo, women are treated as sex objects, and have very limited control over their own personal destinies. Polygynous unions here are rare, partly because female infanticide contributes to a shortage of women. Female infanticide in turn springs largely from the desire of parents to assure themselves of male children to hunt for them in their old age. Polygyny is also kept down by the limitation on the amount of meat a hunter can count on at any one time; usually it is insufficient to take care of more than one set of marital, paternal, and affinal obligations.

Number and Spacing of Children

We have already seen that the spacing of children can affect the survival of foragers. An infant born during a drought or period of severe food shortage is itself unlikely to survive, and its care can endanger the life of the mother. A household with only girls or only boys growing up is at a disadvantage as regards food exchange within the domestic group. Consequently, some kind of control of the numbers of children and the sex of those allowed to live is often found among foragers. We have already mentioned prolonged lactation as a deterrent to conception. Abortion and infanticide are other alternatives which foragers use. Information as to who makes the crucial decisions is scanty.

We assume that the decision can be made by a couple in concert, or by the man alone, or by the woman alone. In the latter case, a woman can cloak abortion or infanticide under a claim of accident as a way of expressing resentment against a husband. Conversely husbands can force wives into infanticide as a means of expressing their dominance, especially in societies like those of the Eskimo where, as we have seen, men's dominance over women is clearly expressed.

I/6   YOUTH AND OLD AGE AS MODIFIERS OF SEX ROLES

Youth

OCCUPATIONS

The allocations of human energies in foraging societies is, as in all other human groups, modified at both ends of the age scale. Children of both sexes contribute to their own food supply as soon as they are old enough to follow their mothers. They pick and eat the easily available fruits and berries. Boys soon start groups of their own and wander near the camp practicing hunting skills, cooking and eating the small animals they catch.

Girls acquire the skills of adult women, and their responsibilities gradually increase as they accompany their mothers, getting the botanical knowledge needing for skilled detection of food sources, and the physical strength needed for digging out roots and carrying ever larger burdens back to camp. From an early age, they also help carry and care for younger children, increasingly as time goes on. For girls the entire process is gradual, with no clearly marked boundaries related solely to food-gathering or child-tending.

For boys the case is somewhat different. Not only are they less freely admitted as apprentices—a false move at a hunt can be much more damaging than any ineptitude of their sisters in gathering—but also, when hunting skills have been acquired, there is a dramatic marker of this fact. The boy makes his first kill of large game and distributes the meat, which in itself validates him as a hunter. In addition, many foraging peoples mark the first major kill of a boy with a small ritual.

PUBERTY RITUALS

For girls the menarche, the onset of the first menstrual period, is an event which is usually, but not always, thought to mark their transition to marriageability as well as to physical maturity. In hunting and gathering societies it is also often the occasion for a ritual, in part public, in which the girl's economic contribution, as well as her sexual maturity, is recognized. Public menarche rituals are found most frequently among those foragers among whom women contribute substantially to subsistence, and especially in North America (Brown 1963).

Group initiation ceremonies for boys at or near puberty, including some form of mutilation such as circumcision, in contrast to rituals directly related to hunting skills, occur among some Australian foragers, but rarely among hunters and gatherers elsewhere. This is an aspect of the ritual elaborations characteristic of Australians which have already been discussed.

The Aged

MARRIAGE AND RESIDENCE

Men and women among foragers are considered marriageable well into old age. Old men can have wives who are in their early teens, and old women, usually widows, can have husbands in their twenties. Widows and widowers also usually have the option of staying with grown sons and daughters instead of remarrying.

ROUTINE ACTIVITIES

Women continue to act as food gatherers well into old age, though they spend more and more time in camp as they grow older, often minding children. Men's occupations in old age converge on those of women: they spend more time in camp, work at sedentary tasks, and to an extent help care for children as well. They are valued as repositories of information and anecdotes, as well as for their services as baby tenders, and they are supported by the young. It is only in extreme circumstances, when bands must move under very adverse conditions, that the old are sometimes abandoned. But people of any age or sex who are weak or injured will in like situations be left to fend for themselves, often with the knowledge that they will die as a result.

SHAMANISM AND DIFFERENTIATION IN RITUAL CONTROL

Men and women who have survived to old age are believed to have the ability to control the supernatural forces which bring both good and evil. It is not uncommon, therefore, for the old to be the only true specialists in foraging societies, the "medicine man" or "medicine woman." In some societies, these specialists are known as shamans: that is, they are believed to be able to control spirits in the sense they can be possessed by them at will. The spirits then assist the shaman to diagnose illness, to effect cures, and to recover lost objects. In the loosely organized local bands of hunting and gathering societies, where there are no leadership positions with institutionalized political authority, the shamans perform some of the functions of political and social control. Illness in these societies is often believed to be caused by the breaking of various taboos, including incest rules. Shamanistic performances in which spirits question the ill person as to his transgressions and elicit confessions of guilt serve to reiterate the rules of the society and to encourage the onlookers to maintain the norms.

Women can become shamans along with men in societies having three of our four patterns of division of labor: (1) those in which hunting is a minimal source of food (Paliyans); (2) those in which men and women jointly participate in large-scale hunts or food collections (Washo); and (3) those in which hunting predominates as a source of food and male shamans are those who are unsuccessful hunters (North Alaskan Eskimo). In the third case, men who are poor hunters are peripheral to the main sources of power in the society, a condition shared by all women, who are by definition nonhunters.

In those societies in which a woman can become a shaman, she is likely to acquire the power after the menopause, which removes her from the procreational aspect of womanhood. She then performs a quasipolitical function like that of the masculine shaman. But not all specialists in the supernatural need be old in order to practice. If men or women have begun functioning in early adult life, not only do they not lose their powers with advancing age but are usually thought to increase them.

For both men and women shamanistic powers can be a source of livelihood. Gifts of meat and other foods, and of trade goods where they exist, are given in return for the exercise of their powers. Men shamans can also acquire wives more easily when they are older than other old men, for women often fear their power and hesitate to refuse them. Women shamans are likely to acquire husbands for themselves and their daughters.

Among Australian aborigines control of ritual knowledge is shown by the expert's ability to stage ceremonial dramatizations of mythical events; this is the counterpart here of possession and shamanism elsewhere. However, here too it is older men and women who are thought to have the special ability and who organize and conduct the elaborate rituals.

I/7   PERSONAL AUTONOMY

We have already discussed, directly or by implication, the relative degrees of autonomy which men and women have with respect to food acquisition and food exchange on the one hand, and sex, marriage, and procreation on the other. There is no real choice of occupation available either to men or women among foragers, with the sole exception of shamanism. But individual decisions are possible for both men and women with respect to their daily routines and the zeal with which they perform their tasks. Men and women alike are free to decide how they will spend each day: whether to go out hunting or gathering and with whom; whether to stay in camp to make arrows or baskets or to tell stories, gamble, or sing and dance; whether to visit neighbors or go off on the trip to relatives who are part of another band.

An important decision which constantly faces a hunting and gathering people is the decision as to travel: when and where to move. This occurs both for the band as a whole and for individual family groups within it. Band movements are apparently influenced by knowledge acquired by hunters or offered by shamans. Those who wish to move try to persuade others to accompany them. Successful hunters are likely to be most persuasive. Women enter into the discussions, since their assessment of the possibility of successful food-gathering must be taken into account. In at least one society a woman can serve as the leader of the band's move. At the household level, husbands and wives join in deciding whether or not and with whom they will go. Failing agreement, the pair may even separate.

I/8 SYMBOLIC RESTATEMENT OF DIFFERENCES BETWEEN MEN'S AND WOMEN'S ROLES

Ritualized symbolic expression is given to the differentiation between male and female activities among the foragers. In a broader sense, these rituals restate concepts which are part of the world view of foragers regarding the relationships between maleness and femaleness, and their place both in society and in the natural order of things.

Menarchical and Hunting Rituals: Blood and Sex Taboos

The high frequency of both private and public rites for girls at menarche among foragers among whom women contribute substantially to subsistence has already been mentioned. Some reference has also been made to the first kill rituals for boys.

The common element which is to be differentiated in these two types of ritual, I believe, is blood. In the case of men the blood involved is the blood shed by the animals they kill. The blood clearly and unambiguously betokens death, as it does in the slaying of an enemy. In the case of women the blood is that of menstruation. The significance of the blood must be highly ambiguous. Until a girl sheds menstrual blood she cannot conceive and begin a new life. After she has finally ceased to menstruate, at the menopause, she can no longer do so. But each monthly flow in between these two points is the antithesis of life, for it means that she has not conceived. Thus, in a symbolic sense, it may be equated with death. Adding to the ambiguity is the fact that women, unlike men, bleed without injury and do not die from the monthly flow.

In foraging societies in which there is a marked separation of the sexes as regards hunting, this separation is restated ritually by keeping the female type of blood—ambiguous as between life and death—most strictly separated from the activities connected with the men's type of blood, that of slaying and death. There is often a requirement that menstrual blood, and women when they are menstruating—

sometimes even between menstrual periods—stay out of contact with men's weapons and even with men themselves. The taboos are usually phrased in the societies concerned as a means of protecting the hunter from harm and keeping his weapons powerful.

The common connection with blood may explain why the first hunt ritual for boys, marking the first blood shed by the young hunter, often parallels in structural ritual elements the menarche ritual marking the first shedding of menstrual blood by the girl. For example, among the Washo a girl during her menarche must give away all the food she collects. In a parallel fashion, a boy after his first kill may not eat any part of the animal himself but must distribute all of it.

A further ritual restatement of the separation of men and women in the sphere of hunting is the frequent taboo on sexual intercourse before a hunt. The taboo is often explained by hunters themselves as an attempt to avoid a man's loss of vital force or energy by the ejaculation of semen.

Deviations from the pattern we have just described exist among foragers who conform to the second of our patterns of sexual division of labor. When men and women customarily join in communal hunts, it is not uncommon for fewer or no precautions to be taken to keep the women's kind of blood out of contact with hunting activities or with men in general. Indeed, among the net hunting Mbuti pygmies, sexual intercourse during menstruation is believed to be beneficial to both men and women.

Male Initiation Rituals

Large-scale initiation rites with circumcision or other mutilation, which keep the initiates and their sponsors occupied for months at a time or even years, are almost unknown among hunters and gatherers. The Australian aborigines form the principal exception.[4] These people differ from other hunters and gatherers in several respects, one of which is in the elaborateness and rich complexity of their cosmology, and the ceremonials in which they enact their concept of the nature of the world. Their view includes the idea that men are responsible for controlling sacred or spiritual aspects of the universe and women the profane or secular aspects. Moreover, men related to each other through males (patrilines) together control particular annual fertility and hunting rituals, "dreamings," as they are called, and conduct secret, all male ceremonies in relation to them. A man among the aborigines, therefore, has the obligation to acquire not only technical hunting skills, with his first kill attesting that he has become qualified for this masculine activity, but also the qualifications for membership in his patriline's "dreaming." This is a kind of cult lodge, the right to the secrets of which the boy must acquire (Meggitt 1972). Australian men must therefore become possessed not only of mundane skills, but

[4] It is not clear why this is so. One hypothesis is that the men spend relatively little time hunting, so that their absence from it does not endanger the food supply of the group appreciably. This means of course only that long initiation rites and other elaborate rituals are possible, but it does not explain why the Australians choose to use their available energies in such a fashion. Another hypothesis is that male initiation rites are expressions and dramatizations of the male solidarity which exists in other segments of the society. Perhaps the importance of ritual knowledge as a means of controlling nature gives Australians a base for solidarity greater than that found among other hunters.

also of complex and sophisticated knowledge in order to play the male role. The Australian male initiation rites where they occur are then not to be understood only or even primarily as rites of passage into masculinity in contrast with femininity (though they include this aspect), but rather as rites of passage which qualify a boy to participate in the ceremonies of his cult lodge. Women, among some Australians, conduct secret rituals concerned with mundane issues such as the acquisition of love magic for attracting mates.

Not all Australians have male initiation rites. For example, there are no such rites among the Tiwi. Here women collect small animals with the help of dogs and distribute their catch to other women to be cooked. Related to this may be the fact that both men and women are eligible for initiation into a Kulama yam cult. The yam cult, somewhat like the European secret society of Masons, has degrees of membership, and inititation takes many years to complete (Goodale 1971).[5]

I/9 SUMMARY AND CONCLUSIONS

The subsistence economy of hunters and gatherers operates in small loosely structured local bands consisting of several conjugal pairs and their dependents. Material resources for subsistence are equally available to men and women in their separate spheres of activity. Failures of skill, industry, or of local environmental resources need not be disastrous for the individuals concerned because of the patterns of exchange and distribution. Leadership roles are limited to the persuasive influence exercised by skilled hunters, by women who are skillful and forceful enough to attract their married offspring to live with them as adults, and by older people who have shamanistic or other supernatural skills. None of these types of leaders have the power to coerce others. Disputes are sometimes settled by consultation with elders, sometimes by public contests between the disputants, with the audience deciding the winner. If the parties to the dispute are irreconcilable—and this includes cases in which husbands and wives are the disputants—one individual or the other, or both, may move off to join another band, though sometimes homicides and feuds cannot be avoided.

In this situation of political and economic egalitarianism, apart from age differences, the only major permanent social division is that between men and women: and men and women each control some of the resources and services required by the other. Economic and sexual cooperation between them is necessary, but their interdependence is full of difficulties. Finding sex partners is not easy; all men are not successful hunters, all women are not industrious gatherers; the actual division of food is always subject to judgment and criticism; not all men and women are potent and fertile; nor are all children healthy. Under these conditions, the cleavage between men and women can be great, and relationships are sometimes hostile. Nevertheless, both men and women have considerable autonomy, and those of each sex have, in most foraging societies, the basis for acquiring self-esteem.

The most important difference between the power of men and women to control

[5] Goodale refers to the Kulama Yam ceremonies as if they involved initiation into the society as a whole. My interpretation, as seen above, is that they concern only initiation into a kind of separate cult group.

others lies in the male monopoly of individual and small-group hunts. This gives men the opportunity for large extradomestic exchanges of meat, a source of power over others not available to women. The general principle that the generous distribution of scarce or irregularly available resources is a source of power, and that men and women differ with respect to their opportunities in this respect, is, as we have already stated, a significant element in understanding the roles of the sexes. (Our discussion of horticultural societies will deal with the issue once again.) Male dominance is greatest where hunting is the sole source of food (Eskimo, pp. 39–45 below); it is least, and equality is greatest, where men and women work together in the major tasks of acquiring subsistence (Washo, pp. 34–36 below).

Before turning to the horticulturalists, we shall give brief descriptions of four societies each of which exemplifies one of the varieties of sexual division in subsistence activities already listed. The emphasis is on the relationship of the sexual division to other aspects of the roles of the sexes.

Illustrative Cultures I

FOUR PATTERNS OF DIFFERENTIAL CONTRIBUTION TO SUBSISTENCE: THEIR INFLUENCE ON SEX ROLES

Men and Women Collect Plants Separately; Male Hunting is Minimal: The Hadza of Tanzania (Woodburn 1968)

The Hadza live in dry, rocky savanna country. Rain falls heavily during six months of the year; the other half of the year is a dry season. In the wet season they gather roots and kill small game like the hyrax, a rabbitlike creature. Their camps are small and widely dispersed.

In the dry season the Hadza collect berries and hunt large game, like rhinoceros, buffalo, and impala. At this time the camps are concentrated near water holes, and there are many more households settled together than during the wet season.

Vegetable foods provide 80 percent of the Hadza diet, meat and honey accounting for the remaining 20 percent. The caloric value of the meat and honey, however, is disproportionally high. There is never a shortage of food. What is eaten depends almost entirely on the amount of effort people wish to expend in the quest for food.

Hadza women collect vegetable food almost every day. They go in groups with their children to spots usually about an hour's walk from the camp. They eat their fill as they collect, eating berries raw, and roasting some roots for immediate consumption. They bring back what they collect only after each woman and her children have satisfied their hunger. Only about half of the food brought back is given to the men in the camp.

Men go off for short periods each day to gather vegetable foods to satisfy their own hunger. Whatever hunting is done is the work of men and boys pursuing game individually, armed with bows and arrows. The arrows are poisoned to bring down large animals. Men eat at the site of a kill and bring back only the meat left over. Meat from small animals is sometimes brought back to camp and eaten by the men (not the women) there. Whatever meat from large animals has not been consumed at the hunting site is widely distributed at the camp and is eaten immediately.

In the dry season men spend more time gambling than hunting (women do not gamble), and those who lose arrows to the winners are prevented from hunting until new ones can be acquired. In any case, it is men up to the age of about 30 that are the big-game hunters, so that most of the large animals are killed by a minority of

33

the men. These successful hunters attract others to their camps to share in the distribution.

Individual Hadza men and women, and even children after the age of 10, are capable each of providing enough food to sustain himself or herself. Thus, except for the case of young children fed by their mothers, only the meat from large game is received from anyone else. Such meat, however, is the most highly prized food among the Hadza. Honey is also greatly relished, but appears to be used mostly as an article of trade.

Apart from hunting, men also monopolize trade. They exchange honey and hides for beads, tobacco, and cloth with non-Hadza neighbors.

Individuals are free to move from one camp to another. Marriage is regarded as having occurred when a man, usually in his early twenties, and a woman somewhat younger live together in the same shelter and travel together for some time. The couple tend to stay in the camp of the wife's mother (and her father if he is still alive and not divorced from her mother). Less frequently the couple join the camp of the husband's mother. A man acquires his initial right to the sexual services of his wife by providing his mother-in-law with a string of beads early in the marriage. After that, he maintains this right by keeping his wife and mother-in-law supplied with trade goods, and by giving them priority in the distribution of meat from large-game kills when this is under his control.

Divorce is signalled by the couple's living apart for more than a few days. The children usually accompany the mother. Divorce rates are high—roughly five times as high as in the United States. In spite of this, marriage is the most stable relationship among the Hadza, in the sense that the affinal obligation of a man to his wife and his mother-in-law is the most binding of any property or other obligation these people have to each other, the mother-and-child (and particularly the mother-and-daughter) relationship alone excepted.

Since a regular sexual bond between a man and a woman is the basis for the only kind of restraint in human relationships among the Hadza, it is also the major source of antagonisms. The cleavage between males and females is therefore by all odds the significant social division among the Hadza.

Autonomy for men, women, and children in this society is probably at its greatest. Masculine opportunities to acquire self-esteem and public recognition are slightly better than those of women, through the men's monopolistic control of the distribution of the proceeds of large-game hunting, limited though they be. Their hunting of game and gathering of honey also gives them a monopoly on trade and the goods derived from it. Older women have an advantage as receivers of trade-goods and meat from sons-in-law, if several live with them; but public prestige is reserved for hunters who distribute their kill.

Men and Women Work Together in Communal Task Forces To Acquire a Significant Segment of Subsistence: The Washo of the Great Basin of North America (Downs 1966)

The Washo inhabited a series of valleys to the east of the Sierra Nevada Mountains, and moved east and west and up 6000 feet to Lake Tahoe as the food search required. Winter was the most sedentary period when several nuclear families and their dependents occupied a cluster of houses. Throughout the winter the men did a little fishing and hunting, but spent most of their time manufacturing hunting weapons, while women wove baskets from willow withes collected in late summer. They lived on the pine-nut flour, grass seeds, and dried meat which they had collected and prepared during the other seasons of the year.

In early spring the young men and boys, and sometimes unmarried girls, left the winter camp for the trek up to Lake Tahoe, which abounded in whitefish at this time, and around which spring bulbs and woodchuck could be found. It was a period for games of all kinds, and when the girls were present for courtship and informal sexual relations. Young Washo from different regions of the wider area came together at this time. Young men were expected to display their hardiness and strength to each other and to the girls, if any.

Later in the spring the rest of the Washo moved up to the lake, and those of all ages—men, women, and children—joined in catching the large runs of sucker and native trout which appeared at that time. Apparently no special skill was required for catching these fish when the runs were on. Surplus fish were dried for future use.

During most of the spring, therefore, the division of labor was organized by age rather than by sex. In the summer this changed as the household groups moved still further up. There the women gathered and ground seeds, and dried and ground berries; the men did difficult and skilled fishing in the smaller lakes and streams. The men also set fish traps and platforms, which were owned by the individuals or households that set them up.

Late summer and early fall were the important hunting seasons. Young boys and old men went after chipmunks and squirrels, which were hunted with arrows, as was the larger game. Women dug gophers and ground squirrels out of their holes. Mature men hunted deer, alone or in groups of six or eight hunters, who left their families to go off on a hunt for two weeks or a month. They might bring back 80 or 100 pounds of deer meat per man, for they were expert stalkers. Some of this meat was dried for the winter. Even more important than the deer were the western jackrabbit, hunted in early fall as the Washo returned to the lowlands. The rabbits were either driven by several men and women into a small area where men could shoot them with bow and arrow, or, a more efficient process, they were driven into the combined nets of several families, who joined together for the purpose of this rabbit hunt. Hunting of antelope was a large-scale event, accompanied by ritual, which depended on the rare appearance of antelope in the vicinity; this, like the deer hunt, was the exclusive province of the men.

The final effort in the fall, before the winter set in, was the gathering of pine nuts, or pinyon nuts, as they are called. A large number of families gathered for this activity, but a husband and wife usually worked as team to knock the pine cones off the trees. The nuts had then to be removed from the cones, and prepared by various cooking processes. After about a month of this work, the final move to winter quarters began. The old people and children were left behind to watch the nut supply, while the mature men and women trekked back and forth carrying the tons of nuts that had been collected, until the whole supply was stored in the winter settlement. To carry the nuts the men used a tumpline around their heads, thus leaving their hands free for shooting such game as might appear on the way, although it was not a good season for game. The women, with no pretensions to hunting, used a tumpline around the chest. Men butchered and dried meat when away on a hunt, and both men and women apparently prepared rabbits for drying and worked over the skins. The sewing of the skins into aprons, blankets, and bedding was woman's work, as was the pounding of seeds into flour.

The nuclear family and its dependents were the separable social units among the Washo. They combined and separated much in the way those of the Hadza do. But the Washo differ from the Hadza in that a substantial portion of the protein supply from game and fish was obtained by many households acting in concert and sharing in the proceeds of the activity. Here cooperation in the collection of food rather than kinship was the basis for distribution. Thus the importance of affinal relationships in themselves as a primary channel for food distribution was greatly diminished.

Moreover, the proportion of protein derived from individual and small-group hunts by men was relatively small. This diminished the importance for nutrition of men's extradomestic distributions of meat. Still, the prestige accorded the deer slayer who did give away his meat remained high.

Men and women were not segregated from each other in many of their daily activities; their networks of association with other persons were relatively similar.

In cases in which no man wished to exercise the relatively slight degree of band leadership accepted by the Washo, a woman could take over the role and make decisions concerning band movements and the like.

Shamanism was open to both men and women in adulthood as well as in old age. Men and women received the same training once they found—as the Washo believed—that they could not resist the call of the spirits.

Life-cycle rituals included a menarche rite for girls, with a public phase in which the girl's economic and sexual role was celebrated. However, at this time the girl's menstrual blood was believed to be dangerous only to the girl herself and not to others, either men or women. Indeed the ambiguous power of menstruation that was stressed in the ceremonies was symbolically represented as beneficent and strengthening, not as dangerous and polluting. After the menarche menstruating women were required to keep away from hunting weapons. A boy's first large kill was marked by a private ritual, after which he was considered marriageable. After the birth of a child the father was subject to ritual activities and taboos similar to those required of girls during the menarchical period.

The two large-scale public rituals which brought Washo from different regions together were the Antelope Hunt which occurred at irregular intervals, and the "Big Time" held annually before the beginning of the pinyon-nut harvest. The hunt ritual celebrated man as hunter; women were excluded from some of the ceremonies. The "Big Time" celebrated the woman as a gatherer. Men were not excluded, but they did not participate in the ritual, except that the leader of the ceremonies had to be a man. All women, by contrast, were required during the "Big Time" to take a ritual bath every day.

The Washo are an example of a society with a balanced interdependence of the sexes for economic and sexual services, and only a limited difference in opportunities for distribution available to each sex. Tensions and hostilities between men and women are likely to have been slight.

!Kung woman carrying child as she gathers food. (Courtesy of Lorna Marshall)

!Kung woman digging for roots. (Courtesy of Lorna Marshall)

Women Gather More than Half the Food Supply; Men's Hunting Accounts for 20 to 40 Percent of Subsistence: The !Kung Bushmen of the Kalahari Desert, Botswana (Marshall 1965 and Lee 1972).[6]

The !Kung Bushmen live in a dry semidesert with heavy rainfalls occurring only during the summer months. Water is scarce under these conditions, and the Bushmen group themselves around permanent water holes, or at the furthest within four or five miles of them. Among some groups of Bushmen the holes and the vegetation near them are "owned" by a man, but his consanguineal and affinal kin can join him, and other visitors are usually welcome to gather or hunt in the area. Alternatively, two or more bands may share in the use of a water hole.

Wild plant foods include a variety of roots and berries, but the mangetti or mongongo nuts, and a particular kind of seed are the most important foods, being rich in oils and vegetable proteins. Game animals are not abundant, and the hunters of a band often do not kill more than 18 large animals (such as a kudu with 100 lbs. of meat, or an eland with 190) in a year. Smaller animals, like the wart hog (35 lbs. of meat) or the springbok (25 lbs.) are also hunted.

Women do the gathering, going out every two or three days. In the morning they walk the five or ten miles from camp to a spot where they know particular foods are available. As we have seen, they carry their children with them, and return in the early afternoon. Men gather food for themselves while on the hunt, and also help women to transport loads of mangogo nuts and seeds when they are abundant and the loads are heavy. The vegetable foods are prepared separately for each household. Although women may distribute some to their kin in the camp, there is no rule requiring them to do so. Among the Bushmen in the Dobe area, by contrast, women apparently pool the vegetable foods, and members of the camp draw from the common source. This does not, however, involve the giving of food by individual women to individual recipients, so that individual reciprocal obligations are not incurred.

Men hunt with bows and poisoned arrows and with spears. They usually hunt in pairs, but occasionally go long distances in groups of 10 or 12. Women sometimes help to transport meat back to camp. Men do not hunt regularly; now and then they take a week or even a month off from the hunt. Meat from large game, as we have come to expect, is shared out in the camp, but in a manner slightly different from that which we have described for other groups. The hunter who has killed the animal makes the initial distribution only if he owns the poisoned arrow which was the first to stay in the slaughtered beast. Arrows are lent and borrowed around, so that often a man uses a missile not his own. In that case, the owner of the arrow receives the meat left after the initial distribution to the task force of hunters, if there has been one. Occasionally even a woman may receive an arrow as a gift and give it to a hunter to use; this entitles her to a moderate share of the meat in the first distribution. Among the Dobe Bushmen this practice apparently does not exist, and men distribute their own kills.

[6] The people here described are the !Kung Bushmen (the sign ! denotes a glottal click) studied by Marshall, with occasional reference to those described by Lee. The differences between the groups will be mentioned only occasionally.

After the first distribution, a man with meat must cut it up and redistribute it, first to his wife's parents, with whom he may be living, then to his wife and children, and then to his own parents. After this, he keeps a portion for himself, and gives some of it to his brothers and sisters and his wife's brothers and sisters, if they are in the camp, and still further to other kin and affines. Each person who receives meat in the final distribution considers it his own, and cooks and eats the piece by himself, not in the nuclear family group.

Aside from subsistence activities and the manufacture of weapons, which they do separately, men and women share many routine tasks. Only men, however, are eligible to become curers, and most !Kung men during dance ceremonies can go into the trances through which it is believed they are able to accomplish cures. Apparently only men can act as headmen of bands and "own" water holes and the vegetation surrounding them.

Residence among the Bushmen involves bride service by a man to his wife's parents for an indefinite number of years, usually 5 or 10, after which the couple may stay or move to join other kin. Among the Dobe Bushmen the core group of members of a band is a set of brothers and sisters joined by the wives of the former and the husbands of the latter. These newcomers sometimes bring their own siblings to join the group.

Girls at an age ranging from some years before to shortly after puberty are married to boys who are slightly older and have not been married before. First marriages are often arranged by parents. In the early years of marriage husbands and wives separate easily on the initiative of either. This also occurs later. However, if several children are born to them, there appears to be a much greater likelihood that a couple will stay together.

Rituals include a menarche ceremony for girls in which they are thought dangerous to themselves and to the hunting skills of men who might see them. Two old men, however, join the women present at the ritual in singing sexually explicit songs, and in dancing erotic dances.

Girls must afterward go through a purification ritual whenever they use a new area of vegetation for the first time after menarche. Subsequent menstruations are, as we have come to expect, thought dangerous to men's hunting weapons. Sexual intercourse at the time of menstruation, it is believed, may make a husband weak and thin. Otherwise, women go about their tasks as usual.

Men go through a private ritual after killing the first male animal, and then after the first female animal. In recent years a form of group male initiation ceremony has been introduced, but it is not obligatory.

Among the !Kung, women as well as men are vociferous in expressing their opinions on all topics. Adultery by either husband or wife can bring on divorce. Men and women, in sum, both have considerable autonomy and substantial bases of self-esteem.

Men's Hunting Provides Almost All Food; Women Process All Food and Skins: North Alaskan Eskimo (Chance 1966; Spencer 1959, 1972; Burch and Correll 1972)

The Eskimo of northern Alaska consist of two different groups. The first are inland Eskimo who travel regularly in search of caribou, their main source of livelihood; the second, the maritime Eskimo, live in coastal villages of some 300 inhabitants each for all but the summer months, and depend on whaling, seal fishing, and occasional hunting for their sources of subsistence. The inland groups depend on trade with the maritime Eskimo, exchanging their caribou hides for whale and seal oil and other coastal products.

Among both groups, men do all the hunting, and move as far from camps and for as long a period of time as is necessary. The women stay at the camps. Women process the carcasses brought in by the men and cut and sew skins, making clothing for the household, and keeping it supple and in repair. Women also cook and care for the young children.

Because of the special skills required to sew fur clothing and to keep it in good repair in an Arctic environment where temperatures drop to 20° and 30° below zero during the winter, it is customary, in discussions of Eskimo culture and society, to emphasize the complementary, interdependent character of the husband-and-wife relationship, and the need of every Eskimo for a wife as an economic partner. What is usually overlooked is the almost complete dependence of the women on the men for all foodstuffs, and for the raw materials, carcasses, which the women process.

Correspondingly, Eskimo men are burdened with the sole responsibility for food provision in an environment in which food sources are so unreliable that periods of famine in which a number of relatives die from hunger are known in every generation.

In place of food exchange between men and women, we have here a system in which, apart from the question of sexual access, a woman furnishes a man with her services as tanner, tailor, cook, and housekeeper in return for her and her children's subsistence.

Among the inland groups men's knowledge of the details of environmental conditions, gained from their hunting expeditions, gives them the information by which to make decisions concerning the necessary movements of the group. Women have neither the knowledge nor the experience to participate in these decisions.

In both inland and maritime groups households consist of nuclear families with dependents or attachments. Several nuclear families whose members are related through close consanguineal or affinal ties usually camp together or form one household.

Meat acquired by men hunting alone is usually distributed to household members and others present. What is left over is cached by inland Eskimo, or, on the coast, is stored in ice cellars. The stored meat belongs to the wife of the hunter. She is responsible for dispensing it at meals. She is also expected to give some to any consanguineal or affinal relative, or trading partner of her husband's who is in need and asks for meat.

The inland Eskimo have two major communal caribou drives each year when the herds come through in large numbers. The coastal Eskimo hunt whale, especially in the spring, in boat crews of four or five men. By his participation in individual and cooperative hunts, and through trading, a man can accumulate private wealth, and thus validate his position as a successful hunter. It is of some importance for Eskimo men, therefore, to have the means of attracting other men to join them in cooperative hunts. Among the inland Eskimo a hunter known for his previous successes and generosity in distributing meat he acquired through his lone hunts is accepted as organizer and leader of caribou drives. When such a cooperative hunt is finished, the meat is shared out among the entire group of hunters, each man then distributing his share to the members of his household.

Among the maritime Eskimo the head of a whaling crew usually owns the boat. The crew are usually not kin, but simply men willing to join the leader, whose skill and experience seem to guarantee success. Whaling crews constitute relatively permanent associations, each having a special *karigi* or men's house, which is used as the ritual center before the spring hunts. It is also used as a recreation center at other times, primarily, although not exclusively, for men. Another trait connected with the whaling crew is the practice whereby the head of the crew may undertake to become the host at a special community feast.

The distribution of whale meat involves first some for the entire community. Then there is a sharing-out among the boat crew or crews responsible for killing the whale, with the choice parts and the surplus going to the head of the crew. He is obligated, however, to give some of his share to those who helped him with the preparations for the hunt, including the shaman who sometimes performs rituals for its success. It is only if a man's crew brings in more than one whale in a season that he can have a real surplus for himself. Otherwise, when his share is consumed, he lives on what his consanguineal kin have available.

Furthermore, even in cases in which the head of a crew does accumulate an actual surplus in his ice cellars, it is customary to require that he empty his cellars of whale meat before each new whaling season, his wife cooking all the meat that is left and distributing it to the young boys of the community who are not yet old enough for whaling.

Among the inland Eskimo a leader of caribou hunts often acquires sufficient prestige to attract men who, with their households, travel with him and form semipermanent bands. The members of these groups tend to follow his advice concerning hunting and traveling, and he often acts as an arbiter of disputes among the men. Among the maritime groups the whale boat owners perform similar functions, except that each settlement usually has several such leaders and arbiters.

These opportunities for achievement among men are augmented by the chance men have to become successful traders through the trading partnerships. As a result, some Eskimo are able to amass wealth in the form of cached meat, seal oil, whaling boats, hunting equipment, and the like, which is available for judicious distribution to their kin and friends. As is common among foraging peoples, no permanent institutionalized leadership exists among the Eskimo, nor is leadership desired for its own sake. The position of social prominence which a successful hunter or whaler achieves seems to be a by-product of his acquisition and generous distribution of goods, rather than the primary goal of his efforts: this goal is to validate his skill as a hunter.

Women, as nonhunters, are obviously excluded from the complex of acquisition and distribution which we have just described for the men. Both men and women can, however, achieve power as shamans; we shall return to this subject later.

All Eskimo men, whether or not they expect to become leaders or shamans, compete with each other constantly in respect to their skills and physical strength, each always measuring himself against the others. The competition is overt in games, in public contests of skill, and in shamanistic combats. Nowhere, however, is rivalry more forcefully expressed among men than in their constant competition for women. And comparatively few women are available. Infanticide, though sometimes applied to new-born boys, is most common in the case of infant girls.

The Eskimo men are interested in women, however, not only as wives with whom they form an economic team, but also simply as sex partners. Both before and after her marriage, a woman's sexual services are considered somewhat like a commodity that men can take, give, receive, and exchange with one another.

Both before and after marriage an Eskimo man tries to have sex with women for two reasons, apart from mere physical gratification. First, he does so as a form of continuing male competition. Second, and more importantly, he tries in this way to establish alliances with other men.

These Eskimo are ready to kill any "stranger." A stranger is defined by them not as a man from a different region, but rather as one with whom no kind of "friendship" or alliance has been negotiated. Men, therefore, constantly make efforts to establish some connection with as many other men as possible.

Routinely, alliances consist of (1) consanguineal and kin connections, (2) longtime association as taskmates in whaling crews, and (3) the relationships established between men to whom children are given or from whom they are taken in adoption. To these three types we can now add a fourth, that of men who have arranged peaceably to share the same woman. This explains the second motivation for sexual activity mentioned above. The agreement to share the woman is made with or without her consent.

After puberty a girl is considered fair game as a sexual object for any man who desires her. He grabs her by the belt as a sign of his intentions. If she is reluctant, he may cut off her trousers with a knife and proceed to force her into intercourse. Whether the girl consents or not, these transitory sexual encounters are regarded as matters of no particular importance among the Eskimo. They are not occasions for vengeful action on the part of her kin, nor do they lessen her desirability as a sex partner or wife, unless she comes to be known as especially promiscuous. If pregnancy results, it is taken as proof of her fertility, and the child is accepted like any other in the household. Physical and verbal aggression among men is frowned on, but sexual aggression against women in the form of abduction or sexual violence is common.

The pattern of obtaining a young woman by direct assault is also followed by older, successful hunters seeking a second wife, or by wife-seeking shamans who, it is believed, can use supernatural as well as physical force in the process. Ordinarily, a girl's first marriage is with a man of her own age, and her agreement is sought. The young groom may come and work with the girl's father for a time, or give him a gift of a seal carcass as a token "bride service." Although once children are born marriages are relatively stable, it is possible for husband and wife to separate at times of economic necessity.

After marriage a man still seeks the wives of other men. Sometimes he succeeds with the cooperation of the adulterous wife; at other times, he resorts to outright rape.

The husband of a married woman who has been adulterous can either ignore the woman and the adulterer with what the Eskimos consider a proper lack of emotion, or he can become "friends" with the other man in one of two ways: either by forcing the man's wife into intercourse in his turn, thus putting the two men in the position of sharing the sexual services of the two women, or by demanding and receiving material compensation. Finally, the two men may fight; if blood is shed, the matter turns into a feud between the close bilateral kin of both.

In more amicable ways men negotiate alliances by exchanging wives with trading partners, by temporarily leaving a wife with a "friend" while the husband is away on a trading expedition, or by giving sexual access to the wife to a visitor with whom the husband wants to establish a relationship.

We have considered economic and sexual relations among Eskimo men and women; we can now turn to the forms of control which Eskimo exercise over their children. Men and women among the Eskimo want children, not only because of the pleasure they take in raising them, but also because their children are the consanguineal kin, sons and daughters, upon whom they can depend for support in their old age. But providing food for children and transporting them, among inland groups in particular, is not easy to accomplish; too many children can threaten the survival of the entire group. An important decision, then, that a couple has to make is whether or not to increase the size of their family. Apparently neither *coitus interruptus* nor mechanical contraceptives are known. Songs sung by certain old women are believed to have contraceptive effects and are sometimes resorted to. Women, with or without the consent of their husbands, sometimes try to induce abortion by leaping from a high place or by applying pressure to the abdomen. Abortion may be resorted to in order to space children, or to prevent a woman from being incapacitated on a long journey. Once born, infants can be killed or abandoned. The decision is probably made jointly by husband and wife; a disagreement between them can lead to abandonment of the wife or separation. Finally, the Eskimo have still another way to reduce the size of a family: that of giving children in adoption, a common practice.

A couple with more children than they feel they can care for can give a child to a kinsman or kinswoman who has few or no children, or to a nonrelative in like case. These decisions are apparently made jointly by husbands and wives both at the giving and the receiving end. Adopted children have all the rights and privileges of natural children in their adoptive families.

We started the discussion of marriage and sex relations among the Eskimo by saying that these form an area of keen competition among men and women. What is the woman's stake in these arrangements, and how much control can she exercise over her own economic and sexual destinies? The answer is not entirely clear. Most evidence suggests that, within the household and in marriage, men make the decisions and women obey orders. However, a woman can leave a husband who is a poor hunter, and ask her kin to raise her children. Women also are free to decide not to accompany a husband on a trading expedition or other travel, although a woman who frequently returns to her parents is subject to her husband's wrath and may be given a good beating. It is primarily in sexual matters that a woman is viewed as if she were her husband's property. She can, however, occasionally participate in an affair on her own initiative, as we have seen.

In any case, a docile and industrious wife can count upon the economic support of her husband and can share in whatever prestige he acquires. Her acquiescence in his disposal of her sexual services is, in the long run, beneficial to her and her children. It is important to realize also that, especially among the inland groups, when the Eskimo are traveling and a woman's consanguineal kin are not in the vicinity, her survival depends on her obeying her husband; she has no alternative.

Shamanism is the one exception to the picture we have drawn. Individuals, men and women alike, who behave erratically are thought to be possessed by spirits who are summoning them to become shamans. If they succumb to the call, they embark on a career of controlling these spirits. The shaman's power over the spirits is demonstrated by spectacular performances. These include, on the one hand, tricks like sleight-of-hand, and escaping from tight thongs by which the shaman is bound; on the other, behavior typical of trance states, such as the ability to stick knives into the body and withdraw them without leaving wounds or other marks of injury. Shamans are believed to be able both to cure illness by revealing the moral transgression which the ill person is believed to have committed, and which caused the malady, and also to cause illness and even death.

If, as we have seen, women are excluded from most material sources of power among the Eskimo, how can we account for their eligibility to become shamans? Among the north Alaskan Eskimos, masculine shamans tend to be those who are unskilled in hunting, and thus barred not only from material possessions but also from the esteem of their fellows. Whether the Eskimo realize it or not, shamanism is a substitute avenue toward prestige and prominence for those men who are peripheral members of the society. Through payments which others make to them of meat, seal oil, and even wives, in return for their performances, the shamans have the means of acquiring what the Eskimo value. In the light of this, it is understandable that women, who are also peripheral to the main activities of Eskimo life, that is, also debarred from the avenues of esteem available to successful hunters, should become shamans. This usually occurs after the menopause, but women can practice shamanism even before the climacteric so long as they are not actually menstruating at the time of the performance. Wives of shamans, in particular, are apt to practice in their own right. Shamanism among the Eskimo is a form of controlled possession, exercised in part in the interests of the norms of the society but by individuals who are peripheral to it.

Symbolic and ritual forms to mark maturity are simple household ceremonies. At the time their voices change boys are given a suit of adult clothing by their women relatives. In late adolescence a father has his son's lip cut to enable him to wear a lipplug or labret. After this he is considered ready for marriage and is expected to behave like an adult, accompanying the older men regularly on hunting parties. In parallel fashion, a girl is given adult clothing when her breasts begin to develop, and is tattooed on the chin (no labret is inserted) at some time during her adolescence.

At the menarche the girl is secluded inside the house for five days. Here symbolic emphasis is placed on the separation of male hunting from female menstruation. The girl cannot touch or eat any raw or bloody meat, and has to avoid touching hunting weapons so as not to impair a man's luck in the chase. The girl and menstruating women in general are believed to be dangerous to shamanistic powers as well.

In contrast with the Washo where the women, important contributors to the nutrition of the people, are presented in a public ritual once the menarche is over, the Eskimo girl is accorded no public recognition either at or just after her menarche or at any other time. During subsequent menstruations a woman is required to wear old clothes set aside for use only during these periods, and is not permitted to urinate inside the house (the Eskimo collect the urine of household members in a single vessel to use in curing skins). Among the inland Eskimo a separate menstrual hut is built; on the coast a menstruating woman is restricted to one part of the house during the day: she can sleep next to her husband, but they are not permitted intercourse. In both groups menstruating women are prohibited from eating raw and bloody meat, but otherwise they can continue all normal household activities, including working on game.

The major communal rituals of the Eskimo are associated not with maturation or with male-female cleavages, but with the spring whale hunt among the coastal groups and the caribou drive among the inland people. We shall limit ourselves to a brief mention of the whale hunt ceremonial. Here, the material function of women as helpmeets of their husbands is clearly replicated by the special ritual functions performed by the wives of the crew leaders. They are believed able to assist in assuring the success of their husbands' hunt by singing special songs, by cooking in ritual fashion, by observing eating taboos, and by maintaining quiet behavior throughout. In this instance a woman's participation as helpmeet of the man is thought so essential that if the wife of a crew leader is menstruating, a substitute for her has to be found.

A final remark may help to place this stark picture of Eskimo male dominance and female submissiveness in a somewhat more familiar perspective. The strong orientation of Eskimo men toward competitive achievement in which skill at obtaining sexual access to women is highly regarded, and the men's virtual monopoly on basic resources, with the strains to which the men are subjected because of the responsibility which this monopoly involves: all these factors put these Eskimo women in a structural position strikingly similar to that well known to us from middle-class life in the United States. Women are more socially isolated than men, they compete and hope for marriage—either temporary or permanent—to a good provider (Eskimo divorced couples, like Americans in similar case, retain some rights and obligations in relation to each other and their children), they run his household for him, they have supporting rights and duties to help him in the accomplishment of his tasks and in his rivalries. The only ways in which they can gain self-esteem are directly from their household skills and their young children's behavior, and vicariously from their husbands' standing in the community.

PART II

Horticultural Societies

The invention of plant and animal domestication, that is, the point at which hunters and gatherers began deliberately to plant roots or seeds and deliberately to feed and shelter animals near their settlements, occurred only about 10,000 years ago. Since that time the system has spread from the centers where it began into a wide variety of environments, and has encompassed the domestication of many different kinds of crops and animals. In the form called agriculture and animal husbandry, it is the subsistence base of contemporary industrial societies.

In this part we shall limit our discussion of sex roles to those societies in which the system of plant cultivation is called horticulture rather than agriculture. In horticulture the preparation of the soil and the planting itself are accomplished with the aid of a hoe and digging stick, and not with a plow drawn by draught animals or machines. Horticulturalists at the time of the first European explorations were the people whom the Europeans found cultivating plants, rather than hunting and gathering, in the Pacific Islands, in Africa south of the Sahara, in North and South America, and in various enclaves in Asia. They are the "tribal" peoples extensively studied by anthropologists, and on whom we have the most plentiful anthropological information.

Horticulture remains today the basic source of subsistence for many of those rural descendants of the original cultivators who have neither been driven off the land by colonial farmers nor become completely dependent on commercial crops and agricultural wage labor. The economy of almost all contemporary horticulturalists, with the possible exception of some Indians in the tropical forests of South America and some peoples of highland New Guinea, is integrated with the world economy, including the use of money. It is with the early stages of this mixed development that we shall be principally concerned.

The planting of crops as a technique for food acquisition resulted in marked differences for horticulturalists as compared with hunters and gatherers, not only in work habits but also in social, political, and religious organization.

The diversity of social and cultural systems which is compatible with horticulture as a subsistence technique is considerably greater than that for foragers. The bases for sex role differentiation and the types of relationships which exist between the sexes are correspondingly more numerous. Indeed, it is from among horticultural peoples that anthropologists have traditionally drawn examples with which to demonstrate cultural diversity in sex roles.

We shall begin this part with a description of horticultural techniques. We shall then describe those basic differences between hunters and gatherers and horticulturalists which accompany these practices. We shall go on to consider what generalizations can be made about the consequences of these differences for the roles of the sexes. The end of the part includes brief ethnographic descriptions of two societies as illustrations of two recurring patterns.

II/1   HORTICULTURAL CROPS AND TECHNOLOGY

Techniques

Horticulture is a technique of cultivation carried on principally in tropical forests and in savannas, that is, tropical or subtropical grasslands. In this type of cultivation land must regularly be cleared of its cover of wild vegetation before it is ready for planting. This is commonly done for wooded areas by the slash and burn method. Trees and underbrush are cut down and then burned on the spot, with the ash constituting the only fertilizer. After a few years of cultivation the land has to lie fallow for as many as eight to ten years before the nutriments which have been exhausted by the plantings return to the soil. The wild plant growth which has accumulated is then cleared again.

Comparatively large tracts of land are required for this system so that population densities remain low as compared with plow agriculture but are higher than those for most foragers. A variant of the slash and burn method just described is one in which each section of cleared land is planted for only two or three successive years, and then allowed to lie fallow for two or three more. This second type requires more labor for each unit of land. It is a slightly more intensive system of cultivation and supports somewhat larger densities of population.

Vegetable Crops and Protein Sources

The two basic types of staple food crops raised by these methods are: first, root crops and fruits such as the sweet potato, taro, yam, and banana cultivated in the Pacific Islands and parts of West Africa, or the manioc (tapioca, cassava) of tropical South America; second, cereal crops like the millets and maize of East Africa and the maize of parts of North and South America, and rice in parts of Asia.

In both systems of shifting horticulture any domesticated animals raised, such as cattle or pigs, are used as prestige objects in exchanges, as repositories for wealth to be saved or exchanged in trade, or as animals for ritual sacrifice. They become a source of meat at whatever point in the ritual cycle they are killed. Cattle also provide milk for some horticulturalists. The animal dung is not usually an important source of fertilizer, nor do the beasts carry or drag burdens.

If the meat of domestic animals is an occasional source of food, how do horticulturalists get animal proteins? Hunting is of limited value because the slash and burn method destroys, around human settlements, the vegetation on which wild animals depend for food, as well as their usual cover. In a few inland South American tropical forest areas, to be sure, hunting does constitute the main source of protein. Fishing is a better source, and many horticulturalists who live on islands or along coasts or near rivers or streams supplement their diet with fish and other marine creatures. In general, however, the level of animal protein in the diet of many horticulturalists is quite low.

The human energy expended by horticulturalists on obtaining subsistence is probably not appreciably greater than that among foragers. An average, over the year, of some three hours' work daily per person is a reasonable estimate.

II/2   MAJOR DIFFERENCES BETWEEN HORTICULTURALISTS AND FORAGERS

There are a number of significant differences between societies dependent on hunting and gathering and those dependent on horticulture.

Permanence of Settlements

Settlements more permanent than those of hunters and gatherers are possible. Women are likely to have to walk less both each day and each year; they need less energy to carry children. As a result, higher procreation rates are possible, though not always achieved.

Size and Density of Population

The range of population size and of population density is therefore much greater for horticultural societies than for foragers. Some horticultural peoples are numbered in the millions, though small groups of several thousand are also found. Settlements range in size from villages of forty or fifty people to cities of several hundred thousand.

Exchanges

ADAPTIVE VALUE OF INTERLOCAL EXCHANGE SYSTEMS

We saw that among hunting societies it was the distribution of meat to units larger than the household which was essential for survival. In parallel fashion, among horticulturalists the food distributions that seem to have assured survival are those which occur in exchanges among different local groups or communities. The occasional failure of land resources to keep pace with expanding population, the vagaries of rainfall, winds, and temperature, the intermittent appearance of insect pests, all subject the horticulturalist to periods of food shortage. Any system by which different local groups can claim rights to the food of those in neighboring areas who have not been affected by disaster at the same time obviously has great adaptive value.

PATTERNS OF RECIPROCITY AND REDISTRIBUTION

There are several principles in accordance with which exchanges between localities can be arranged. One is the expectation of generalized reciprocity among kin living in different settlements which we saw operating among foragers. Though the unit of *production* for this exchange remains the household, consisting of a nuclear or extended family, and some exchanges continue among these groups as such, a more common unit of *distribution* is the kin group, organized as a corporate body. The transactions can take the form of *redistribution*, either egalitarian or nonegalitarian, in which foodstuffs and other valuables are accumulated in large quantities by persons who have the obligation to redistribute them.

In egalitarian systems the distributor gives as much as he gets, and in the long run gives it back to the original donors. In nonegalitarian systems, persons of an institutionalized higher status receive a great deal more than they expect to redistribute, and maintain permanent reserves of imposing size.

In horticultural societies redistributive exchanges can be elaborated into great ceremonial feasts, in which one person or category of persons, such as a clan, organizes the labor to produce a large quantity of food and valuables and then acts as host to another group. The guest group is expected eventually to reciprocate as hosts on another occasion. Such redistributions frequently occur on the occasion of life-cycle ceremonies, where the activities of participants and contributors are determined by kin obligations, or as part of religious rituals, in which the obligations are defined by the assignment of specific roles to various persons.

Where the rights to organize such exchanges and redistributions are institutionalized and become the prerogative of named officials, such as a chief, a king, or a queen, we have the elements of nonegalitarian political organization of a type generally unknown to hunters and gatherers. Here, for example, the chief of a clan is expected to collect tribute from constituents for distribution at periodic ritual occasions or in time of stress. The recipients of this distribution, the guests, may be either the constituents alone, or groups of outsiders, or both. The total situation also creates opportunities for exchanges of objects of use other than food and valuables. Pottery, baskets, clothing, implements, and other products of crafts can be included in exchanges and in trade.

Trade operates on the principle of balanced reciprocity; an equivalent return of goods or services is expected within a short time. Those with whom trade is permitted depends among some horticulturalists on prior social relationships such as kinship, or specific trading partnerships, but in others trade with anyone who have the commodity one wants is among the possibilities. The medium of exchange used in trade varies. In some societies there is no medium and direct barter suffices. In others special purpose monies are used. These consists of objects like shells or beads or brass rods, which have a standard value but which can be exchanged for only certain specific commodities, such as cattle, pigs, or wives. Among some few horticulturalists ordinary all-purpose money, cash as we know it, is available for trade.

Crafts

A variety of craft skills unknown among hunters and gatherers, including weaving, wood carving, and metal-working, is common among horticulturalists, who also make and use pottery vessels of various kinds.

Land as a Strategic Resource

Among horticulturalists a major strategic resource is the land itself, which is employed as a base for planned production and not merely as a territory where the natural flora and fauna can be exploited. As a result some system of apportioning land for cultivation is customary. The most common system in horticultural societies is for corporate enlarged kinship groups such as lineages or clans, rather than nuclear families, to be considered the owners of the land. They are owners only in the sense that designated elders or officials of the group have the right to allocate plots for cultivation from the corporate holdings to members of the group who are heads of nuclear or extended family households. (The domestic group, or household, as we shall refer to it, is usually the basic social unit for producing food and making ordinary equipment.)

In some societies a man can gain rights to land by merely clearing a new area himself, but once the initial period of cultivation has been completed, even such land reverts to his corporate kinship group.

The land to which a corporate kin group has rights is frequently widely scattered, with holdings of other kin groups intervening.

Some system of inheritance is usually provided for, if only because a man or woman may die while the land he or she has been allotted for use still has several years of productivity before the next fallow period. Use rights can be inherited laterally in the same generation (e.g., by brothers and sisters) or vertically (e.g., by offspring, nephews, or nieces).

Principles of Reckoning Descent

Principles by which people are entitled to rights in corporate kin groups vary among horticultural societies. In some, descent and rights to inheritance and succession are reckoned through men only (patrilineally), in others through women only (matrilineally). These unilinear systems are more common among horticulturalists than among foragers. In other horticultural societies the principle of entitlement is that it is traced equally through men and women (bilateral or cognatic descent). It should be noted that matrilineal descent-reckoning the world over is rare, but to the extent that it occurs, it is found in higher proportion among horticulturalists than elsewhere. Why this should be so is not understood.

Warfare and Alliances

Corporate kin groups (lineages or clans), local groups composed of members of different kin groups, or aggregates into which such groups are organized (tribes) have the obligation to protect the land which they control and its crops from encroachment by others. The critical areas are likely to be at the boundaries of a clan's or tribe's territories, as its members seek to clear new land which may run over onto that about to be used by a neighboring group. Organized warfare for the purpose of defending or expanding territories is endemic with these societies. Once established, the patterns of warfare are extended to include fighting for revenge and for women. Among horticulturalists, then, a considerable portion of the energies of men is usually devoted to training and to preparation for war.

Warfare leads to the need for allies, so that any extension of kin relationship, in addition to providing economic aid and goods and services involved in exchanges, now has the function of furnishing possible assistance in combat. Thus marriage, a source of alliances in warfare as well as in economic matters, is of concern to entire corporate kin groups—to clans, for example, where there are clans—as well as to lineages and their constituent family units.

Marriage

Corporate kin groups are normally exogamous: men and women of one kin group get their wives and husbands from another. Women's procreative functions are considered by kin groups as valuable for increasing the population strength of the corporate group. If, in addition, a woman moves physically at the time of marriage to the household or village of her husband (virilocal residence), and thereby provides, in addition to sexual access and procreative ability, her household services and sometimes horticultural labor for her husband's kin group, a bride price is often paid by the groom's kin to the wife's kin in return. The pattern prevails not only in patrilineally organized but also in matrilineal societies in those cases in which the bride moves out of her parents' household.

The bride price never takes the form of land or the rights to land. Cattle, pigs, shells, hoes, metal rods, or other special purpose monies and, in recent times, cash itself constitute the main types of property. In other words, the movable woman is replaced by movable property.

Bride price can also be paid in the form of labor performed by the groom for his wife's household. (This is similar to what we called bride service among the foragers.) Such labor occurs most commonly in matrilineal societies in cases in which the groom goes to live in the bride's household in a different village (uxorilocal residence). Bride price in goods or services is a feature of marriage transactions most frequently among sub-Saharan African and Melanesian horticulturalists, among whom unilineal kin groups also predominate. On the Polynesian islands a system of relative ranking for both individuals and kin groups results in equal exchanges between the two parties arranging a marriage contract, rather than a transfer of wealth from one party to another.

In Polynesia, individual men and women are typically ranked in each household on the basis of seniority, so that the eldest child, whether girl or boy, has more rights and privileges than the other children, male or female, and so on down. Kin groups reckoned as descendants of elder ancestors outrank those considered to have descended from younger. Here it is important to conserve high rank for future generations, not to mar it by a union with a lower-ranking group. This is accomplished by arranging marriages between senior children in equally high-ranking kin groups, and so on down. Transfers of moveable property at marriage, when they occur at all, are in the form of an equal exchange between the kin of the bride and the kin of the groom of mats, tapa cloth, grass skirts, canoes, and foodstuffs. In Polynesia, these transactions symbolize the equality of rank between the participants.

The causes of the difference in patterns between bride price cultures and those which have equal exchange at marriage are not clear; the matter requires further investigation.

Polygyny is practiced more frequently among horticulturalists than among foragers. This corresponds to the substantially greater accumulation and distribution among horticulturalists of all forms of wealth; women may be considered in the category of valuable possessions.

Residence and Cooperation

In the relatively permanent settlements which we have seen are characteristic of horticulturalists as contrasted with foragers, more than one kin group can be found in any one settlement. Where kin groups are widely separated, relationships between non-kin in a given locality, such as a village, can sometimes be useful. This occurs when the local membership of a kin group does not provide sufficient manpower for the defence of landholdings or when the labor force of a kin group needs to be augmented at peak periods of economic or ceremonial activity.

Rituals

Corporate kin groups and tribes among horticulturalists are concerned with the protection of land not only from encroaching human beings, but also from the disfavor and wrath of gods and spirits. Leaders of kin groups, villages, and tribes (such as lineage priests, headmen and headwomen, and chiefs) conduct rituals at various times in the cultivation cycle for the protection and growth of crops.

In addition, large-scale communal rituals designed for promoting human fertility and welfare, and for helping to achieve success in warfare, are more frequent among horticulturalists than among hunters and gatherers. These are conducted not only by leaders of kin and local groups, but also sometimes by members of special cult associations.

Large-scale initiation ceremonies for both boys and girls are also more frequent among horticulturalists than among foragers; see below, pp. 112–114, 131–133.

Political Organization

Allocation of land for cultivation, the existence of large-scale exchanges, and internal and external warfare, all create situations which would seem to lend themselves to the establishment of formal political controls. In spite of this, some horticulturalists have no more institutionalized leadership roles which include the right to control others than do hunters and gatherers, though even such horticulturalists often assign quasi-judicial functions to the elders of a kin group. Many other horticulturalists, however, have well-developed institutions of political control. Some live under hereditary clan or tribal chiefs with some coercive powers; still others under despotic "paramount" chiefs, often called kings and queens, who have the power of life and death over their subjects and control an administrative structure of lesser chiefs and officials with executive and judicial functions. It was to this last type of political organization that we were referring when we earlier discussed nonegalitarian systems of distribution.

Summary

The salient traits which differentiate horticulturalists from foragers allow in a general way for a larger number of social positions with specific rights and duties and increased opportunities for power over people and events.

It is only against this background that we can understand the much greater diversity that exists among horticulturalists as compared with foragers in the structural positions possible for men and women, in the options available to them with respect to activities and approaches to power, and in the variations which these societies display in the quality of the relationships between the sexes.

II/3 SEXUAL DIVISION OF LABOR

Cultivation

CLEARING THE LAND

The basic characteristic of the division of labor among foragers which was significant for noneconomic sex roles was the male monopoly of hunting. Among horticulturalists men also have what is close to a monopoly: it is the clearing of the fields. Typically, men do the work involved in preparing the land for cultivation, such as felling trees and cutting and firing the underbrush. I suggest that the assignment to men of the initial clearing of the land is a response to conditions in which at least once or twice in every generation some new land requires clearing at the frontiers of a people's holdings. Here the possible need for defense, or for aggressive fighting to acquire new territory, and the opportunity to exploit chances for hunting in the bush areas probably contributed to making the slash and burn process largely a man's task.

Once the land is cleared there does not seem to be an adaptive advantage, of the kind we described for male hunting, in having either one sex or the other perform the subsequent horticultural tasks: planting, weeding, harvesting, and transporting crops. Lactating women can carry infants to the cultivations and return carrying loads of foods and children in much the way gathering women do. This is just as true of pregnant women up to the time of delivery. Men are also free to carry burdens on their return to the homesteads. The only impediment to their doing so occurs in societies in which there is the possibility of enemy attack between gardens and settlements. Interestingly enough, men can also take weaned children with them to the cultivations, so that small boys accompany their fathers more often than they do among foragers.

The male monopoly over clearing land has one important consequence, however. Women among the horticulturalists are never able themselves to initiate the process of cultivating new or long-fallowed land; they must depend on men literally to prepare the ground for them. But the men's clearing of the land does not give the men the same kind of basic advantage that the male hunter has. The preparation of the soil does not automatically give a man the ability to distribute highly favored food outside his domestic group in the way a big kill of game does. Labor is required to raise crops first, and enough has to be raised to permit distribution in accordance with cultural standards for proper feasting and exchange before any acquisition of prestige or power is possible.

PATTERNS IN CULTIVATION

Let us then consider some recurring patterns in horticultural societies for sexual division of labor in the work of cultivation.

Men Clear; Men and Women Cultivate. Men clear land; both men and women raise substantial crops. This pattern is the most common among horticulturalists, and has several variants.

(1) Men raise only prestige crops used in exchanges; women raise staple food crops. This pattern is common in highland New Guinea. Among the Gururumba, for example, men raise sugar cane, taro, and bananas. Although sugar cane is a regular if minor source of food in every household, the root crop, taro, is used only in exchanges, as are bananas. Women raise sweet potatoes, which constitute the main staple food for human beings as well as for pigs (Newman 1965).

(2) Men and women cultivate both staples and prestige crops; women raise additional staples and trade with their surpluses and with other goods.

This pattern is common in West Africa. Among the Ibo of eastern Nigeria, for example, men, helped by women, cultivate yams. These are a favored daily food and furnish the bulk of nutrients during the eight or nine months of the year that they are available. Men may receive honorific titles ("yam titles") by the ritual distribution of yams along with other goods to those outside the household. Yam titles carry with them valuable social prerogatives. Women, working alone, grow taro and cassava, which furnish the bulk of the family's subsistence in the months when yams are not available. The portions of taro and cassava not eaten by the family are not, however, distributed as donations outside the household for the purpose of achieving honorific titles for the women. Instead, they form part of a stock in trade with which women engage in commercial activities. Women also trade in peppers and okra which they raise, in palm oil which they press from palm kernels, in breadfruit, plantains, and kola nuts derived from trees growing near their house compounds, and in cooked foods of various kinds. Sometimes the trade is extended to cloth and other craft products. Some women even buy goods at wholesale and become virtual entrepreneurs. Women who acquire wealth from trading may use it to help their husbands get titles of honor. They may even, if quite wealthy, acquire similar titles for themselves. These would never have been available to them as a result of direct distribution with the household as a base (Uchendu 1965).

(3) Men and women raise the same crops, working either together or separately. This is a common pattern in Central and East Africa. Among the Bemba of

Zambia, men and women work together cultivating finger millet, although only the women reap the crop. Women also gather wild vegetables as relishes to be eaten with the porridge which is made with the millet. Millet thus eaten provides sustenance for the family, but neither enters into honorific exchange nor becomes an object of trade. That which is distributed outside the household to fulfill obligations and to gain prestige is beer, brewed exclusively by the women from the millet grown by both sexes (Richards 1939).

Among some South American growers of manioc in tropical forests, women help men in both planting and harvesting. Some spend considerable additional effort and time in preparing manioc flour. Where flour is an article of trade, however, the man who cleared the field on which the manioc was raised and who organized its production owns the product and receives trade goods in exchange for it (Murphy 1960).

(4) Among systems in which both men and women raise crops, there remains a fourth theoretical possibility, an arrangement whereby women would raise prestige crops and men staples. This does not occur among horticulturalists. At our present state of knowledge we can only speculate on the origins of this anomaly. Prestige crops are those involved in extradomestic distribution. Men as hunters had an advantage in such exchanges. Perhaps as foragers took up horticulture in regions in which men and women for unknown reasons began cultivating different crops, the men retained the practice of distribution outside the household, so that their crops acquired the connotation of prestige.

Men Clear; Women Cultivate. Men clear the land; only women do the work of cultivation. This pattern was common among the Indians of the eastern United States. Among the Iroquois of New York State men did some hunting to contribute to the food supply, but women raised corn, which was the staple food, on land cleared by the men. Households consisted of several nuclear families, related through women, who occupied a single "long house." Each family had its separate fire, but cooked food was distributed to all the occupants of the long house through the head matron of the group. No significant patterns of food distribution outside this extended household existed, except that hospitality was offered to strangers, who were fed by the women. It should be noted, however, that Iroquois male warriors were sometimes away from home base for months or even years, and that they themselves depended on dried corn and other provisions supplied by the women to see them through their expeditions (Brown 1970a).

Among some East African societies such as the Tiriki of Western Kenya we also find women as the sole cultivators of the ground cleared by men. Apart from some distribution of beer, the food raised by the women does not enter into extradomestic exchange. The men, however, carry on some cattle raising and use the animals for prestige-conferring distribution (Sangree 1965).

Men Clear and Cultivate. Men clear the fields and do most of the work of cultivation, with women as minor assistants. This pattern is rare; the Yąnomamö of the jungles of southern Venezuela and Brazil are an example (Chagnon 1968). Here hunting and the gathering of honey by men, the gathering of wild plants by women, and fishing by those of both sexes occupy considerable time and energy, but

Yąnomamö man carrying plaintains out of his garden. (Courtesy of Napoleon A. Chagnon)

Yąnomamö man cooking plaintains in a clay pot. (Courtesy of Napoleon A. Chagnon)

the bulk of the food supply comes from the gardens cultivated almost exclusively by men. Their main crop is plantains, a bananalike fruit. Hunters constantly search for sites for new gardens. Each man has several plots in different stages of development. Clearing is a frequent and heavy task. Wives and daughters accompany men to the gardens and assist them in planting and weeding.

A pattern similar in many respects to that of the Yąnomamö, of having men both clear and also cultivate, occurs in a very different environment. Among the Hopi Indians, in the dry land area of Arizona where clearing is a minor task but a simple form of irrigation is practiced, men do the clearing, the irrigation, and the cultivation of staple crops, corn, beans, and squash. Women do not assist in these tasks, but have their own small gardens near the villages, atop the mesas, where they raise a few vegetables and relishes.

POSSIBLE EXPLANATION OF PATTERNS

How can we account for the fact that after the initial clearing of the land there are three major patterns of participation by men and women in cultivation? As we have already suggested, the work of women at cultivation easily parallels their tasks as food gatherers and may well represent a continuation of that work. Indeed, the suggestion has been made that women introduced plant domestication as an outgrowth of their experience with the collection of wild foods. That men should join in cultivating crops, whether staples or prestige crops, makes sense as a continuation of male efforts to gather plants to feed themselves on the hunt, and of their contribution to large-scale food collection during seasons when wild plants, nuts, or seeds are especially abundant.

The puzzling pattern is the third, the one in which men do all the cultivation, and women participate only in the harvest or as incidental assistants. In other words, we need explanations, not for why women contribute to subsistence among horticulturalists, but rather for why, when they do *not* do so, this should be the case. I suggest two possible solutions to this problem, the first based on ecological considerations, the second on patterns of warfare.

Ecology. In the inland tropical areas of South America, where hunting rather than fishing provides the protein in the diet (the Yąnomamö are an example), the vegetation near the ground is sparse: the trees create a canopy which effectively shuts out most of the sunlight. Thus there are few food plants available for gathering. Among people who are not horticulturalists but who depend solely on hunting and on gathering in such forests, women as gatherers can contribute very little to the food supply. Men not only hunt, but also climb trees or fell them in order to reach sources of honey or the marrow of palm trees (Clastres 1972). When horticultural techniques were first introduced to such peoples by their neighbors, it is possible that, without a tradition of major food collection performed by women, men simply added the cultivation of crops to their other forest activities, and continued to spend considerable time hunting as well.

Warfare. In the inland tropical forests of South America the purpose of warfare from the standpoint of the peoples themselves is to capture women from neighboring tribes, or to avenge earlier losses of their own women through enemy raids. It has been suggested by an anthropologist that such constant raids have the consequence of spacing populations so widely that the proper environment for wild game, the significant, scarce, and, in the tropical forest, sparsely placed source of protein, is not destroyed by expanding cultivation (Siskind 1973). But with women as the prize and with raids a constant danger, it becomes hazardous for women to work unprotected in the cultivated lands. Men, therefore, do most of the work, occasionally with women as protected assistants.

In a parallel way, among the Hopi of Arizona the need for men to protect water sources in the bottom lands from aggressive incursion by outsiders might account for the absence of Hopi women from the work of cultivating the staple crop.

It is noteworthy, however, that the practice of warfare can also take men away from home base for long periods of time, as we have seen. When this happens, women's participation in cultivation may increase relative to men's (Ember and Ember 1971). The Iroquois furnish an example of this pattern.

Provision of Protein Foods

As we would expect, the hunting of game and deep-sea fishing, to whatever extent these occur among horticulturalists, are done by men. Women, however, as among hunters and gatherers, kill small animals, and collect small fish and other sea creatures in shallow water and streams. Where domesticated animals are raised, the nature of the animal seems to affect the division of labor. If pigs are domesticated, it is usually the women who feed and care for them; if sheep, goats, or cattle are raised, young boys and men usually have the prime responsibility. Why the difference? I believe the reason is that pigs are largely raised on such vegetables as sweet potatoes which are fed to them directly; they root for other food in the vicinity of the home compound. If straying pigs cause quarrels, these are between neighbors. Cattle, sheep, and goats, by contrast, do some grazing at a distance from horticultural settlements. Their straying can give rise to more serious conflicts between different settlements, and different kin groups are more likely to be involved. The possibility of such situations of physical strife may account for the fact that the work of herders of animals other than pigs falls most often on the boys and men of the household.

Transportation and Processing of Foods

The burden of transporting crops from the plantations to the homesteads falls on both men and women in horticultural societies, as can be seen from the foregoing account. But although there are some societies in which men are largely exempt from this task, in almost all of them women are involved in some part of it. Even if they are only minor assistants in other phases of cultivation, as among the Ya̧nomamö and the Hopi, they are likely to help substantially in bringing home the harvest.

The major work of cooking and other food processing for daily meals is done by women, but men assist in some societies. For example, in Polynesia men regularly extract coconut cream, which serves as a relish for the evening meal. The heavy work of pounding certain root crops and of grinding all grains is, however, everywhere done by women and sometimes requires two or three hours each day.

Although in some societies women have a monopoly of cooking daily meals and men are excluded, in others men and women join in the task. In no horticultural society, it should be noted, are women wholly excluded from routine cooking. Why this should be so is not clear. It is possible to speculate that women's lactation and the subsequent feeding of infants establishes the pattern of the woman as food giver, which is then extended to her performance of the function of food prepraation for all the members of the household.

Food preparation for large-scale extradomestic feasts or ceremonials is another matter. Among growers of root crops and fruits, this kind of cooking is often the work of men. In New Guinea, as among the Gururumba, men prepare the earth ovens, butcher the pigs, and fill the ovens with pork and with roots and other vegetables. In South America, as among the Yanamamö, men prepare huge vats of plantain soup in preparation for the arrival of guests from other communities.

Among grain growers such as the Bemba, however, where the ceremonial food is beer, the normal household process whereby women do the brewing is continued for large ceremonials, the only difference being the number of women employed. Nevertheless, even among these people men cook porridge for a chief when he is passing through.

The right to command cooks or brewers, male or female, for ceremonial large-scale feasts is an aspect of the control over the labor of others in horticultural societies: a control over men when they are the main cooks; over women where their work is required. We shall consider this matter further in our discussion of the management of large-scale exchanges.

Warfare

Men are the principal fighters and defenders in horticultural societies as in all others; it is mostly the energy of the male members of the society which is expended in the preparation for war and in actual fighting; it is the men who account for the majority of deaths in warfare. That this is so can probably be accounted for by many of the factors by which we explained the male monopoly of hunting: the need for unpredictable absences from the homestead which is incompatible with the nurture and transportation of children, and so forth. But there may be an additional adaptive factor at work here, related to the maintenance of the population. The number of children that a woman can bear is severely limited, particularly where the average spacing is frequently one child in every three years. Under these circumstances a woman can scarcely have more than a dozen children between menarche and menopause. One man, on the contrary, is capable during his sexual maturity of impregnating an extremely large number of women. Therefore, for the maintenance of a population, men's lives are decidedly more expendable than women's.

These factors have not, however, prevented some horticultural societies from using women in warfare to a limited extent. In at least one African society, the Dahomey, a special corps of women fighters is known for its fierceness in battle. Among the Kapauku of the highlands of West Irian in New Guinea, women go along on war parties, acting as advance scouts, and, while the fighting is going on, running in among the men retrieving their own relatives' fallen arrows (the cultural rule here is that they will not be harmed by the enemy) (Pospisil 1963). In some societies women accompany warriors to the site of battle as burden bearers and cooks. By and large, however, fighting is a male task, and the power and recognition derived from success in warfare is almost entirely limited to men. As a nonroutine, highly emotional group activity which endangers life, warfare acquires great value and contributes to the belief in many societies that men's activities have greater prestige than those of women.

Crafts

For crafts there is no obvious adaptive advantage in the choosing of either sex for training in the requisite skills or for their actual use. Horticultural societies vary as to which sex is assigned which craft. In some men weave and sew garments, as among the Hopi, and women do not; in others it is the other way around. Pots can be made by men or women, or both. Among the Yanomamö, men do not let women handle pots in the making, on the ground that they are too clumsy with their hands.

Metal-working is an exception. It is almost entirely a man's skill, especially when iron is involved. This may be related to the earliest use of metals for hunting weapons and implements of war, which men were accustomed to fashion for themselves.

Child-Rearing

Here it suffices to say that the absolute biological constraints which allocate child-bearing and lactation to women are not the only determinants of division of labor for rearing children, even infants. Although mature women as mothers always have some responsibility for very young children, actual child care can be shared with slightly older children, sometimes with small boys as well as with small girls, with other women who are relatives or neighbors, and also with old women, old men, and often for extended periods of a day with men of mature age.

Since men train boys in male skills, wherever little boys of four or five or somewhat older are not in danger and do not get in the way, they are taught by men and spend much time with them. This parallels the training which girls get from women.

The specific amount of time and energy which any woman spends on the care of infants and young children is allocated, as I suggest in the Introduction, under the constraints imposed by other functions which the particular woman is expected to perform in a particular society, rather than the other way around. In other words, women's work as traders in Africa, or as horticulturalists in many parts of the world, is not made possible by the compatibility of such tasks with child-rearing; it is rather that cultural norms with respect to family size and systems of child care are arranged to conform with women's customary work requirements. We have already seen that the collection of noncultivated food by women among some gatherers is not suited to child-rearing, and seems to coincide with small family size. Fertility rates also tend to be low in societies where women do very heavy and prolonged horticultural labor, as in parts of New Guinea.

II/4   DIFFERENTIAL CONTROL OVER EXCHANGE
AND POLITICAL POWER

In our discussion of hunters and gatherers we have already presented the point of view that rights of distribution and the control of the channels of distribution of goods and services, rather than rights and control over production, are the critical elements for the understanding of differences in power between the sexes. We shall now turn to this matter for horticultural societies.

Domestic

Because there is no simple division of labor in horticultural societies, with men producing one kind of food and women another, and no universal pattern in which women produce craft objects of one type and men another, the variation in patterns of domestic exchange is great. The situation is made even more difficult to describe by the diversity in postmarital residential patterns, in household composition, and in the arrangements which exist for the control over household goods and budgets.

We can say, however, that in societies in which women cultivate crops for household consumption, in contrast to those in which they do not, they have more to exchange with their husbands. Conversely, where men's part in cultivation is confined to the clearing of the land, they obviously produce no vegetable food to exchange.

General reciprocity in marriage among horticulturalists, however, always includes the clearing of the land by men and the preparation of food by women, and sexual access by the men to the women and by the women to the men. But even the procreativity of the couple and the child-tending services of the wife need not be part of the domestic exchange. In societies with matrilineal descent-reckoning, as we shall see, the children are assigned to the descent group of the wife and her brothers, not to that of her husband. Her nurturance of the children is then not primarily a service to him. Control and management of food once it has been brought into the household is usually a woman's task, but even here, prestige foods grown by men stay outside the sphere of domestic exchange, as may some of the foods which women sequester for trade. The routine physical care of the homestead, housekeeping in its literal sense, although usually in charge of wives, is again not a significant aspect of domestic exchange in societies in which married men sleep and spend most of their time in communal men's houses which they maintain, while each man's wife and her small children spend their time in the wife's own separate house.

Patterns of domestic exchange must be examined separately, with great care, for each society. Some of these will become apparent in the descriptions of particular peoples at the end of this part.

Extradomestic

EGALITARIAN AND NONEGALITARIAN REDISTRIBUTION

The labor of a household is rarely sufficient to provide an abundant surplus over the household's own nutritional and other needs. Extradomestic, long-range exchanges require that the organizer have the right to ask those outside his or her household either to work directly on the organizer's land, or to give him or her part of the product of their labors, food and other valuables, or both.

The crucial question in determining sex differentiation in the control over economic resources among horticulturalists is, therefore, which sex has the right to command the labor of others or the product of their labors, and to organize and control the distribution of the resulting accumulation.

What is the relative participation of men and women in managing the accumulation and distribution of goods in longe-range exchanges? The role of men as organizers differs, depending on whether the exchanges are egalitarian or nonegalitarian.

In societies with egalitarian distribution and little or no balanced reciprocity resembling commercial exchange, such as that of the Gururumba, all mature men who can accumulate sufficient foodstuffs and other valuables are free to organize distributions and to compete for the status of "big man." Here competition for the limited degree of economic and political leadership available is open rather than restricted.

In societies with nonegalitarian redistribution, such as the Bemba, among men only those who *a priori* hold positions of rank (chief or ritual leader), usually through inheritance, are entitled to organize large-scale extradomestic exchanges.

In other words, distributions among egalitarians validate the right to prestige and rank, while in nonegalitarian societies, with restricted access to positions of power, distributions are among the entitlements of rank, the rank itself being validated on other grounds, such as membership in a royal clan.

For purposes of clarity we have given an extreme view of the bases for distribution systems. In fact, some competition for status positions exists even in more stratified societies, particularly (1) where a large group of lineage or clan members is eligible to succeed to offices, or (2) where some appointive political or ritual offices are available. Here men, as in egalitarian societies, use distribution as a means to demonstrate their wealth and connections, and to achieve personal prominence even if they fail of appointment or succession to formal office. In such cases, where women's trading, which we shall discuss later in this connection, exists to a substantial degree, wives often help their husbands through the profits of their trade in this pursuit of titles.

As for women, in societies in which men conduct egalitarian redistributions and by so doing gain noninstitutionalized positions of prestige or rank, women are by and large precluded from the entire procedure. In other words, if there are no hereditary political or ritual positions of power, and such positions of prestige or rank as do exist are achieved individually for the life-span of the achiever, women are at a distinct disadvantage, regardless of the extent of their participation in food production.

Far different is the situation of women in many of the societies with nonegalitarian distribution. Here women, by the acquisition through inheritance of institutional political or ritual rank, can participate significantly in extradomestic exchange.

Horticultural societies with nonegalitarian distribution systems, as we have seen, often have institutionalized political and ritual positions based on inheritance, either in the male or in the female line, or bilaterally. Where this is so, women, like men, are often eligible to acquire such positions through their consanguineal kin connections. The mothers, sisters, or daughters (but rarely the wives) of chiefs or kings, especially in Africa (e.g., the Bemba) and Polynesia (e.g., the Tonga), may become persons of high rank during the lifetimes of their powerful male relatives, exercising in their own names the power to command resources and arrange distributions. Sometimes such male connection is not necessary, and rank is passed down from woman to woman, as among the Lovedu of Africa (Krige and Krige 1943). Women may hold the title of queen, or queen mother, or princess, or chief. They may rule in conjunction with a male relative (king and his mother jointly), or a woman may have the paramount and only rank of queen. The parallels with royal women in Europe and Asia, both ancient and modern, are obvious, and point up the fact that in societies with hereditary institutionalized leadership membership in the royal or aristocratic lineage often overrides whatever impediments may routinely separate women from the acquisition of power. In these societies women can compete for power with their male kin and even with their husbands (Hoffer 1974).

TRADE
A second basis for women's participation in distribution, apart from institutionalized positions of rank, is trade. This occurs in those societies in which commercial exchange, especially but not exclusively in food, raw and cooked, is a significant part of the economy. Such societies are mostly found in West Africa. Among some of these peoples, women monopolize trade in all commodities, and participate both in exchanges in local markets and in long-distance trade with other tribal groups. In others men control trade in some commodities, such as cattle, or specialize in long-distance trade. Wherever women are traders, they not only sell or barter their own horticultural produce and craft items, but also buy supplies from other women for resale. Although most women are petty entrepreneurs, some become wealthy merchants. Their trading accounts are kept separate from those of the household, and they are free to use the profits as they please. Customarily, after the provisioning of the household, which is their first responsibility, women use trading income to increase the scale of their operations: they "plow it back into the business." They can lease land, buy labor either by paying for it directly in food or in cash, or by paying bride price for "wives" for themselves. These "wives" take over domestic cooking and other household duties, and help with the care of children, thus freeing the women for trading activities. This may help to relieve the friction between husband and wife inherent in her double role as homemaker and merchant, however beneficial the latter activity may be financially.

With the profits of trade which are neither contributed to the household for food, clothing, or the education of the children, nor used for mercantile expansion, a woman can independently of her male kin enter into extradomestic distribution and exchange in her own behalf. She may fulfill kin obligations to her own lineage members by bringing gifts on occasions such and births and funerals, she may contribute to women's organizations such as a market control committee composed of all the women married into her village, or a society comprising all the mature women of her lineage. By other extradomestic distribution she may even acquire honorific titles for herself, with corresponding status. In some societies, such as the Yoruba of Nigeria, women distribute wealth accumulated by trade by organizing or joining women's religious cult societies (Bascom 1969). Trading women can also use the leverage afforded by their influence in the competition for political control within their own or their husbands' kin or residential groups.

We have already seen that women traders sometimes help their husbands in the men's competition for titles and positions. They may do so either by outright gifts or by loans. We shall revert to the tensions between men and women caused by these practices when we discuss the quality of the relationships between the sexes.

The independence from male control of a woman's trading activities is probably to be accounted for by the need for her working decisions about prices, quantities to buy or sell, and the like to be made right at the market place or on the way to it, where there is no opportunity to consult with a husband or other male relatives. Furthermore, it is only by permitting a woman to retain control of her capital that men have found it possible to reap maximum advantages from their wives' and daughters' trading activities (Mintz 1971).

II/5   DIFFERENTIAL CONTROL OVER LAND ALLOCATION AND OVER MOVABLE PROPERTY

The patterns here are similar to those which we discussed in our account of extradomestic exchange. In societies with egalitarian distribution systems land is allocated by men in their capacities as heads of lineages or clans. In societies with nonegalitarian systems, where women acquire status positions, they participate in land allocation. Strangely enough, these generalizations hold true even for societies with matrilineal descent-reckoning, where one might imagine that women would be in control. In fact, however, perhaps because men are primarily engaged in clearing and defending new lands, the allotment is done by the men who are members of the matrilineal kin group.

Personal Property and Special Purpose Monies

Among horticulturalists much movable property is owned and inherited by whichever sex has use for it. Clothing and ornaments are obvious examples of personal property usually associated with one sex or another. But shells, beads, cloth, mats, cattle, pigs, and the like which are used as special purpose monies, and cash itself where it is used, are controlled and inherited by whichever sex has the right to use them in organizing exchanges or trade.

Woman as Movable Property

Thus, in egalitarian societies most of the movable property except for personal items belongs to men, whereas in nonegalitarian societies there are opportunities for women holding political office to control a wide range of possessions. Women traders can do so as well. Through bride price paid in exchange for women, women themselves become a form of movable property in their status as wives. As we have seen, this occurs in societies with both patrilineal and matrilineal descent-reckoning, where at marriage brides move to their husbands' kin's household. Ordinarily men control the movement of women as wives, accumulating and giving bride price in return for rights to their sexual and procreative services. Moreover, like other movable property, women can be inherited, except that a man never has the right to inherit his own biological mother as a wife.

In the same way that women with the political status of chief or queen and women with independent access to wealth through trade can organize large-scale exchanges, they can also, as we have seen, acquire wives in their own right by paying bride price for them; this occurs only in some African societies, and not elsewhere in the world. These payers of bride price are legal husbands, though female; they do not have homosexual relations with their wives, but rather engage consorts for them, or allow them sexual freedom, or are paid by men for sexual access to them. The female husband is none the less the legal parent of any of her wife's offspring. A female husband is usually herself married to a man. She may take on wives for a variety of purposes. As we have seen, women traders' wives are used to relieve their female husbands of household chores. They are also available for work in the fields. Sometimes, as substitutes for a female husband, they are available as sex partners for the latter's male spouse for the purpose of procreation, if the female husband herself is barren or has not produced male children. Among the Lovedu, where, as we have seen, the queen never marries a man, but has numerous wives; these share the burden of producing children for the royal lineage through arranged sexual contacts.[1]

In both egalitarian and nonegalitarian systems, women can be treated as a form of movable property in the sense that they can be captured from enemies and taken as wives. Indeed, raiding other groups for women or avenging the loss of women to an enemy are, as we have seen, avowed reasons for warfare among some horticulturalists. The Yanamamö furnish an example.

II/6 MARRIAGE, DOMESTIC LIFE, AND SOME SEX ATTITUDES

In the course of our previous discussions we have mentioned two situations in which the population's energies have to be organized in horticultural societies for nonroutine enterprises: warfare and exchanges between localities. The bases upon which military alliances are created; the labor force organized for exchanges; the constant interplay and overlapping between categories of people who are potential allies or enemies, hosts or guests, donors or recipients; all these factors are most important in giving shape to the economic and social structure of these peoples.

Relationships between Affinal*

It is in this context that in these societies marriage and subsequent affinal connections are always important. They are ways of bringing two groups together. Hus-

[1] This discussion has benefited from the suggestions of Denise O'Brien.

bands and wives are not easily detachable from their natal kin groups. In a sense they bring these groups into the marriage with them, and subsequently impose them on their children.

Altogether apart from the personal qualities of the human beings concerned, and the varied personal adjustments which men and women make in marriage and parenthood, their relationships are influenced by the cultural expectations as to the network of relationships which each husband and wife and each father and mother has separately outside the conjugal unit. In horticultural societies these significant outside relationships are those which a person has after marriage first with his or her consanguineal kin group, and second with his or her affinal relatives, that is, with the consanguineals of one's spouse. The third element is the relationship of the two in-law groups with each other. The first two are best discussed a little later in connection with patrilineal and matrilineal descent systems. As for the third element, in societies in which the separate consanguineal kin groups have no obligation the one to the other but that of providing spouses, the quality of relationships between husband and wife is likely to be only slightly affected by the relationship between the affinal groups. In those societies, however, in which affinals are expected to support each other in exchanges, politics, and war, the process of negotiating the proper arrangements always leaves room for debates, disputes, and conflicts which are likely seriously to strain the husband and wife relationship as well. To get a feeling for this situation, imagine that in a middle-class family in the United States the bride's grandparents and all her aunts and uncles on both her mother's and her father's side had joint responsibility for arranging and paying for the wedding!

Relations as Affected by Descent-Reckoning and Residence

Patriliny and matriliny, the principal forms of descent-reckoning among horticulturalists, have up to now not figured largely in our discussions. We have not needed to distinguish societies from the standpoint of descent-reckoning because this factor is not significantly interrelated with such matters as the sexual division of labor, with the presence or absence of some stratified distribution and with men's and women's consequent opportunities for holding inherited political office, with the control over property, nor with the participation of the sexes in warfare. But rules of descent and succession in corporate kin groups, especially as they are combined with residence rules for a married couple, do have weighty consequences for the relationships between the sexes in domestic life and, indeed, for the relationships with extended kin as well. It is possible to describe some patterns of strains and tensions on the one hand, and devotion and loyalty on the other, between husbands and wives, adult brothers and sisters, and parents and children which are different for societies with patrilineal and matrilineal descent-reckoning. In addition, the expectation of which kin will be loyal, which of doubtful loyalty, and which antagonistic has undoubted influence upon attitudes and beliefs regarding sexual intercourse and maleness and femaleness in general.

We have space in this book to discuss only unilineal descent systems, and these only in their simplest forms: patrilineality with virilocal residence, and matrilineality with uxorilocal residence. But the general principle that inheritance, succession, and residence rules and patterns influence the quality of relations between men and women holds for all societies.

PATRILINEALITY WITH VIRILOCALITY

The vast majority of societies with patrilineal descent-reckoning have exogamous corporate kin groups, that is, the members of one patrilineal kin group must find spouses in another such group. They also have virilocal residence: the bride comes into her husband's household from another community or another part of the same community. She is highly valued for her share in procreativity; she will add to the population strength of her husband's kin group. This value does not, as we shall see, automatically carry with it a position of power.

Incoming Bride's Position. In these societies a bride coming into her new dwelling finds herself in a situation in which the men of the patrilineal group, at least her husband and his father and brothers, have been in close proximity all their lives, and continue to be so after the marriage. They control, as we have seen, the allocation of the patrilineal group's resources. To the new bride these men are apt to be utter strangers or at most mere acquaintances. Nor are the women of her husband's household (his other wives, if any, his mother, his unmarried sisters, or the wives of his brothers) likely to be people well known to her before her marriage.

Apart from the obvious loneliness of a young girl coming into a strange household, what strains does a new bride face? Even her husband who might seem to be the one member of the household who is her natural ally is, especially in the case of a first wife, in the throes of transferring his loyalty from one woman, his highly supportive mother, to another, his new and unknown wife. For the rest of the household she is the woman from outside, in exchange for whom the patrilineal group has parted with significant resources in the form of a bride price. All eyes are upon her to see if she will perform her part of the bargain. Is she a hard and willing worker at home or in the plantations? Will she quickly become pregnant and produce a son to add to the male population strength of the patrilineal group? If she fulfills these expectations, some of these strains may ultimately be lessened.

In polygynous households the second and subsequent wives must compete with their predecessors for their own advantage and that of their children, when they arrive. If co-wives are located beneath a single roof, or in separate houses in the same compound, jealousies among them are greater than if they are settled in widely separated residences.

All these strains are intensified by the competition among themselves for the patrilineal group's resources carried on by the men of the group: at the least, by her husband, his father, and his father's brothers. These resources can include land, livestock, the political and ritual offices in the patrilineal group, and the control over the marriage of the sisters and daughters of the men. The bride price which the marriage of these women brings in can be used to acquire additional wives for the older men who already have one or more, or for the younger men who have none. Occasions for dissension among the men are thus manifold; yet the men must retain some degree of unity if they are to be effective in their relationships with other groups.

Faced, then, with these strains and tensions, and with only the lukewarm support of her husband, what resources can the wife command to bolster her own position and ultimately to secure advantages for her children?

If her natal patrilineal group is bound to her husband's by reciprocal ties of exchange, political support, or military alliance, or by its obligation to complete the payment of the bride price, she can count to a certain extent on the intervention of her father and brothers to support her in stressful situations. Such support is easier to obtain if her kin live nearby. In the absence of such favorable circumstances, she can expect little help from her own patrilineal group.

A second source of strength may be the possession of property of her own over which she has personal control. She may have this kind of property as a result of independent trading activities, in which a woman may also get help from other women organized in local trading associations or in lineage sisterhoods. Women can also have independent property where the subsistence contributions of husband and wife are budgeted separately, and each controls the distribution of his or her own.

Failing either of these kinds of kin or economic support, and even to an extent where they exist, one source of power available to a woman rests in the members of the patrilineal group who are her own children, mainly her sons. It is when her sons grow older that her motherhood assumes real importance in her struggle for some degree of autonomy.

By supporting her son, who is a full-fledged member of the patrilineal group into which she married, in his competition for wives and other resources against her husband, her husband's brother's sons, and her co-wives' sons, a mother gains some power through her son's reciprocal devotion to her and dependence on her advice and encouragement. She may even lead her son to try using her own brothers to support him against his father and other members of his patrilineal group. In the process, she intensifies the conflicts among the men already inherent, as we have seen, in the patrilineal structure, sometimes causing the premature separation of brothers. She thus contributes to the tensions between herself and her husband (see Collier 1974).

Attitudes of Sexes toward Each Other. In societies reckoning descent by patriliny, then, as in some degree in all societies, the feeling of the sexes toward each other cannot be understood as a monolithic attitude of all men about all women or vice versa. Rather, men view women in the role of wives (and by extension all women sexually available to them) at best as of doubtful loyalty, at worst as hostile, recalcitrant creatures, often even as witches. Women are apt to have the same view of themselves, and some do indeed practice witchcraft.

Men consider women in the role of mother, sometimes of sister, that is, those not sexually available to them, as friendly, supportive, and generally admirable. In some cases a man has a special relationship with the sister whose marriage produced the bride price used in obtaining a wife for himself (see Collier 1974).

The attitude of men toward women sexually available to them appears to color their attitude toward sex itself. They may regard sexual intercourse as dangerous, especially to their own health and manhood. In extreme cases they believe that intercourse should be practiced as infrequently as is compatible with the necessities of procreation.

A woman, in the mirror image, views men sexually available to her, principally her husband or potential husbands, as men to be manipulated in the women's own interests. They use their rights to grant or withhold food, and sometimes also sexual accessibility, as sources of control. Men not sexually available to her—her sons and her father and brothers—are possible sources of help and support.

Tensions between men and women, whether they are potential sex partners or not, often grow out of the activities of women as traders, and their consequent achievement of income, positions, and wealth in their own right. When the women traders live in patrilineal systems, as they do in much of West Africa, such tensions may even impair, though they do not destroy, the benign relationships between mother and son. In some societies hostility of men toward women traders is intensified because men fear that their control over the distribution of resources is threatened. The men often accuse them of using their absence at the marketplace to indulge in adultery or in outright prostitution. This increased hostility is reflected in the men's attitude toward sex. Instead of merely regarding intercourse as an external element of danger to health, they turn their fears inward. They are beset by anxieties regarding their own sexual potency. Impotence would expose them to the ridicule of their wives, and indeed to that of the whole marketplace if their women are gossips (LeVine 1966; Nadel 1952).

To summarize, from the standpoint of domestic authority and control, egalitarian, politically unstratified societies with patrilineal descent groups and virilocal residence have the greatest potentiality for strong overt dominance of husbands over wives. However, it is possible even in these societies for women to have sources of countervailing power indirectly, either through their own patrilineal kin groups, or their sons, and directly through their control of food and sex, and possibly through their commercial activities.

The situation is somewhat different in more stratified societies. Women who hold political office outside the household, as we have seen they can do in this type of society, exercise a degree of domestic control as well, a control which for the most part is not dependent on the factors mentioned above.

In nonegalitarian systems the normal domestic functions of the head wife of a chief or king can involve significant control of major resources and so elevate the wife to a position of public power. Supervision of the dozens of wives who serve as a chief's agricultural work force, of his slaves, and of the distribution of his food stores, is a base for real extradomestic political control (Hoffer 1974). Even in such societies, however, the position of the ordinary wife of a common man is likely to be similar to the general pattern for patrilineal societies which we have described.

Our model of patrilineal, virilocal systems is useful because it provides a first set of expectations as to the quality of sex relations in any society which is known to be organized along patrilineal, virilocal lines. But this fact does not exempt us from the necessity of examining the particular social, economic, and political arrangement of each patrilineally organized society before drawing conclusions with respect to the nature and quality of relationships between the sexes. For example, if men marry women from clans that are potential enemies, then sons, as members of their fathers' clans, are potential enemies of their mothers' male patrilineal relatives. In such a situation the supportive relationships between mothers and sons which we have described in the model are somewhat impaired (see Gururumba, pp. 101–115).

MATRILINEALITY AND UXORILOCAL RESIDENCE

Matriliny is a system of reckoning, as we have seen, in which women serve as markers of descent lines. This situation must not be confused with matriarchy, a form of governance existing perhaps only in theory, in which women are the sole rulers. On the contrary, in societies reckoning descent matrilineally it is the men of the matrilineal group, that is, the men counting their common descent through women, who allocate land, combine in warfare and defense, and have the main political and ritual functions.

Rules for residence after marriage vary in matrilineal groups, but uxorilocal residence, the system in which a groom comes into his bride's household, is far more frequent under matriliny than under patriliny. To provide the greatest contrast with the patrilineal, virilocal situation, we shall concentrate our attention here upon the uxorilocal situation.

Incoming Husband's Position. How does the position of the incoming groom compare with that of the incoming bride? Sometimes, like his opposite number, the incoming groom is a stranger (although men in matrilineal systems usually marry women of the same local community, they do not necessarily do so). He finds himself among a group of women—his wife, her mother, and her sisters—who have lived in close proximity all their lives. He, too, is obligated to work for the permanent members of the household, and to increase the strength of the spouse's line, here by fathering children. He is subject to the close scrutiny of these women and that of their male relatives in his fulfillment of these obligations, through probably not as intensively as if the matrilineal group had parted with some of its resources to secure him. There is no groom price corresponding to bride price. (That the groom is not, as we shall see, absorbed into his wife's matrilineal group to the extent that it is possible for a virilocal woman to be into her husband's patrilineal household may account for the absence of groom price.) Nor, again, is a man's wife his natural ally in the domestic situation. Her loyalties have always been and remain with her mother, her sisters, and her brothers. These last continue to have at least a standby responsibility for her economic support and that of her children. A man's relationship with his sons parallels that of a woman with her daughters in patrilineal situations. He lives with and trains his sons in economic and political skills, but the sons leave the households at the time they marry, and he has little or no legal control over them. They obtain their rights from their mother's brothers, the men of their matrilineal group. So much for the similarities.

There are striking differences. A man remains a full and active member of his own matrilineal group, sharing the responsibilities, regularly fulfilled by men rather than by women, for the allocation of the group's resources. As we have seen, he has responsibilities in regard to the maintenance of his sister and her children. Thus, there is always a place where he is a person in his own right. This cannot help but strengthen him in his dealings with his wife's kin, and remains true regardless of the kind of mutual obligations which exist between the two affinal matrilineal groups, his and his wife's.

Furthermore, the in-marrying husband does not have to fear competition from fellow-husbands of his wife. Polyandry, the marriage of one woman to more than one man, is even rarer in these societies than in those of other types.

A third difference is the lack of competition among the permanent members of the household into which the groom has moved. Such competition as may exist does not go on among the sisters and their husbands, but among their mature brothers, who are not members of the household and may not even live nearby. In the absence of groom price, there is no rivalry among the sisters living together over the expenditure of matrilineal resources to procure them husbands; nor when their sons marry do the women have occasion to quarrel about the distribution of incoming wealth. Where women are traders, they retain individual control over their incomes.

Whatever tensions exist among the women are likely to be concentrated on the possibility that a brother may favor one rather than another of the sisters. On the whole, the strains among the women of a household which counts descent by matriliny are relatively slight.

This assessment of the relative absence of rivalry among women in a matrilineal virilocal situation makes sense in light of the structure of the group and is supported by the scanty data we have. The very meagerness of the information is not without importance. It bears evidence to a lack of concern with the relationships among women, which should be remedied by further research.

If this relative lack of contention relieves the incoming husband of stress and strain, it also deprives him of any chance to gain power by playing one woman against another. A man gains nothing by working toward and controlling his daughters' interests against those of this wife's sisters' daughters in the way in which a woman in a patrilineal system works through her son to gain power. In other words, an in-coming husband's relationship to his opposite-sexed child, his daughter, here is substantially different from that of a woman with her opposite-sexed child, her son, in a society with descent based on patriliny.

In these matrilineal systems the major conflicts for a man in his own generation are those between his marital obligations to his wife and his consanguineal obligations to his sisters; in the next generation, those between his paternal obligation to his own sons and his avuncular (uncle's) obligations to his sister's sons.

In his own matrilineal group he depends on his sister and her husband to produce children to add to the strength of the group and to become his heirs. As we have seen, he retains an obligation to guarantee his sister's economic support. But he lives with his own sons and his own wife; his routine labor is directly aimed at feeding them and is performed on his wife's matrilineal land. Claims upon him, then, are twofold: his sisters' because her sons are his heirs and successors to the matrilineal prerogatives belonging to men; his wife's in that she is entitled to his labor on behalf of herself and her children. His wife's claims can cause difficulties with her brothers, who may feel that he is not doing enough for their sister's children. They have a right to interfere in the matter. Thus a man's relationship with his brothers-in-law, his male affines in his own generation, are likely to be somewhat tense, though to be sure he does not live in the same household with them.

Attitudes of Sexes toward Each Other. What are the consequences of this situation for the relationships between husband and wife? In general, in societies with matrilineal descent-reckoning and uxorilocal residence, women have a greater chance of domestic equality with men in household control than do women in patrilineal, virilocal systems (Schlegel 1972). On the whole, relations between the spouses are less tense than in patrilineal systems, partly because they are of less practical importance to either side of the marriage.

A woman's procreative capacity is in the service of her own matrilineal group; she works on her own matrilineal land, and her husband and his kin paid no bride price for her. His labor service to her kin replaces any groom price and is given in exchange only for his right of sexual access to her.

Since from a man's point of view she is only a wife, as it were, and not important to him either for working his land or as mother of his own descent group's children, she cannot in any sense be considered a piece of valuable movable property of his, as women can often be counted in patrilineal systems. This situation goes hand in hand with the rarity of polygyny in matrilineal systems. (The few instances which do exist are those in which men marry a group of sisters living in the same household.)

For the wife the husband is a worker, a sex partner, the necessary father for her children. It is in the woman's interest first to acquire a husband, then to hold on to him. If she cannot, or if she is dissatisfied with him, she can eventually find another. In case of divorce neither the wife nor her children move to another household. The husband can easily go back to his mother's and sister's establishment.

What about mothers and sons in matrilineally organized systems? Here women, as we have seen, are entitled to economic and social support from their brothers, as well as from their fathers with whom they continue to live. They also have the advantage of long-term cooperative relationships with their mothers and sisters. In this context, control over their sons is by no means their only source of influence in the world of men. Sons, in their turn, have two sets of men concerned with their welfare, their fathers and their mother's brothers. Their dependence on their mother's maneuvering in their behalf is decidely less. Consequently, mother-son relationships lack the intensity which they have in patrilineal systems.

It is possible now to see that the sharp line which we drew in patrilineal systems between the relationships of men and women sexually available to each other, on the one hand, and men and woman not sexually available, on the other hand, cannot be as clearly drawn in matrilineal systems. Apart from a husband's right of sexual access to his wife, and her brothers' lack of such right, a woman's husband and brothers have similar and overlapping interests in relation to her. In the same way a wife and sister have similar and to an extent overlapping interest in a man who is husband to the first and brother to the second. As a result, I believe, the total situation in societies with matrilineal descent-reckoning and uxorilocal residence is conducive to less hostility and tenseness between men and women sexually available to each other, just as there is less emphasis in this situation on the benign qualities of mother and sisters.

It should come as no surprise that attitudes toward sexual intercourse here indicate fewer stresses and strains than do those encountered in patrilineal descent systems. There have been no systematic investigations of the matter, but I have some tentative suggestions as to the form of sexual anxiety more likely to occur in matrilineal than in patrilineal systems.

I suggest that instead of a man's worrying that sexual intercourse may be dangerous to this manhood and physical strength, or that he may be impotent to perform the sex act, both husband and wife are worried about the man's ability to father strong and healthy children, one of his prime obligations to his wife's matrilineal group, and essential to its future growth. The death of infants and children is attributed to the father's moral infractions or even to his malevolence. Further, although sexual intercourse itself is normally believed to be pleasurable and desirable by both men and women, from the standpoint of the wife's matrilineal group the intercourse of one of its members with an outsider is tinged with a certain amount of ambiguity as to its results for the health and welfare of its next generation. This may account for the attribution of a mystical power to sexual intercourse in some matrilineal societies of this kind, but if the power is dangerous it threatens not the sex partners themselves, but children and others in a vulnerable position.

We have presented a somewhat simplified model of a society with descent-reckoning through women and uxorilocal residence. In fact, only about half of the actual societies with matrilineal descent groups have uxorilocal residence rules. The rest show a variety of patterns which variously affect the internal relationships of the households.

One variation exists among the Bemba, in which a husband, after some ten years of uxorilocal residence, may choose to leave his wife's household for one of several other locations. The consequences of this variation we shall discuss in our separate sketch of this society later on. We have space here to mention only three other residence patterns associated with matrilineal descent-reckoning.

(1) Residence is virilocal, and matrilineality operates only in the control of land and the flow of inheritance (Ndembu of Africa); (2) there is virilocal residence for a woman when she marries, but her husband at the age of 12 or 13 has moved from his father's household to that of his mother's brother (avunculocal residence), and it is into this maternal uncle's house of her husband that the new bride moves (Trobriand Islands); (3) a man has the option of either moving into his wife's household, or of remaining in his mother's, performing his sexual duties toward his wife and his labor service to her kin group as a commuter. In the latter case, his children, living with their mother, can often be seen carrying cooked food to their absentee father (Ashanti of West Africa).

Relations as Affected by Population Control Strategies

The attitudes of the sexes toward each other and cultural concepts about sexuality have thus far been discussed as consequences of men's and women's positions in relation to kin and residential groups. Another basis for variations in cultural ideas about sexuality among horticulturalists is the degree of population pressure on land resources. Our example will be drawn from New Guinea.

In the highlands of that island striking differences are found in the degree and types of hostility between the sexes. Among peoples who have long been settled in the area, have little new land available, and for whom an increase in the population could threaten the adequacy of the food supply, sexual intercourse is believed to weaken men, and women are considered dangerously polluting. In contrast, peoples newly settled in a previously uncultivated area, for whom population increase is needed to add to the group's numbers both for labor to cultivate new lands and to enable them to gain and maintain a foothold in new territory against the pressure of aggressive neighbors, sexual intercourse is viewed as benign, and relatively little pollution is attributed to contact with women (Lindenbaum 1972). For the first group, fear of coitus and of the power of menstrual fluid to harm both men and crops (the sex act must not take place in a garden) is accompanied by living patterns which segregate adult males in men's houses. Marriage for men is delayed as a consequence of the difficulty of accumulating bride price, and permanent bachelorhood is an allowable status for men. These beliefs and practices limit the frequency of sexual intercourse among both the married and the unmarried, and probably result in low reproduction rates.

In the contrasting group, sex relations are believed to have a revitalizing force for men, and the sex act is performed in gardens to encourage the growth of plants. Nor are men's living quarters segregated. Here, if men have any reservations about their contact with women, it is because they are uncertain about their ability to be as sexually active as custom requires and women would like. Reproduction rates over the long run are higher here.

The kin and residential arrangements we have already discussed as influencing sex attitudes are themselves not unrelated to population pressures, so that the two kinds of explanation are mutually reinforcing. At least in highland New Guinea, where land resources are diminishing, relationships between neighbors are hostile. Marriages between neighbors are made in an effort to establish alliances so as to diminish the danger of attack and to provide allies in fights with still other groups. But the alliances are precarious; there is always the danger that one or the other side will not fulfill its obligations and hostilities will break out.

In this situation wives partake of the ambiguity which exists in the relations between the intermarrying groups; sex antagonism is high on this account.

Among peoples for whom land is abundant and labor is scarce, affinals are more likely to be regarded as unambiguously beneficent; husbands and wives represent and convey these benign relationships. Here sexual intercourse is not deemed dangerous, women are thought to be less polluting, and sex antagonisms take different forms.

Summary

A great deal of further research is needed to confirm and elucidate the interrelationships among population pressures, warfare, social structure, and cultural beliefs and practices concerning sex relations and the nature of males and females. Whether the analyses just set forth are entirely accurate or not, the main idea we want to convey is that sex antagonisms and beliefs about the nature of the sex act and its consequences are not disembodied cultural peculiarities of one society as compared with another, but have a systematic relationship to nonsexual phenomena.

II/7 DIFFERENTIAL PARTICIPATION IN AND CONTROL OVER RITUAL

Properly to understand the differential participation of the sexes in ritual among horticulturalists would require an examination for each society of (1) the timing and purposes of each ceremony; (2) the rights of men and women to participate in the different roles available in the ritual drama: producers, directors, actors, and audience; (3) the economic, social, and political situation of the society, and (4) the specific cultural system of ideas, beliefs, and symbols through which the nature of the world and of men and women are understood. For horticultural societies, to a far greater extent than among foragers, the permutations and combinations of these elements are so varied as to make useful generalizations difficult, and we shall attempt only a few. (Brief analyses of a few rituals in specific societies are included in the ethnographic descriptions given at the end of this chapter.)

We shall concentrate particularly on generalizations concerning the differential opportunities of men and women to act as ritual specialists, either as producers or directors or as leading actors in the ritual performance.

Public Rituals for Group Welfare

Although it might be expected that the sex of the ritual leaders would be related to the sex of the gods, goddesses, or spirits whose propitiation, or the manipulation of whom, is the purpose of the ceremony, this is not the case.

As we suggested in the introduction to this part, in public rituals undertaken for the benefit of an entire group such as lineage or clan, a village or a tribe, rituals held either at regular intervals or at times of social crisis, the rights to play roles of producers and directors parallel the rights to roles in the political organization of the society. Entitlement to political control over others is, among horticulturalists, always connected with supernatural power. Leadership and authority are backed by the assumption either that political leaders are capable of controlling and manipulating supernatural beings, or that they themselves, in their own persons, are sacred. Political and economic leaders are thus also, in effect, priests or priestesses.

In societies with egalitarian distribution systems, where competition for economic power and for whatever small degree of political power exists is limited to men, only men are entitled to take the responsibility for initiating and organizing major rituals meant to insure the protection and welfare of the group. Among the Gururumba of New Guinea, for instance, men organize the clan pig festivals that take place about every five years. Here "big men" finance the affair by paying ritual experts and by calling in, somewhat as we call in an open loan in our society, the pigs, other foodstuffs, and valuables owed them from previous exchanges.

In societies with nonegalitarian redistribution systems and institutionalized, inherited political office, women and men are entitled to initiate and conduct rituals as functions of the offices which they hold. The Lovedu queen who is the main political personage in her tribe is responsible for regular rain-making ceremonies. These are believed to be the most vitally important rituals for the welfare of the entire population. In this the provision of beer, the performance of labor, and the actual presence at the rituals of members of the tribe are thought to be owed to the queen by virtue of her special spiritual powers. She is, in turn, expected to use these powers for the benefit of all her subjects (Krige and Krige 1943). In a similar way, when eligibility for clan or lineage headship is inherited, rituals involving the worship of deified ancestors, or local gods or spirits important to the kin group, are conducted by a headman or headwoman. In patrilineally organized systems, women closely related to the lineage head—for example, his sisters and daughters—sometimes organize and lead the rituals (Ibo of Nigeria). In matrilineal, uxorilocal systems, women who are the eldest matrons of a household own the lineage and household shrines and have power to perform rites for the protection of these places of worship. Here, in a fashion parallel to that which we have just seen in patrilineal societies, some lineage rituals are conducted by the brothers and sons of the lineage head (Iroquois and Hopi). What might be called establishment gods and spirits are celebrated in rituals organized and conducted by establishment personnel, male and female.

Life-Cycle Rituals

PRIVATE DOMESTIC RITUALS

Rites held at the scene of childbirth are usually conducted by women; men are frequently but not always barred from attending. Where midwifery is treated as a ritual specialty, women are usually the midwives. In some societies male curers are called in for difficult births. Subsequent rituals for infants and young children, such as naming, first haircutting, and the like, are conducted by the men and women of the household, and ritual specialists are not usually involved.

PUBLIC INITIATION RITUALS

Here we shall consider only those rites of passage which are mandatory for a society's population in all-inclusive categories, such as those for all men or all women at some point in their lives. We shall not be concerned with initiation ceremonies into special cult groups or associations.

General initiation rituals take a variety of forms. They may be held for individual boys and girls or they can be conducted every few years for all boys and girls who have reached the appropriate age. When rites are held for individual young people, the seclusion or separation phase of the rite (see Introduction) is often a domestic affair. Here the dramatization of the "coming-out" of the person in a new guise is the public, extradomestic event celebrated by rites and feasting. Initiation ceremonies for girls frequently take this form, but in some societies individual boys are initiated in this way also.

Group initiations held for several children at the same time, and therefore extradomestic in character, are not all sex segregated, nor are they necessarily held for young people at or near the time of physiological puberty. Among the Hopi, for example, both boys and girls are initiated together at about the age of six, with part of the rite including the whipping of the children by the Katchinas, the male masked impersonators of the Hopi ancestor gods. After this ordeal the initiates discover the secret, previously withheld from them, that the Katchinas are only human beings disguised as gods. Among the Ibo initiation is for boys only, but occurs in a form similar to that found among the Hopi. It takes place when the children are about eight years old. Here all boys initiated into the masquerade society at the same time form a cohort or age-grade category with special social functions for these initiates for the rest of their lives.

The most spectacular initiation rites are those held for groups of adolescents of one sex only. These last at least several days, sometime weeks or even months or years, during which the young people and their sponsors paticipate jointly in the various phases of the ritual.

The period of seclusion, however long it lasts, frequently includes a time of formal instruction by elders, sponsors, and ritual specialists: these are men for male rites and women for female. The teachings, in the form of mythological tales, songs, dances, music, lectures, and harangues, are likely to deal with general moral precepts and with what we would call sex education. But the last named is by no means the exclusive concern of this instruction; also imparted at this time is information on the kind of work expected of adult men and women respectively. Often secret information is communicated, and the initiates are warned never to divulge the secrets either to the uninitiated or to the opposite sex. The rites are believed to confer on men the strength to be warriors, and indeed the essence of manhood itself; on women, the strength to bear children, and the very essence of womanhood. From the standpoint of the participants in the ritual and of the audience, the overt purposes are, however, related not only to manhood and womanhood; the rites are expected to convey the ideals of responsible adult citizenship in the society.

We have already stated in the Introduction that rites of passage usually include a form of social degradation or physical pain, like the Hopi whipping of the children. Pain is inflicted presumably to increase the emotional intensity of the experience, and thereby to make the transition from one social role to another more decisive.

Operations on the bodies of initiates are often performed. These include incisions in the forehead, face. chest, arms or legs such as to leave visible scars or cicatrices, the knocking out or filing down of teeth, and sexual mutilation (circumcision, clitoridectomy). All these are methods of both inflicting pain during initiation and also of creating a permanent change in the body which forever differentiates the initiates from the uninitiated. (The operations do not necessarily take place as aspects of the initiation rituals; in some societies they are performed for individual boys and girls either at or long before puberty as purely domestic events.)

It must be emphasized that, with or without painful operations, initiation rites are dramatic affairs, charged with emotion, especially when the boys or girls, having been symbolically killed and resurrected, reappear in special clothing and ornaments to be greeted by the assembled community. Initiation rites of this kind occur somewhat more frequently for men than for women.

Whatever the specific content of public large-scale group initiation rites, the question arises as to why they occur in some societies and not in others. More specifically, why are there rites for men in some societies, for women in others, and for both in still others? Why are bodily operations included in some and not in others? Why are secret rites totally absent among some horticulturalists? We do not have wholly satisfactory answers to these questions, but a variety of explanations have been proposed.

Psychological Explanations. Psychologically oriented explanations are based on the assumptions that (a) initiation rites are designed consciously or unconsciously primarily to provide sex identity for their participants; (b) certain social conditions and cultural practices make it difficult for individuals to acquire a sense of their own maleness or femaleness; and (c) in such cases initiation rites help to establish sex identity, so that men and women can function as adults with less sex role conflict.

What conditions are believed to make the acquisition of adult sex identity difficult? For boys and men, one answer proposes a chain of circumstances beginning with (a) low protein sources, which make mother's milk and long suckling periods crucial for infant survival; (b) a cultural rule which prevents the conception of a new child while the first is still nursing: the so-called postpartum sex taboo, the prohibition of sexual intercourse for a year or more after the birth of a child; (c) a cultural rule which has infants and young boys sleep with their mothers while fathers sleep elsewhere as a concomitant of the postpartum sex taboo; and further (d) it is suggested that the consequence of mother-son sleeping arrangements is that boys identify with their mothers, the only powerful sources of gratification for them in their earliest years. But in adult life it is the males that have the power; initiation rites are thus needed to help boys to make the necessary transition from identification with the powerless female to that with the powerful male. Cross-cultural studies of correlations between initiation ceremonies for boys including some form of sexual mutilation, and each of the other traits (sleeping arrangements, sex taboos, and low protein diets) seem to bear out these psychologically oriented hypotheses, at least for societies in Africa and the Pacific, though not for South America (Whiting 1964; Saucier 1972).

Initiation rites for girls which include some mutilation have been correlated with situations in which girls sleep with their mothers exclusively, and then move into virilocal marriage arrangements where men dominate (Brown 1963). Here the argument is that girls also identify with their mothers as the sources of power, and need to be reconciled to their own loss of power as females in order to acquire a new adult female identity. The greater the difficulty of making the transition, it is assumed, the greater the trauma required, which accounts for the mutilation.

Sociological Explanation. Sociologically oriented explanations are based on the assumptions about ritual that we have preferred in this book, that initiation rites are restatements of social structural characteristics and convey messages concerning them. For example, cross-cultural studies demonstrate high correlations between male and female initiation rites viewed as dramatic expressions of male and female solidarity, and societies which show other evidence of sex solidarity as well (Young 1965).

Female puberty rites also occur more frequently where women contribute to subsistence, especially among North American Indians (Brown 1963). Presumably when women are not only producers of children and purveyors of sexual satisfaction but also work at providing subsistence, their enhanced value is marked by rituals celebrating their femaleness.

High correlations have also been found between initiation rites for girls and uxorilocal residence. Here, it has been suggested, the connection is that rites signal adult female status for girls in a situation in which, because they do not leave their mothers' households at marriage, their transition to female adulthood might otherwise remain socially ambiguous (Brown 1963).

To return to male rites, another hypothesis, one not yet tested by cross-cultural statistical analysis, is that male initiation rites dramatize male solidarity in local communities in which men from several different kin groups live together. Here loyalties to the village or district are required in the competition with other localities and need therefore to be reinforced (Murphy 1959).

The attempted explanations just described have been based on information from societies at all technological levels and not merely on that from horticulturalists. No one hypothesis alone, at this stage of our knowledge, is sufficient to explain the presence or absence of initiation rites or the various forms which they take.

MORTUARY RITUALS

Mortuary rituals are believed to be significant for the community as a whole in many societies, especially those with ancestor gods for whom large-scale public rites are held. The most elaborate rites are held at the death of a prominent man or woman, and are conducted by whatever ritual specialists—priests, priestesses, or the like—conduct other ceremonies. Both male and female kin of the dead also always participate.

Curing Rituals

RESTORATION OF HEALTH

Curers, both men and women, as part-time specialists among horticulturalists, can acquire their skills and powers in several ways.

Ascribed Curing Roles. In nonegalitarian societies, where eligibility for political and concomitant religious leadership is inherited, headmen and headwomen, male and female chiefs, kings and queens are believed to include curative powers among their other abilities.

They deal with epidemics or unusual bouts of severe illness which strike a kinship group or a district. They do this by conducting conciliatory rituals to propitiate their own ancestor gods or other major gods and spirits.

Achieved Curing Roles. Among all horticulturalists there are individuals who do not necessarily have other kinds of prominence, but who achieve the role of curers. This role, when conceived of as dependent on expert knowledge, can be learned through apprenticeship to skilled practitioners. Budding diviners are taught various techniques for diagnosing illness, budding herbalists can be shown where to find medicinal plants and when to prescribe them. Both men and women function in these roles among horticulturalists, and there is no discernible pattern as to why one or the other sex or both do these kinds of curing in any one society.

A second type of curer common among horticulturalists is the shamanistic curer, like the shaman among foragers, who acquires power through possession by gods and spirits. As we have seen, trances or odd physical manifestations like trembling or convulsions are interpreted as being signs of seizure by spirits. Such an episode is often construed as a message from the spirits bidding the person seized to become a healer or diviner. The supernaturals concerned in the possession are likely to be different from those controlled by the political leaders of the group. They are usually lesser gods, demonlike creatures, or the gods of neighboring peoples rather than the major ancestral or native deities of the community.

Attempts to cure illness among horticulturalists are carried on not only through rituals conducted by individual practitioners, but also through the ceremonials of curing cults or associations. Members of these cults are often those who are thought to have healing powers as a result of having themselves been cured of severe illnesses. In many such cases the illness cured is again thought to have been caused by lesser spirits or foreign gods. Women figure prominently in these possession cults both as patients and as organizers and directors of the ceremonies once they have become members (Lewis 1971, *passim*). The men who are active as shamanistic curers and as cult members are often noticeably not otherwise in dominant or powerful positions in the society.

Why then are women and less favored men likely to be involved in cults in the societies in which these exist? It has been suggested that, under the stress of social deprivation, these men or women, consciously or unconsciously, develop those illnesses the symptoms of which are ascribed to the intervention of lesser gods or spirits. Since they cannot control the mainstream deities of the society, these persons develop the symptoms of possession by peripheral spirits (Lewis 1971).

But such supernaturals, minor though they are, are still believed to be dangerous to the society as a whole. The kin of the patients feel compelled to mobilize resistance by hiring individual curers, or, if the divines so recommend, by paying for a cult ceremony to put a stop to the evil. From the standpoint of the attitudes of the sexes toward each other and of the differential opportunities of men and women, the symptoms and the cures of these illnesses are particularly interesting.

Often the "familiar," the possessing spirit or demon, is of the opposite sex from that of the patient, and the ecstatic possession state is viewed as a form of sexual congress. Male cult shamans sometimes dress or behave as women during possession in order to impersonate their spirits. Another common feature is the pattern by which the gods and spirits believed to be possessing women patients in their trance states demand male objects to effect a cure of the ill woman. The objects include phallic symbols, fine clothes, jewelry, or special foods from distant places that are normally acquired only by men, and indeed that are difficult and expensive for a husband or other male relative to procure. In societies in which such symptoms occur, the cultural rules of proper behavior for the sexes prevent women from acquiring many coveted privileges and material objects themselves in the ordinary course of events. Consciously or unconsciously, it is through illness that these women make demands for special attention. The cures enable them to exercise a measure of indirect control over the behavior of their male kin. Less favored men in a similar situation can often control their elders and others upon whom they are ordinarily dependent.

I suggest that women are likely to be more prominent in possession cults among egalitarian horticulturalists where men compete for the control of the distribution of wealth like cattle or prestige crops, and where women have material opportunities neither for ascribed political or religious office nor for success in extradomestic trade.

In North America similar phenomena affecting both men and women occur through what are believed to be spirit visitations in dreams, in which the spirits command the performance of specific acts or the acquisition of specific objects. Under this bidding a patient or his kin may commit incest or other sexual transgressions, or acquire objects normally forbidden (Wallace 1958).

CREATORS OF ILLNESS: WITCHES AND SORCERORS

Among many horticulturalists illness and death are believed to be caused not only by gods and spirits, major, minor, or foreign, but also by the deliberate mystical acts of human beings. In some societies all deaths, in fact, are attributed to witchcraft or sorcery. Witches and sorcerers, however, have benign functions as well: they are thought to be the necessary curers for illnesses caused by the withchcraft or sorcery of others. The same people are believed to have the power to kill and to cure.

In this book we have discussed beliefs about whether men or women or both are capable of, and are actually practitioners of, witchcraft in a particular society from the standpoint of the social strains under which each sex functions, and the degree of strain between them (pp. 67–73; Marwick 1970). A distinction between capability and practice is necessary here because people's statements about their beliefs as to what category of persons are witches and sorcerers, and their explanations of who and what caused particular cases of illness do not always coincide. For example, Marwick in the article just cited found that among the Cewa of East-Central Africa there was general agreement along hypothetical lines that virtually all deaths were due to sorcery, and that 80 to 90 percent of the sorcerers were women. Marwick also collected explanations of about 200 actual cases of misfortunes, mostly involving deaths. Among these cases he found that only 55 percent of the misfortunes were attributed to sorcery, and among these, 58 percent of the alleged sorcerers were male and 42 percent female (Marwick 1970:284). In other words, when it came down to cases, men predominated as witches, but both sexes in this society indicated a belief that it is the women who desire to kill by the use of mystical power. The situation resembles the contrast in the United States between the contempt frequently expressed for women drivers and the statistical evidence showing that their safety record is better than that of men.

Most anthropological reports seem to involve generalizations made by informants, and are not based upon a systematic counting of cases. With this understood, we can use the limited information available to suggest that the expression of attitudes about harmful mystical powers and their use is a reflector of social strains. A by now classic demonstration of this point of view is Nadel's (1952) study of witchcraft in several African tribes. He compares two neighboring peoples and raises the question as to why in a similar ecological setting, with similar political, economic, and religious organization, only women are accused of witchcraft in one society, while both men and women are said to be witches in the other. Nadel concludes that in the first, as a result of changes brought about by colonialism, women have expanded their participation in trade, and by their increased mobility and economic independence are threatening the degree of control their husbands can have over them. Thus arises the attribution of witchcraft to women alone. The change has not occurred in the second of the two societies; here neither sex is singled out for the attribution of mystical destructive powers, which are attributed equally to both.

II/8   AGE AS MODIFIER OF SEX ROLES

As was the case in our treatment of the foragers, our discussion up to this point has dealt with the roles of the sexes primarily as mature adults. Age, at both ends of the life cycle, of necessity modifies these roles.

Differential Socialization of Children

TASKS

The tasks assigned to boys and girls, beginning when they are five or six years old, seem to depend on the nature of the work done by the adults of each sex, the preoccupations of the children's mothers, and, although evidence for this is not conclusive, on the labor needs of the society.

If children are given responsibilities at all, these are likely to consist of a form of preparation or training for the adult roles of the sexes. The chance that children will be given actual responsibility is greater where mothers spend time away from the homestead and have a great deal of work to do elsewhere. As for adolescents and young adults, whether or not they form part of the work force seems to be related to the labor needs of the society.

Boys. As among the foragers, where the presence of young boys on a hunt is an impediment to the men's efficiency, so among horticulturalists: if the major work of men is clearing land and engaging in warfare, small boys do not actively assist their fathers. Any substantial participation in land clearing and fighting requires, among other things, full physical maturity.

Where men cultivate crops, on the other hand, it is possible for them to take their children to the gardens. In some societies men customarily do so. But small boys can have tasks involving real responsibility. Where cattle rearing is combined with horticulture and cattle exchanges are controlled by men, preadolescent boys take cattle out to graze each day and are responsible for their care. In the process slightly older boys act as supervisors and tenders of the younger brothers or cousins who accompany them.

It is also possible for small boys to have no work responsibilities whatever, as we shall see for the Gururumba of New Guinea, among whom men do not do serious work in the gardens until after their marriage. Neighbors of the Gururumba, the Bena Bena, whose men also wait to cultivate gardens until after marriage, believe that children up to eight years of age are so immature that they do not even have dreams. Children of the Bena Bena are brutally pushed away, boys and girls alike, from the localities of such adult activities as the butchering of pigs, the preparations for ceremonies, and the religious rites themselves. Indeed, these people thought the European quite foolish for putting children of six or eight in school at all, since it was quite obvious to the Bena Bena that these children were too young to learn anything whatever (Langness 1965).

Among other horticulturalists, as we indicated in passing in our discussion of initiation, boys and men are grouped into formally recognized and named age grades. The responsibilities of each cohort change as the boys and men get older and move from one grade to another; a common basic pattern is one in which boys before the age of 12 or 13, under the direct and sometimes severely enforced orders of the next older cohort, are responsible for duties like herding sheep, goats, or cattle, or for cleaning up the village. The next age set of boys and men from 12 to about 30, who sometimes but not always undergo an initiation ritual marking the entrance into the set, are considered the warriors of the community. They practice athletic skills like wrestling and martial skills like spearthrowing, have sex relations with unmarried girls, and are in general considered to be at the height of their physical powers.

A third grade comprises men between 30 and 50: mature, married adults who are expected to father children, and to do the men's work of cultivation. They are responsible for the civic administration of the community.

Finally, the fourth grade consists of elders over 50, who either are ritual specialists of some importance or have no assigned tasks at all.

Changes in grade are marked, apart from rituals, by shifts in residence. Those in the grade of warrior, for example, often live outside the village in separate camps and return when they marry. An unusual form of residential shift is found among the Nyakyusa of East Africa. There, boys aged between 11 and 16, or thereabouts, set up their own villages. Each cohort continues to live as a group in the village thus established, bringing their wives in when they marry. When the last man dies, the village dies with him (Wilson 1960).

Highly structured male age grade systems, in which all males of a society are fitted, are most common among African horticulturalists who combine the cultivation of crops with cattle herding. The causal connection, if any, is not clear.

It is apparent that the age grade system described results in some degree of population control, since under it the warrior grade of young adult men has sexual access only to pubescent girls who are relatively unlikely to conceive. But detailed information required to established and test any hypothesis on this subject is lacking.

Girls. For girls and women formally structured age grades are rare, if they exist at all, although status changes related to age are sometimes described by a definite descriptive word. Girls may be referred to as belonging to the "preadolescent" class or the "unmarried" class, in much the way that the term "teen-ager" is used in the United States.

The responsibilities given small girls seem, as we have said, to be related to the work assigned to their mothers and to other mature adult women. If adult women work in distant fields, or engage in trade, small girls of five or six may be left in the village to care for infants of five or six months or more, with or without much adult supervision. Mothers nurse infants in the mornings and evenings; supplementary food is given by the child tender in the meantime. Boys in many societies can act as substitutes when girls are not available, and, at least in one African society, it is usual for boys to take care of younger brothers, girls of younger sisters (Bohannan 1965).

Young girls (and boys) also assist at household tasks such as gathering wood and water or tending fires. Girls only are likely to assist at cooking chores. Girls also accompany their mothers and other women to the cultivations, where they help in planting, weeding, and harvesting crops.

Almost to the extent that it does for boys, full capability in handling household tasks depends for girls on the maturation of physical strength. In societies where grain or mealies must be pounded, or where heavy loads of sweet potatoes are harvested daily, strength and endurance beyond the reach of small and even of adolescent girls is required. In a fashion similar to that of boys, girls among horticulturalists sometimes have a period free from significant subsistence activities and household chores for some months or even for a year or two. This period in their case occurs between menarche and marriage. Girls who enjoy such a respite spend their time in the company of other girls, primping, dancing, and visiting. They are often sought out by would-be lovers, with whom they flirt, and, in some societies, are permitted to have free sex relations.

SYMBOLIC MANIFESTATION OF SEX DIFFERENTIATION IN CHILDREN

Clothing, body decorations, and ornaments are used to distinguish males from females in all societies. The age at which infants and young children are differentiated in this way varies among horticulturalists, but by the age of five or six children are certain to be wearing sex-distinguishing marks of some kind.

Although less widespread, another mode of differentiation, beginning in childhood, as a symbolic statement of differentiation in tasks and responsibilities is the spatial separation of boys and girls for sleeping and eating. Among some horticulturalists it is between the ages of five and eight that boys and girls are sent out of the parental homestead for sleeping. If, as sometimes occurs, only boys are sent to grandparents or into men's houses, this means nevertheless that a significant daily routine pattern differentiates boys and girls early in life. If girls are also sent away, as they are among the Bemba, then they share with their brothers the experience of separation from their parents and also from siblings of the oppostie sex. It has been suggested that these "extrusions" are more significant markers for sexual identity than are rituals at puberty, but this view is not widely held. It is also between the ages of five and eight that, if adult men and women of the society eat separately, a child will begin the lifelong practice of eating only with persons of the same sex, whatever may have been the patterns of eating previously; this cannot fail to have some effect on sex role identification.

ACQUISITION OF FULL ECONOMIC RESPONSIBILITIES FOR MEN AND WOMEN

Neither the acquisition of adult physical strength nor biological evidence of full maturity is sufficient basis for according either men or women full adult responsibilities, in whatever way these are defined among horticulturalists.

A man's social maturity may have to be delayed until his father's death, or until he has fathered two or three children, or until he has proved his ability either at warfare or at economic exchanges. A woman may not attain the right to run her own household and control its food resources until the death of her mother-in-law or of her elder sisters-in-law. It is interesting that marriage and motherhood in and of themselves do not "naturally" provide an adequate basis for the independent control of a woman's domain any more than marriage and fatherhood do for a man among horticulturalists.

Old Age

There is probably less information on the changes in roles of either sex in old age than on any other subject related to sex roles; patterns are difficult to discover. I suggest that, in societies in which social maturity comes when a man or woman already has grown children, both men and women who live into their fifties and sixties and beyond are likely to retain power and control as long as they remain mentally active. Where ritual leadership and political power coincide, it is also likely that the control of the supernatural is not believed to diminish with old age.

Where cattle raising and warfare are important, if the elders have no clear administrative and political functions, the loss of physical vigor is felt deeply by men, and they make an effort to keep up with athletic activities, even at the risk of incurring ridicule.

The Mesakin men of the Sudan are an unusual example, but they illustrate the point. Here there are three male age grades, of which only the middle one comprising the boys and men from 17 to 25 is highly valued. The men of this grade live in cattle camps; they compete with each other in wrestling and in the practice of fighting with spears. After 25 they are abruptly moved out and into the grade of elders. Here there is no additional grade for men over 50. In this situation, men in their 40s are reluctant to transfer a gift of cattle to their sister's sons at the time of the boys' first sport event after puberty (a form of anticipated inheritance in this matrilineally organized society) regarding this gift, perhaps without realizing the fact, as a symbol of their own aging. Among the Mesakin a man's mother's brothers are frequently accused by the man of witchcraft, an index, as we have seen, of the tensions involved (Nadel 1952).

Among horticulturalists the chances are that if there is a change in the prestige and power of men with age, the change will be in the direction of a decline in power. This is not necessarily true for women. Often, after the menopause, women already in control of a household may gain added power and prestige by the acquisition of new spiritual and supernatural powers, powers from which their menstruation and their giving birth to children had previously barred them.

Among the Ibo, for example, elder women conduct lineage rituals from which they were barred in their earlier years; they can even be initiated into some men's associations. It is usual to stress in this connection that women lose their female sexual ascription after the menopause, and are therefore entitled to take on male pursuits. Another way to look at the situation is to note the fact that in a woman's lifetime entirely new roles can be acquired in old age, while, among horticulturalists, this is rarely the case for men. In consequence, old women can sometimes have more public extra-domestic power than old men, thus reversing the balance of a lifetime.

II/9 DIFFERENTIAL OPPORTUNITIES FOR AUTONOMY AND SELF-ESTEEM

Subsistence and Occupational Roles

From the standpoint of the autonomy of the individual, we can now summarize much of what we have said about horticultural societies. As among foragers, basic subsistence tasks and the ages at which they are undertaken are not matters of choice for either men or women. Specialized occupations such as crafts or trade are usually also sex typed in any society, so that men can aspire to pursue only those usually followed by men, and women those by women.

Political and Ritual Roles

We have seen that in egalitarian societies men have options as to whether or not they will compete for roles as leaders, and women on the whole do not. In stratified societies eligibility for political roles, as we have seen, may extend to both men and women who have certain kinship or seniority qualifications. Autonomy here is often possible when there is more than one candidate eligible for a position, and men or women can decide whether to compete for it or not, or whether to accept it if offered. For example, a patrilineal lineage priest among the Ibo has the right to designate his eldest sister as the Head Daughter of the lineage. The woman can refuse the office if she feels that its ritual or economic duties will interfere too much with her other interests, or if she fears that she will not get sufficient cooperation from her lineage sisters. In this society her right of refusal parallels that of the male elder of the lineage, who may not wish to take on the duties of patrilineal priest (Henderson 1969).

Marriage and Sexual Activity

FIRST MARRIAGE
Whether to marry for the first time or not is rarely a true option in horticultural societies, since the acquisition of full adult status is dependent upon the acceptance of responsibilities as wife or husband. Nevertheless, as we have seen in the previous discussion of highland New Guinea, permanent bachelorhood is a recognized status in some societies. It is sometimes a free option, but what more often occurs is this: a few men find themselves unable to marry because their elders cannot assemble a bride price for them, or because there is an actual shortage of eligible women. Such shortages can be the result not only of differential death rates for the sexes from disease or illness but also of cultural practices. For example, if the sex ratios are equal, polygny practiced by some men lowers the number of women available to others, or, if the killing of widows is the cultural rule, this fact diminishes the number of women available as wives.

Women, unless they are excluded from marriage by ritual office, also regularly marry. In a few societies an unmarried state for some women results either from physical disability, or from the father's exercise of his option to keep a daughter in his household.

The decision as to when to enter into a first marriage is sometimes made by the couple concerned, even where their personal decision has to be ratified by their elders.

The decision as to timing is not in the hands of bride and groom in cases in which they represent two intermarrying kin groups which are actual or potential supporters of each other in economic or political affairs, or in which a substantial bride price is involved. Here the chances are that the timing of the first marriage is in the hands of the elders, often but not always with little consideration for the desires of the prospective bride and groom. Indeed, some of these marriages can be contracted for while both are infants or children. The exact point at which a marriage occurs is often dependent upon how successful the elders have been in accumulating sufficient wealth to support a male initiation ceremony, where this is a prerequisite, or to furnish the bride price, where this is necessary.

That individual boys or girls in many horticultural societies have little power to choose their own spouses in first marriages should be expected from our previous discussion. As we have seen, marriage in many of these societies is entered into not primarily to provide mutual sexual access to husband and wife, nor primarily so that they may procreate children for the married pair to cherish as a couple, nor primarily to provide for mutual companionship for husband and wife in work or recreation. Rather, the marriage is often entered into primarily to enable a kin group to perpetuate itself through the children born to the couple, to establish relationships between affinal groups, and to secure the labor of a spouse.

Where there are no property transfers at marriage and the relationships between affinal groups are unimportant, by and large boys and girls choose their own marriage partners. Apart from these considerations, the choice of a spouse by or for an individual is always circumscribed by the marriage rules of the society.

LATER MARRIAGES

Second or later marriages of those whose spouses have died or who have been divorced are not necessary to validate a person's adulthood. Whether an option to remarry or not exists depends on the cultural rules of each society.

The decision to remain unmarried is not open to widows in societies in which a levirate rule exists. Here the widow is required to become the wife of a brother of her dead husband; the men can negotiate among themselves and with her as to which brother will take her. In other societies inheritance rules require that a widow marry her deceased husband's male heir, whether he is one of his brothers, or one of her co-wives' sons. Neither the man nor the woman is likely to have an option in the matter.

In the case of a man whose wife has died, of a widow where no remarriage rules exist, and of a divorced person of either sex, the decision whether or not to remarry rests largely with the individual man or woman.

Men and women remarry more frequently when no children were born of the first marriage. In general, women past the menopause are more likely than women at the earlier stage to choose against remarriage. A man's decision to remarry, aside from his personal inclinations, is likely to depend on whether he has another wife or wives, and, in cases where it is necessary, whether he can himself accumulate a bride price—for he can no longer look to his elders to do this for him.

Whom and when to remarry are for both men and women frequently a matter of personal decision. For both, the same prohibitions and prescriptions obtain as for first marriages. A divorced woman who had a liaison with another man is likely to marry him. A widow, or a divorcée not involved with another man may look to her own kin or the kin of her husband to help find her a new husband, but she usually retains a degree of freedom of choice greater than that of an unmarried girl. The widow's or divorcée's new husband, however, must certainly consent to the match.

PREMARITAL SEXUAL ACTIVITY

Degrees of Sexual Freedom. The degree of sexual freedom before marriage permitted both boys and girls in horticultural societies varies considerably. In many Polynesian societies, for example, free sexuality for both boys and girls is the rule, and is often accompanied by the belief that sex is a proper and enjoyable pastime in adolescence, to which boys and girls may devote considerable time and energy, making every effort to perfect their skills. At the opposite extreme are societies like the Gururumba, in which girls are expected to be virgins at marriage, and boys are discouraged from having casual encounters. In such societies a girl's premarital loss of virginity entails social disapproval; the practical effect may be the lessening of the bride price she may be expected to bring. A rare variant pattern is found among the matrilineal Kaoka of Melanesia (Hogbin 1964). Here, if a girl loses her virginity, her mother's brother can grant further sexual access to her in return for payments to him by her sex partners. The girl also receives gifts as a result of these liaisons. A period spent in this sort of life is usually ended by her marriage. That positive advantages are permitted to accrue to both uncle and niece from this arrangement would seem to show that a decision to engage in premarital sexual intercourse is at least a marginal option for a girl in this society.

In between the two extremes are patterns in which (1) premarital sex relations are permitted as long as a girl does not become pregnant, or (2) premarital sex relations for girls are precluded by marriages contracted before the girl's puberty, while boys are either forbidden premarital sexual activity altogether, or are restricted to adultery or to liaisons with widows and divorcées. There are also a few societies in Melanesia where free sexual activity between unmarried boys and girls is prohibited, but boys are drawn into homosexual relationships with men in the men's house where they all sleep. In these cases the boys have no choice in the matter.

Reasons for Variations. The reasons for these variations in premarital sex rules are not clear. Nevertheless, there are some conditions which appear to be related to the different patterns.

Controls on the sexual activities of the young either in the form of outright prohibition or early marriage for girls occur most frequently, although not exclusively, in societies with substantial bride-price payments at marriage, accumulated not by the groom himself but by his father or by others who are members of his corporate kin-group or the local community. Elders control the movable valuables, and through them, the ability of a man to acquire a wife; elders also control the giving of a wife in return for the property. That kin-groups in this situation should limit the sexual activity of the young so as to increase the value of sexual access to a young woman and in this way her total value as well makes sense. The prohibition of sexual intercourse for young girls is easier to enforce than that for boys, since a girl's virginity has a physical manifestation and transgressions can be detected. However, controls on the sexuality of young men, however difficult to enforce, are not uncommon. We have stressed the part played by bride price in this matter; large-scale equal gift exchanges at marriage have the same effect and for analogous reasons. In other words, free premarital sexual activity is apparently related to the absence of large-scale property transactions at marriage.

Another correlation between premarital sexual activity and other domains of a culture has to do with beliefs about sexuality and attitudes toward it. Wherever sexual intercourse is viewed as potentially severely damaging to health (as among the Gururumba) or safe only between married partners who can take ritual precautions against harm to their children (as among the Bemba), premarital sex relations are likely to be disapproved of. We have already seen that such beliefs are in their turn related to other characteristics of the societies which hold them.

Restrictions on premarital sex relations do not appear to be significantly bound up among horticulturalists with a concern which has traditionally been a deep one in the United States, the question of to whom children born out of marriage will be assigned and from whom they will get economic support. One reason for this is that the number of children conceived outside of marriage is likely to be small in the societies which we are discussing, even where boys and girls are equally free to engage in sexual activity. This is so because there is apparently a period of low fertility for human females during the year or two immediately following the menarche. Under the nutritional and environmental conditions of horticulturalists, menarche occurs later (age 16) than in contemporary industrial societies (age 12½ to 13). The girls in a horticultural society are usually married no later than a year or two after their first menstruation and sometimes before that. Where a child does result from the premarital intercourse of a young girl, it can be assigned to her kin-group or can be adopted.

SEXUAL ACTIVITY IN MARRIAGE

Reciprocal Accessibility. In ordinary routine marriages among horticulturalists reciprocal sexual services and sexual accessibility are among the rights and obligations of husbands and wives. Each spouse has a prior but not necessarily an exclusive right to the sexual services of the other. Variations from this pattern occur when, as we have seen, female husbands take women as wives, and no reciprocal sexual rights are involved. Mutual sexual accessibility is limited when polygynous kings or chiefs have from 10 to 100 wives, and the husband is not obligated to provide regular sexual services to all these women. In ordinary polygynous marriages, where cultural norms do not require that a man rotate his sexual services among all his wives equally, older women in some societies do not expect to have the same frequency of access to their husbands as do the younger ones. In some, however, the first wife, regardless of her age, may retain a prior right to her husband's sexual services. Where rotation is required, a man's neglect of the prescribed order can be viewed by the neglected wife as a serious infringement of her rights. She can demand indemnity, exactly as if she were a man expecting to be recompensed by another who had committed adultery with his wife, in a pattern which we shall soon discuss.

Still other limitations on autonomy in sexual activity for husbands and wives are those derived from ritual prohibitions on intercourse, or from their opposite, the requirement of a ritual act of intercourse. Both the prohibition and the requirement are often associated with periods in which individuals or the community are believed to be in a vulnerable state. As we have seen, the most frequent prohibition is on intercourse while the woman in menstruating. (In a few societies, on the contrary, intercourse during menstruation is thought to be beneficial).

Another frequently occuring restriction among horticulturalists is that which prohibits sex relations for some period immediately after childbirth, the so-called postpartum taboo. This restriction lasts, among some of the societies we are discussing, especially in Africa, but sporadically elsewhere as well, for more than a year after the birth of a child, and sometimes for as long as two or three years. We have already discussed this taboo as a possible antecedent for male initiation ceremonies; we shall now consider it further as a form of restriction on sexual freedom.

Why should any people put themselves in the position of prohibiting sexual activity to women for such long periods, thereby requiring either abstinence or extramarital sexual activity for monogamous men? Even where men and women customarily engage in sexual intercourse outside of marriage, the practice still limits the number of mature women available. Does the practice imply control of men over women, and accompany other kinds of male control? Or is it best understood as a device for spacing children thus limiting population under certain conditions? If this is the case, why use abstinence as a method, instead of another like abortion, which is actually the more common method in South America? And what consequences does the postpartum taboo have for relationships between husband and wife?

Efforts to discover conditions under which postpartum taboos, long or short, are to be expected have been made mostly by anthropologists using the cross-cultural technique of searching for statistically significant correlations (those greater than can be expected from chance occurrence). Correlations are sought between the existence and length of the taboo and a series of other physical, environmental, social, and cultural traits (Whiting 1964; Saucier 1972).

One such correlation has been established for Africa and the Pacific. It is that tropical horticulture with low levels of protein in the diet has more than a chance correlation with long postpartum taboo. The correlation between the two traits has been explained as resulting from the lack of adequate protein, such deficiency being especially harmful to young children after they have been weaned. In such an environment, the long period of breast-feeding permitted by the postpartum taboo might have had the biologically adaptive value of improving the nutrition of young children. There are, to be sure, societies living in low-protein environments, especially in South America, which have survived without the benefit of this adaptive mechanism, if such it be; but it should be noted, as we have seen, that abortion rates are high in South America. It would then seem to be a matter of choice between two methods of achieving a like result.

Another set of independent correlations has been found, showing that the long postpartum sex taboo is associated with societies in which it is the elders who exercise power (Saucier 1972). These correlations, however, tell us who exercises the control that enforces the taboo rather than why a postpartum taboo should be instituted in the first place. The same may be said for a correlation that has been established between long postpartum taboos and the isolation of wives in separate locations. This again shows how distance, social and physical, between husband and wife lends itself to the maintenance of such a taboo, but it does not explain why the taboo exists.

A more pertinent correlation is that between the postpartum taboo and the heavy use of women's horticultural labor. Here child spacing is the significant factor. Perhaps freedom of sex relations for both men and women is sacrificed in order to cut down on women's work as child-tenders by decreasing the frequency of pregnancy and childbirth. This makes the absence of the long postpartum taboo in South America intelligible: women contribute less horticultural labor in many societies there than they do in Africa and the Pacific. If the spacing of children relieves women of excessive burdens, women might favor the long postpartum taboo for this reason, and the need for controls might be the need to put restraints on the men.

However explained, a long postpartum sex taboo has differential effects on the sexual autonomy of husbands and wives. In polygynous societies, where such taboos are more frequent than in others, a man can hope to have another wife who is not under taboo, so that he is not restricted in his sexual activity, as is his wife with her recently born child. Even in monogamous societies, the man is not always under taboo, so that he does not suffer from ritual compulsion to avoid adultery or other illicit intercourse. Thus the woman under postpartum taboo is at a distinct disadvantage in comparison with her husband in regard to freedom of sexual action.

Initiating Sexual Activity. In horticultural societies do men or women initiate sexual activity within marriage? The ethnographic material on this subject is scanty. We may tentatively suggest that husbands appear always to have the right to initiate sexual activity (subject to the taboos already discussed), and wives are expected to acquiesce, although they need not always do so. In two types of cultures wives are likely to have the same right and may even be thought to be more eager for sexual activity than their husbands. The first is the type of culture in which sexual intercourse is viewed as a form of recreation, and a man's or woman's skill as a sexual partner is admired; this occurs in parts of Polynesia. The second is found where women have some economic independence, enabling them to support themselves and their children, as in parts of West Africa.

Control over Number and Spacing of Children. We have already seen among foragers that some control over the number of children a woman will have and at what intervals she will have them may be exercised by the methods of abortion and infanticide. Infanticide is less frequent among horticulturalist than among hunters and gatherers. It is likely to be used to eliminate infants who are thought to be anomalous in some way: twins, for instance, or those born with physical defects. In such cases cultural rules are so explicit that personal decision plays a relatively small role.

Abortion, on the other hand, is preponderantly a matter for the woman's decision, and is resorted to under a variety of circumstances. In societies with a short postpartum sex taboo, a woman already tending an infant may abort simply to avoid the work of caring for still another. Such abortions, as we have seen, are sometimes disguised as miscarriages. Abortion may also be used by a woman as retaliation against a husband, in a society in which men want children, but husband and wife relationships are hostile.

Outside of marriage there are two major purposes for abortion. The first is to conceal pregnancies resulting from illicit intercourse. The second is to allow a woman to postpone the end of free sexual activity, which the birth of a child, even out of wedlock, would entail. In both of these instances the decision rests with the woman.

Some horticulturalists, like some foragers, have a pattern of adopting children, or of giving them foster care. Adoption usually gives children the same rights as the natural children of a couple, while fostering is often a kind of child-lending pattern. Decisions as to whether to give children in adoption appear to be made jointly by husband and wife, usually for the purpose of establishing or maintaining an alliance with the receiving couple. Receivers of a child in a patrilineal descent system may want a son as an heir if they have no sons of their own, or a daughter who may serve by her marriage to establish an affinal link with a patrilineage elsewhere. In one Polynesian society, on Bellona Island in the Solomons, a mature man who has remained unmarried often adopts a son both to achieve the adult status usually gained only through marriage and also to acquire an heir. Here unmarried and divorced women may also adopt children, but they are restricted to girls; under their system of inheritance an adopted son would not be eligible as an heir to landed property.

In the West African trading societies, especially among the Yoruba, women, whether married or single, independently adopt or take in as foster children either boys or girls. The children perform household duties, care for other children, and help in trading activities. In return their education is sometimes provided by the foster mother.

Adoption gives both men and women an optional mode of increasing or decreasing the number of their children.

Extramarital Sexual Relationships. An option to have sex relations with a person other than a husband or wife is usually open to both mature men and mature women in horticultural societies, but adultery is frequently thought to be risky for the sex partners engaging in the act. For a married man or a married woman the result may be punishment or divorce. A husband may beat a wife caught in adultery, with varying degrees of severity; a wife may scold her husband in similar case, or even use physical force upon him.

Among the Ibo, the women of a man's patrilineage (his "sisters") are responsible for seeing to it that his wives do not commit adultery. If a wife is caught doing so, she is ostracized by her husband's "sisters" and by the other wives of the village as well. Apart from the unpleasantness of such social exclusion, the ostracism can impair the offender's trading capabilities, because the women of the village control trade.

The third party in an adulterous affair is treated differently depending on whether the offender is a man or a woman. In some societies, where the male adulterer is viewed as having usurped the husband's right of exclusive sexual access to his wife, he is required to pay compensation to the husband. Moreover, if a married man chooses an unmarried girl as a lover, he can be subject to the wrath of her father or her mother's brother, and may also have to pay compensation.

If a husband commits adultery, a wife can rarely exact a penalty from the woman involved. This would seem to indicate that a woman is not regarded as having as firm an entitlement to her husband's exclusive sexual services as he has to hers.

As we have seen, supernatural or mystic penalties are believed in some societies to result from adultery. Here the dangers of sex relations outside of marriage lie in the harm these relations are believed to cause to the health of the man or woman engaged in the illicit intercourse, of their respective spouses, or of their children.

In general, sexual jealousy is apt to be strong, and adultery to be the focus of restrictions and penalties, in situations in which either the social structure itself makes for hostilities between husband and wife, or the individual couples are incompatible on other grounds. It is under such circumstances that adultery is particularly risky, and constitutes at best a marginal option for men and women.

DIVORCE
Societies in Which Women Contribute Horticultural Labor. Divorce among horticulturalists is a realistic option for both men and women. The rates of divorce (although our information is sketchy) appear to be very high in comparison with those in the United States.

PROPERTY AND LAND-USE RIGHTS   Where significant bride price or substantial gift exchange is involved in marriage, the movable property is usually an element to be considered in deciding upon a divorce. In some societies divorce can entail the return to the husband's kin of the bride price received by the wife's. Especially in Africa, this can mean expensive legal proceedings for both parties. Still, divorce is not seriously handicapped by these complications.

Why not? There are two factors by which the return to the husband's kin of a bride price originally received for a woman is rendered less burdensome. First, the woman's labor services and trading activities, where these occur, are scarcely less valuable to her kin group than they were to her husband. Second, though the bride price for second and subsequent marriages is usually less than that for a first marriage, a divorcée's kin can, by a later marriage, recoup at least part of the wealth they had to return. In societies where women have independent wealth, they themselves can accumulate the equivalent of a bride price for the purpose of financing a divorce and thus completely avoid burdening their kin.

In societies in which substantial mutual gift exchanges accompany marriage, the return of the gifts, if necessary, is facilitated by their being very nearly equivalent in value.

In patrilineally organized horticultural systems with virilocal residence, a divorcée can call upon her father and brothers to grant her land for cultivation until she contracts another marriage. Thus her subsistence is assured, and the question of alimony does not arise.

In matrilineally organized societies with uxorilocal residence, as we have seen, a divorcée can continue to enjoy the use of her own kin group's land, and may eventually bring in a new husband to help her work it. In such a marriage the divorced husband, leaving his wife's household, may return to his own kin group to work an allotment of the land there, to which he has never lost the right.

KIN GROUPS   We have seen that marriages among horticulturalists usually involve not only the husband and wife, but their kin groups as well. In a high proportion of such societies first marriages are entirely arranged by the kin groups. It might seem that divorce, entailing the dissolution of ties between the two groups, would meet with considerable resistance from one or the other or both. The problem is, why, after all the trouble involved in setting up these marriages, do the kin groups seem to acquiesce rather readily in their dissolution?

It is suggested here that the very involvement of the two groups is the basis not only for marriage, but for divorce as well. Kin groups rarely relinquish all their rights in their daughters and sons when they marry. A divorced spouse has continued to be at least a partial member of his or her kin group, and the return to it does not mean a complete change.

In sum, blood ties between parents and children, and brothers and sisters, provide a residual source of support, which makes the affinal tie between husband and wife looser in some horticultural societies than those to which we are accustomed in industrial cultures.

CAUSES OF DIVORCE   What are the common causes of divorce in these societies, and which sex has the right to intitiate the process?

Childlessness. A couple's inability to have children frequently triggers divorce. In most societies such failure is assumed to be the woman's fault, and a husband is entitled to divorce her on that account. A woman may attempt to avert this action by persuading her husband to take another wife, or, as we have seen, if she is engaged in trade, she may provide her husband with children who are born of a union between one of her "wives" and an outside lover or her husband himself.

In patrilineally oriented societies a woman cannot divorce her husband because of the couple's childlessness.

In some societies with matrilineal descent-reckoning, however, if no child has been born of a marriage, it is not assumed that the woman is blameworthy, and she may divorce her husband and acquire another.

Other Causes. Apart from childlessness, divorce is the result of serious dissatisfaction on the part of one or both of the spouses with the way in which the obligations of the marriage are being fulfilled.

A wife may become dissatisfied because of her husband's inability or unwillingness to provide sufficient land or other goods, because of his refusal to call curers when she or her children are ill, or his lack of proper attention to her kin. A husband's sexual impotence, or, in societies, as in much of Polynesia, where sexual compatibility is an important aspect of marriage, his lack of sexual skill can also cause her to be dissatisfied. His flagrant adultery may be a major source of complaint if it results in the economic neglect of her and her children.

A husband, in his turn, may be dissatisfied with his wife's services to him. He may accuse her of stinginess with food for him and his guests, of laziness at her field or household tasks, of spending too much time visiting her relatives, of neglecting the care of their children, or of spreading gossip about him. A husband may also, in some societies, accuse his wife of repeated disobedience which publicly challenges his stance of dominance. A wife's known adultery is the most flagrant example of this.

Problems in marriage can also arise from jealousies among co-wives. These conflicts are not necessarily the result of sexual competition among the wives. They may arise from a suspicion that one wife is being given better economic treatment than the others, and that her children are favored by the shared husband. The quarreling between co-wives and the complaints which they bring to the husband can completely disrupt the tranquillity of the household.

As we have seen, all these instances of domestic discord can be transformed into accusations of mystical attack. Wives can accuse their husbands of using bad medicine, or sorcery, or witchcraft to harm them or their children; husbands accuse wives of using supernatural means of harming them or getting them into compromising situations.

A wife's dissatisfaction may be caused by her husband's decision to move his household to another village in search of advantages such as proximity to a political leader, or to resources of his own kin group. A husband may be irritated by his wife's efforts to engineer such a move for the purpose, for example, of being nearer her own kin.

INITIATIVE IN DIVORCE   If the level of irritation reaches the point at which a permanent separation seems the only solution, are men and women equally free to initiate a divorce?

It appears that wherever formal legal procedures before lineage or district elders or specially designated officials are required, men are more likely to initiate the suit for divorce. In such cases women are usually represented by male kin, more rarely permitted to speak for themselves. In any event, the arguments are likely to center upon the property transactions involved in the marriage, which are usually the concern of men. But there are some societies in which women can file suit for formal divorce and speak for themselves in court. What the conditions are which are conducive to one sex or the other or both having the right to initiate divorce is not understood.

Wherever divorce is less formal, a husband may on his own initiative send his wife away, and, unless the cause is barrenness, he and his kin forfeit any bride price that may have been paid. In the same informal situations women can leave their husbands on their own initiative. In some societies a woman sometimes does so in order to join a lover, who then takes her as a wife.

A woman who does not wish to appear to take the initiative in a divorce may use one of two subterfuges. She may go on longer and longer visits to her relatives, until finally she does not return at all. Or she may deliberately behave so badly as to force her husband to send her away. Sometimes, under these conditions, a woman's kin are suspected of encouraging her to pursue this course of action so that they may not have to return the bride price.

CHILDREN AS A DETERRENT   Whatever the autonomy of men and women in initiating and carrying through a divorce, a partial deterrent in horticultural societies may be the reluctance of a parent, where father or mother, to part with the children, when this is necessitated by the patterns of the culture.

In a patrilineal virilocal situation a mother contemplating a divorce must face leaving all her children except one still being suckled, for the other children stay with her husband, and even the suckled one goes back to him when it is weaned. In a society of this type a husband sending his wife away faces no such loss.

Where matriliny and uxorilocality prevail, the anxieties of husband and wife are reversed; it is the husband who must face the loss of the children. Other residential patterns entail similar deprivations. All this constitutes one factor in the slightly decreased rate of divorce for parents with children.

That the prospective loss of children is not a more powerful deterrent to divorce may be accounted for by the cultural patterns among horticulturalists which frequently separate young children from parents, thus lessening for the latter the trauma of a permanent separation. In the normal course of events, children visit kin living in other communities for several months at a time. Under some arrangements boys eat and sleep in a men's house from the time they are five years old. In others, once weaned no child sleeps in a hut with parents who are sexually active, but goes to sleep with grandparents or widows. Furthermore, as we have seen, some residential arrangements involve the movement of boys to the households of their mother's brothers (avuncular residence) at the age of 12 or 13. At about the same age, girls are frequently married or about to be married, so that they will leave their parents' residence in any case. Patterns of adoption and foster-care also result in considerable movement of young children. Though the children of a divorced couple have no personal autonomy in the matter, the patterns of movement which we have described probably tend to lessen the trauma of the separation for them as well.

Societies in Which Women Do Not Contribute Horticultural Labor. We have thus far discussed patterns in all of which women contribute labor in cultivation, and in some of which property transactions are involved in marriage arrangements as well. In a few horticultural societies in which neither of these traits exist the situation is far different. Here the woman's physical person as a sex partner and a mother often becomes a major source of value in the society.

Among the Yąnamonö, for example, women become pawns in the competition among men. Here there is no peaceful mechanism for handling cases of adultery. Instead, violent fights between the wronged husband and the adulterer are the rule, conflicts in which each is backed by his kin-group and its allies; nor is there any institutionalized divorce for either party.

Women try to run away from excessively cruel husbands, and their male kin may take them back, but here again fights break out between the two affinal groups, each bolstered by its allies.

On the other hand, if a man abandons his wife, she apparently returns peacefully to her male kin. Here certainly men have far more autonomy in the breaking of a marriage than do women.

Tactics of Indirect Control

We have discussed the differential autonomy of men and women, their freedom to control their own activities and the right to control those of others. In whatever spheres of life men or women have legal or jural rights, their ability to enjoy full use of them always depends on some degree of cooperation, or at least of acquiescence, on the part of the other sex. Men and women are everywhere interdependent.

In situations in which men have the jural rights, the more common pattern as we have seen, what tactics are open to women? Put in another way, how do those without direct power exercise an indirect influence on events, and in deciding to use or not to use this influence, in effect enjoy a small measure of autonomy themselves?

When men are in competition with each other, woman can resort to any or all of three tactics. First, if their own kin are involved, and they have retained relationships with them, they can choose one side or the other to support; second, they can act as links mediating the dispute between the two in the interest of harmony; third, without openly espousing the cause of their menfolk's adversaries, they can engage in what might be called subversive activities, like sullenness, nagging, complaints, ridicule, gossip, and, in the extreme, witchcraft.

Even where no external conflict is involved, and it is merely a matter of a woman's getting what she wants from her menfolk, she can use the third of these tactics, or, as we have seen, a modification of the first: she can appeal to her male kin for help. In this situation she has an additional resource. On the unconscious level, if our interpretations are correct, she can join possession cults, or fall ill as indirect ways of obtaining attention and recognition of her needs.

These tactics sometimes influence a wider circle than that of her household and kin group. In New Guinea at the point in the pig-raising cycle at which a large number of pigs have reached maturity since the time of the last general ritual slaughter, it is the crescendo of complaints from the women about their workload in raising yams for all these animals which impels men to decide that the time has come for the next ritual pig festival.

Among the Yąnamonö, women's fears that they will be abducted by enemies while they are gathering wood lead them to encourage the men to engage in warfare.

When women use illness consciously or unconsciously as a weapon to achieve their own ends, they set in motion the mobilization of domestic resources to conduct a curing ritual. This ritual may consume wealth which the husband might otherwise use for his own aggrandizement and thus cause him to feel frustrated.

Besides working in these ways through husbands and kin, women themselves participate in a form of indirect social control through gossip. The desire to avoid gossip can often influence the activities of those who hold the jural power in a society.

Because these women's tactics may, on the one hand, force the dominant men into actions which they do not wish to take at a particular time, and, on the other, may frustrate them in the accomplishment of their own plans, they create feeling of deep hostility.

We have attributed these tactics to women because of the preponderant frequency of situations in which men are dominant and women subordinate. Where the situation is reversed, and men are subordinate to women or to other men, they often resort to similar tactics.

When a wife cooks badly or refuses to cook for a man or his guests, or otherwise neglects her household duties, the levers a husband may use to exact compliance are complaints and ridicule. Men use sorcery or withcraft on powerful elders who control them. Where a man through his lack of success in the terms of his own culture is particularly dependent on others for support and protection, he may use the tactics of possession and illness that we have described for women.

Thus the use of these tactics, whether by men or women, can be viewed as illustrating the general principle that the structural situation in which people are placed in any society influences the means they use to achieve their ends.

II/10 SUMMARY AND CONCLUSIONS

Horticultural societies differ from hunters and gatherers by their dependence for subsistence upon domesticated plants. They use a system of shifting cultivation; their tools are the hoe and the digging stick. Plant foods are supplemented among some horticulturalists by proteins derived either from domesticated animals or from hunting and fishing or both.

Here the range of variation in (1) settlement and population size and density, (2) patterns of domestic and extradomestic exchange, (3) sexual division of labor and occupational specialization, (4) political centralization and authority, (5) domestic and kin organization, and (6) ritual forms is considerably greater than that which we found among hunters and gatherers, making generalization difficult. Still some consistent patterns may be discerned.

Control over land and its allocation is a source of disputes; warfare is endemic among horticulturalists. Interlocal exchanges of food, valuables, and marriage partners contribute to survival but are also a source of causes for warfare.

Consistency in the sexual division of labor among horticulturalists is found in the male monopoly over the initial clearing of land, and the male responsibility for fighting wars. That these are virtually exclusively male tasks can be attributed to the technology of shifting cultivation, and to the interregional exchanges and conflicts which this technique engenders.

The cultivation of cleared land is not a monopoly of either sex. It is most frequently the work of both men and women. In some societies it is assigned to women alone; in a few, to men alone. Other subsistence tasks and craft skills among horticulturalists are not consistently allocated to either sex, except that routine domestic cooking is most frequently done by women, and metal working is a male specialty.

Child tending is not exclusively an adult female task, although women are responsible for its assignment to others. The number and spacing of children appears to be regulated to conform with the subsistence activities allocated to women, and not the other way around.

In the spheres of extradomestic exchange and political and religious affairs men more frequently than women have rights of organization and control. Women nevertheless have similar rights among some horticulturalists, especially those with nonegalitarian systems of economic distribution and political control. Women have access to inherited positions of authority and power far more often than they have the right to enter into open competition for them. Another source of extradomestic economic and political power for women lies in their participation in trade.

Marriages here constitute exchanges of men and women between corporate kin groups or local communities or both. Moveable property in the form of valuables like shells, mats, pigs, and cattle is commonly given to a bride's kin by the groom's kin (bride price) when a woman moves out of her natal household into that of her husband or his kin. In another system, both sides exchange equal amounts of property at marriage.

Among horticulturalists marriage does not sever the ties of the spouses with their natal kin groups. The quality of personal relationships in marriage, the attitudes of men and women to those who are sexually available to them in contrast to those who are not, and the ideas and beliefs about sexuality prevailing among the people of a given society are at least partially dependent upon the nature of the customary relationships between affinal groups in that society.

Affinal relations are in turn affected by the systems of reckoning descent, succession, and inheritance in a society, and by the location of married people's residence. The patrilineal descent system with virilocal residence and the matrilineal descent system with uxorilocal residence have been described in some detail as types in order to outline the way in which the social structural positions of men and of women influence their behavior toward each other, and affect cultural beliefs and values concerned with the relationships between the sexes.

In those patrilineal virilocal systems in which women are neither traders nor public officials, it is only indirectly through their sons that they can gain power. In this situation a woman's maneuvers tend to create conflicts between her husband and his brothers. Women as wives, and indeed all sexually available women, are viewed with suspicion and antagonism; men are afraid of sexual impotence. Women not sexually available (mothers and sisters) are admired and respected by young men as allies against their male elders.

In matrilineal uxorilocal systems, on the other hand, the matter of sexual availability or nonavailability is not as compelling a factor delineating friendly from hostile relations between the sexes. Women both affinal and consanguineal (wives and mothers and sisters) can under some circumstances be allies or at least neutrals, and in others can place demands upon men which create conflicts with other men. Here the loyalty of young men, having little or no power in their wives' matrilineal groups, is regarded as questionable, and the young men tend to be viewed as fickle and emotional. Because these men have no personal interest in strengthening their wives' matrilineal groups, their real interest in the health and welfare of their children can become suspect; women sometimes fear that male sexual transgressions will harm their children and therefore keep children away from the pollution of sexually unclean men.

Whether men or women or both are suspected of being witches is also related to their differential structural positions.

The descriptions of the patrilineal Gururumba and the matrilineal Bemba which follow this summary are designed among other things to demonstrate specifically how (1) the tactics used by men and women to gain control over others are a consequence of the direct or indirect power available to them in in their economic and social situations; (2) how cultural beliefs about the personal characteristics of the sexes and about sexuality itself are related to these tactics; and (3) how certain rituals restate these relationships and beliefs.

There is a possibility that social structures and attitudes toward sex are together a consequence of strategies of control developed, sometimes unconsciously, by members of a society as a means of regulating the ratio of land and food resources to population.

Finally, the degrees of autonomy and self-esteem available at different ages to men and women with respect to occupation, politics, ritual, marriage, divorce, sexual relations, and the spacing of children vary greatly among horticulturalists. For each society the differential degrees of autonomy enjoyed by the sexes can best be understood in relation to the economic and social structure of the society.

On the following pages we shall give two examples of horticultural societies in which men clear the land and in which both men and women cultivate it.

Illustrative Cultures II

TWO PATTERNS OF DIFFERENTIAL CONTRIBUTION TO SUBSISTENCE: THEIR INFLUENCE ON SEX ROLES

Men Raise Only Prestige Crops Used in Exchange; Women Raise Staple Food Crops: The Gururumba of Papua and New Guinea (Newman 1965; Read 1965; Strathern 1972)

The Gururumba, 1121 strong, live in six villages at an altitude of 5500 feet in the upper Asaro valley of the eastern highlands of New Guinea. They make their gardens on the slopes of the surrounding mountains at altitudes of 6000 to 7500 feet, and as a protection against raids and sorcery, they also have some cultivation at 7500 to 8200 feet, and collect pandanus nuts at that level.

Australian government control of the region has put an end to local wars, but the structure and culture of the society developed under conditions of native warfare.

Land is the major productive resource. Two kinds of gardens are cultivated: first, those in which the crops (sugarcane, taro, bananas, and yams) are planted and tended by men, and, except for sugar cane, used as food primarily in ceremonial exchanges; second, those in which the crops (sweet potatoes and green vegetables) are planted and tended by women, and used as ordinary daily food for human beings and for pigs. There is a shortage of the type of land on which men's prestige crops grow best, but apparently none of the type needed for staple foods.

The division of garden crops into those raised by women for daily food and by men for ceremonial exchanges is adaptive for a situation in which men traditionally engaged in warfare and spent more time than women in travelling to other communities as guests at exchange ceremonials. Neglect of men's gardens on occasion does not affect the basic food supply. It is interesting that pigs, the major source of protein in this society (hunting here is unimportant), are tended by women and are fed with food grown by women. From the standpoint of the long-term nutritional requirements of the population, the eating of pigs on special occasions and at times of stress provides the needed protein balance in an otherwise largely vegetarian diet.

Cultivable lands are controlled by patrilineages. The senior man of the oldest group of lineage siblings has the right to assign plots for the use of the members of the patrilineage, all of whom are entitled to share in the land available. Husbands apparently assign plots to their wives, but a woman, even after marriage, has the residual right to work land and to use the fruits of land belonging to her own patrilineage. Thus, in theory at least, a woman has access to a wider range of land than does her husband. Men assign pandanus nut trees to their wives for tending; distribution of the nuts is subject to the husband's approval.

Both men and women own their own garden implements and net bags, as well as some magic spells believed to be helpful for the growth of the plants. The net bags are especially connected with women, who carry babies, produce, and pigs in them.

In order to prepare a new garden, men break the soil, build fences, and dig drainage ditches. (Once the soil is broken, women prepare it for planting.) The lineage rights to land are reinforced by the obligation of the men of the lineage (brothers and cousins) to assist each other cooperatively in the labor of preparing each new garden assigned to one of the lineage members, and by the subsequent right of the lineage mates to share in the first harvest of the new garden.

Next to gardens, pigs constitute a second important form of productive property. Pigs are owned by individual men, who at the appropriate times castrate, kill, and butcher them, but, as we have seen, do not tend them. Those who care for and feed pigs do so in their roles as wives and daughters of the animals' owners. The women are referred to as the pigs' "mothers," and they mourn for the animals when they die or are carried off to be slaughtered.

Pigs are never killed or eaten to supply food for routine meals; they are used only in ceremonial exchanges and on ritual occasions.

A man usually acquires his first pigs at the time of a ceremonial exchange in honor of one of the ritual crisis periods in his life. From that time on, he personally creates the necessary alliances through exchanges which will enable him to increase his herd. A man may farm out a pig to another, to be raised by the latter's womenfolk; the pig remains the property of the original owner, but the other man retains a portion of a litter in return for his family's services.

Let us now consider routine food and labor exchange between men and women. Women daily harvest staples from the gardens (in this climate sweet potatoes cannot be stored) of which they are the cultivators, and distribute the produce, cooked, to the men of their household and to their children. Through raising fodder for the pigs and actually feeding them, the women enable men to gain prestige through exchanges. In return women receive sugarcane from men, but no other routinely eaten food. The major item which they do receive is the men's labor in the initial preparation of the garden and occasionally in routine cooking.

On ceremonial occasions women receive a portion of the pork distributed by or to their husbands as part of a ceremonial exchange.

To sum up, among the Gururumba, tasks performed by women in the production of raw food are dependent upon the performance of prior tasks by men. The control over the resources required for food production, namely the land, is also in the hands of men. Within the framework of this basic situation, men depend on women for labor, and for a certain amiable willingness to assist them in the completion of the projects they begin, control, and cherish: the ceremonial pig-feasts and exchanges.

In addition to vegetable food and pigs, the Gururumba have another kind of property: valuables consisting of shells, feathers, ornaments, and the like, which are used for personal adornment and in trade. These are owned by individual men and women, but only men use them in trade and exchanges.

Finally, there are houses, which are subject to two kinds of ownership. Most are owned by the man of the nuclear family whose women and children are their permanent residents: these are usually referred to as "women's houses." There is also a men's house in each section of the village, owned by the men who inhabit that part of the settlement. It serves as a combined clubhouse and men's residence. For building all these houses the help of the men who are owners, of members of their lineage, and of all other men living in the same village is expected. Only a token return in food and valuables is given to the helpers.

A husband and his wife or wives constitute the major working members of a household. Sons of the conjugal units assist very little; they go to the gardens with their mothers until the age of seven, after which they begin to wander about with other boys their own age. As young adolescents they are involved in a long initiation process, and later in courting, so that they often do not become usefully functioning members of the labor force until after their betrothal and subsequent marriage. This situation may be a consequence of pressures on land. Daughters accompany their mothers to the gardens from babyhood until puberty, and at the age of ten start contributing significantly to the accomplishment of routine chores, such as the transportation of sweet potatoes. But, like the boys, girls have a period of free time after puberty and before betrothal, during which they are courted and sleep in a separate girl's house, one of the "women's houses" being assigned for the purpose.

Let us consider more fully the spatial distribution of men and women engaged in routine tasks. Men sleep in the men's houses, and after eating a little cold food left over from the night before, they proceed to their gardens or to errands outside the village. However, as we know, their gardens do not supply daily food requirements, so that the men often spend some of the day sitting around in the village. They do go for wood, however, which is used to fuel the fires needed to prepare the evening meal. This meal is eaten at the women's houses; it has been prepared, usually by boiling, with both men and women working together at the task.

Women, with their young children, go to their gardens daily. The plots are more distant than those of the men, and women sometimes have garden houses where they can stay overnight.

Thus, men and women are separated during most of the day, and usually at night. Men make special visits to their wives for sexual intercourse. A husband and wife, therefore, are actually together only while food for the daily meal is being cooked, while the meal is being eaten, and occasionally for sexual activity.

The major focus of economic activity from the point of view of the Gururumba men themselves is not the provision of daily sustenance, but the accumulation of food and valuables for the purpose of entering into exchanges. These exchanges arise, in their most important form, out of continuing obligations to give material property to someone as part of the fulfillment of a kinship duty. They also occur in the form of a return for some service rendered. The assumption is always that giving implies an obligation to reciprocate on some appropriate occasion (hence our constant use of the term "exchange"). The larger the number of recipients, for example, as guests at a feast, the larger the number of people upon whom a man can call for return gifts. Women are providers; men are transactors (Strathern 1972).

A "big man" is one who so manipulates his reciprocal obligations as to be the host on occasion to large groups of guests, so large that to fulfill his obligation he needs to muster the labor of, and to collect contributions from, not only the members of his nuclear family, but a wide circle of those who are indebted to him for previous benefactions. The status of "big man" is not hereditable, and women cannot aspire to it. The Gururumba are an egalitarian society.

The main occasions for exchange are rituals of various kinds: first, those connected with the life-cycle of a man's own and of his sister's children; second, those associated with the great pig festivals held every four or five years; third, those centering upon warfare. In the last named, allies are repaid by the exchange for joining the fight, and for sheltering and protecting the warriors of those who are conducting the ritual.

Even when exchanges are on a small scale, they usually require organizing the event with the help of kin and other assistants drawn from outside the nuclear family. In these situations it is the men rather than the women who are responsible for preparing the large cooking pits, and actually cooking pigs and vegetables in them. The men also heap up lavish displays of raw food for distribution.

In the course of their conduct of economic affairs and in their search for wives, Gururumba men travel a great deal through the countryside. Such travel is not possible without safe stopping places in the villages along the route. A man has to find villages in which someone will feed and shelter him from possible enemies.

Men's need to acquire allies and protectors for themselves stems from the Gururumba political system which, unless it is otherwise stated, refers to the period before Australian control. Law and order (that is, social control) are not maintained by the acceptance on the part of the Gururumba and their neighbors of a political authority, such as a chief, with the function of adjudicating disputes and the right to use force to gain compliance with decisions. Instead, a precarious peace is maintained, both among the Gururumba themselves and between them and their neighbors, by the understanding that property will be accepted as recompense for injury if an agreement between the disputants can be reached, and also by the threat of physical reprisals if the negotiations are unsuccessful.

A man expects to be aided in the settlement of disputes either during negotiations or in actual combat, if necessary, by the same groups of people as those to whom he expects to give and from whom he expects to receive assistance in the form of labor and contributions in preparation for exchanges. Those concerned in this reciprocal relationship fall into four categories: (1) his consanguineal kin, (2) his affinal kin, (3) his fellow-villagers, and (4) his age-mates, that is, those with whom he goes through his initiation ceremony. We shall take these up in order.

(1) *Consanguineal kin*

Paternal consanguineal kin are grouped into

> (a) patrilineages, as we have seen; several patrilineages whose members trace descent agnatically to a distant common ancestor consider themselves joined in a
>
> (b) patriclan: the three patriclans of the Gururumba constitute a
>
> (c) phratry, which is coterminous with the Gururumba as a whole. Again, we shall take up these subdivisions of consanguineal kin in order.

(a) *Patrilineage*:   The members of a man's patrilineage are divided into, first, those senior to him, that is, they are ahead of him in the succession to the headship of the patrilineage; second, those on his own level; third, those junior to him. Senior male patrilineage members can be counted on to allocate land to a man, as we have seen, and to arrange his marriage. The women elders of his lineage and his own elder sisters (who have married into other communities) are expected to shelter him and provide him with food on his travels. The men on his own level are expected to collect the bride price for him, to help with his first garden, and to support him in any dispute. The junior members of his patrilineage are under his tutelage. These men, his younger brothers and sons, may be ordered to perform various menial tasks. The women in this group, his younger sisters, his daughters, his nieces, and the daughters of his younger brothers are valuable to him because he may bestow them as wives, receiving bride price, and cementing alliances thereby.

A man's mother's patrilineage (not his own) can also be counted on for various purposes: his mother's brothers support him in his life-cycle ceremonies; his mother's sisters, like the elder women of his own lineage, are available for shelter and food.

(b) *Patriclans*:   A man's patriclan exchanges women as wives with members of another patriclan. The patriclans are also military units, mobilized, for example, to avenge the death of any patriclan member. Since the Australian control took effect, these wars have been fought only with sticks and stones, but previously they had been fought with arrows, spears, and axes with intent to kill. The clan members sit together as guests at ceremonial exchanges for mutual protection against attack; they serve as hosts jointly at pig feasts held every four or five years and at smaller food exchanges held annually.

We have noted that patriclans serve as units for interchange of women as wives; in Gururumba warfare, it is patriclan which is pitted against patriclan as enemies. In other words, the source of affinals is also the potential source of enemies.

(c) *Phratry*:   The three patriclans of the Gururumba, constituting, as we have seen, a phratry, are obligated by that fact to attempt the peaceful settlement of interclan disputes. All members of the phratry are responsible for assistance to their fellow members in disputes with nonphratry clans and in wars with such clans. All three patriclans join in religious rites performed for the ancestor of the phratry.

(2) *Affinal kin*. The rules of the Gururumba require that a man marry a woman from a patriclan other than his own; it is expected that eventually his patriclan will give a bride in return.

A man's male affines include, most importantly, the men to whom bride price was paid in his behalf by his elders, and to whom small "payments" (as if in supplementation of the bride price) are made on the occasion of his children's life-cycle ceremonies. A man can in return call on affinals to help him in arranging food displays for any of his exchanges, for cutting large stick props for his sugarcane gardens, and for similar enterprises.

A man's female affinals, the wives of his junior and senior lineage mates, all function in the way his consanguineal women relatives do; they are available to provide shelter and food when he is away from home. The same is true of a group of quasi-affinals, the wives of his age mates.

But, save for the quasi-affinals just mentioned, all affinals—men and women alike—are potentially dangerous. As members of patriclans different from one's own, they are always capable of becoming enemies in disputes and in wars, as we have said. The relationship with affinal relatives is therefore always ambiguous; a man needs to count on them for help for himself and his children, but he is always wary of their response.

This situation strongly influences the relationships between husband and wife, and those between all men and women who are sexually available to each other.

(3) *Fellow villagers.* A village is physically divided into sections based on the affiliation of its initated men with a particular men's house. Patrilineages of different patriclans can live in one village.

The majority of men in a village have some men of their own patrilineage as fellow villagers; their wives usually come from elsewhere. A minority of men are without patrilineal kin in the village, either because they are living with the patrilineage of their wives, or because they have decided to join a "big man" not of their kin. A village, therefore, always includes men and women from different patrilineal kin groups.

As common residents of the village, they have certain rights and obligations. These include moving jointly into the forest to gather pandanus nuts, and performing joint rituals meant to insure the growth of these nuts; sitting as an audience and otherwise participating in court cases; assigning a "woman's house" for village courtship use; acting as hosts and organizers (and hence complementarily as guests) in exchanges; conducting the funeral of a resident none of whose clan members live in the village; and participating in giving bride price for the male inhabitants.

(4) *Age mates.* For any man his age mates are those who are initiated into the men's cult at the same time as he. No one of these men is expected to consummate his marriage until all his age mates have at least been betrothed. As adults, they frequently engage in economic exchanges with each other. The wives of age mates afford a man shelter and food on his travels.

From among the four categories just listed, a man's affinal kin are the least secure source of assistance, while at the same time they are potentially the most useful, because if so disposed they can serve as allies in a hostile territory. A Gururumba man acquires the whole range of affines (his wife and her patrilineage, his sons-in-law and their patrilineages, and the wives and sons-in-law of his junior lineage mates, and their patrilineages) through the operation of the Gururumba marriage system, which we shall shortly discuss.

Unlike the men, the women, participating as principals neither in exchanges nor in war, have much less need of assistance outside their own natal patrilineages and their nuclear families, though their potential sources of assistance are comparable to the men's. But they do need at all times the support of their patrilineage.

A woman expects the elder men of her patrilineage to arrange her marriage. If she should avail herself of her privilege to claim some of the patrilineage land, it is they who will assign it. The senior members of her patrilineage are expected to back her in disputes with her husband. Her brothers also help her in the life-cycle rituals of her children.

On her side, she is responsible for offering shelter and food to her younger brothers and her brothers' and sisters' children when they are away from home.

In the circle of her affinals (her husband and his kin) apart from her gardening and cooking tasks, a woman has the important function of bearing and rearing children to strengthen her husband's patrilineage. She also functions as a link between him and her kin.

In disputes between her husband and his patriclan on the one hand and the members of her patriclan on the other, a woman is in a position to try either to pacify her husband and her kin, or, if she has a grudge against either side, to exacerbate the difficulties. This ambiguity in a woman's loyalties between potentially hostile kin groups creates considerable tension in husband-and-wife relationships.

In fewer than one-third of Gururumbu marriages, the husband, instead of taking his wife to his village to live, comes to her village to live with her patrilineage. In such cases the woman acquires some of the privileges of the men of her lineage. She can give public evidence in court cases, and eventually, when she is old, she can become custodian of ritual objects associated with her village section's men's house —an astounding privilege, because other women are not even supposed to know that the objects exist. It would seem as if, by not physically leaving her patrilineage and by having her children grow up in the vicinity of her own lineage, a woman acquires the reputation of having complete, unambiguous loyalty to her own lineage and clan, and she is therefore treated almost as if she were a male member of it. We shall discuss other implications of this system of residence later.

We now turn to marriage among the Gururumba. At the completion of a boy's initiation into the men's cult, when he is in his midteens, his elders are expected to arrange a betrothal and marriage for him. The most likely source is a clan to which the boy's patrilineage has already given women in marriage, but a "big man" tries to widen his affinal alliances and seeks brides in other clans as well. Once a promising bride is discovered, negotiations concerning the size of the bride price the girl's kin will accept from the groom's are undertaken. The atmosphere is rather hostile; each side has prestige at stake. The groom's kin must give a respectable amount, but they must keep in mind their other exchange obligations and the total extent of their resources. For the bride's kin the larger the bride price, the more they believe themselves respected; they cannot accept too little.

When the preliminary negotiations are satisfactorily completed, the betrothal has taken place, and the collection of the bride price, often a lengthy process, begins. The girl in her late teens is, however, immediately brought to the groom's mother's house. Between this time and the actual public ceremonial payment of the bride price, which constitutes the marriage, the young couple are expected to abstain from sexual intercourse. Such a period may last two to five years. The bride price, collected mainly by the groom's lineage mates and supplemented by his fellow villagers, is distributed by them in turn to their kin and their fellow villagers.

An interesting aspect of first marriages is that a majority of the men (63 percent) are unable to keep their betrothed wives with them. The girls either run away on their own, or are sent away because they are sullen and insubordinate. Even the second wife of 40 percent of the men does not remain with her husband. Why should young women want to leave their husbands, or behave in such a way as to force the men to send them packing? The situation seems particularly odd, because if a girl returns to her mother's house, the bride price must be returned by her patrilineage, which is never a pleasing prospect. Why then is there not more pressure on her from her kinsmen to stay married? Again, husbands are entitled to beat their wives in this society, and actually do so from time to time; why, then, do they not simply beat their wives into submission instead of sending them away?

To attempt to understand the situation we need to consider several conditions both antecedent and subsequent to the marriage. From the time of a girl's first menstruation ritual (to be discussed later) until her betrothal, she is freed from garden work and household tasks, and spends her time primping and dressing in preparation for the courtship parties that take place at night. As we have seen, a woman's house in each village is used for these. The girls gather inside the house after dark and wait for the young men to come to them, often from distant villages. There is considerable fondling, but apparently sexual intercourse does not occur. A girl can always reject a young man's advances; he, on his side, tries to entice the girl directly with gifts of valuables and indirectly with magic spells. For the girl, it is advantageous to prolong this period in her life. On the one hand she has few responsibilities and no hard work, and on the other the active, direct power to control men's relationships with her.

Her betrothal can be a severe shock to her, particularly when, as is often the case, her elders choose her husband not in accordance with her preference for one or another of the boys who have been courting her but to suit their exchange obligations and aspirations. In addition, upon betrothal her removal to her husband's village, often distant from her own, and the beginning of her work in her mother-in-law's garden and with her husband's pigs, under her mother-in-law's eye, come as an abrupt and painful change from her immediate past. She may feel badly treated also in that the inception of her sexual gratification is delayed too long while her husband waits until all his age mates are affianced before he consummates the marriage.

It is expected that the bride will attempt to ease the transition by paying visits back to her own village; this practice is sometimes continued even after the marriage has been consummated.

It should be noted in this connection that this kind of visit is one of the few occasions on which women travel any considerable distance. Their need for multiple sources of shelter and food en route is much slighter than that of the men, and women have correspondingly less need than the men to activate the kin connections to which they could, if necessary, lay claim.

To return to the young wife visiting her home village, such visits can become so frequent and prolonged as to constitute abandonment of her husband. It is usual in such cases that the girl has not yet become pregnant, and so has not begun to fulfill her child-bearing obligation to her husband's lineage for which, in large part, the bride price was paid. As a result, her kinsmen have to repay the bride price to those from whom it was received. However reluctantly, her own patrilineage members accept her return, perhaps because there is a shortage of women available for marriage (10 percent of the marriages are polygynous, and 4 percent of the adult men are bachelors), and the chances are excellent (there are no spinsters among the

Gururumba) that she will eventually marry and bring them a bride price which they can keep. The pressure on a woman to stay married increases as she gets older, and eventually she remains in a household as a permanent wife.

But what of the young man? It is usually after this first betrothed has left him that he goes to courting parties in the hope of enticing a girl to elope; this done, he hopes that his elders will arrange the bride price. The young man knows which girls are eligible, whose acquisition would be advantageous to himself and his kinsmen. He courts one of these. She teases him, promises to elope, and then does not go with him; she requests more gifts, and upon getting them may turn to someone else, so that he has to start all over again with another girl.

The young man's situation is further complicated by the Gururumba belief that sexual intercourse, through contact with women, depletes a man's energies, and can inhibit his growth: chastity is the best policy! This point of view conflicts with equally strong cultural emphasis on the need to father children to strengthen his patrilineage and patriclan, and with his realization, acquired partly through the joking and teasing of the elder men in the men's house, that he will not attain his full masculine strength until he has either managed to have sexual intercourse secretly or has consummated a marriage.

After the stressful period for both men and women, there usually follows a period of relative stability in marriage. Once children are born the transfer of property from the husband's kin to the wife's, begun by the bride price, continues: the husband must now give food and valuables to his wife's patrilineal kinsmen, such distribution occurring at the time of the life-cycle rituals of his children. These rituals include those connected with birth, naming, the child's first steps, the assumption of hair ornaments by pubescent girls, nose-piercing for boys, the onset of menstruation, male initiation, and death. In return, the wife's lineage through her brothers is expected to contribute labor in such ceremonies for the children. It must be stressed that although these gifts are considered obligations, the opportunity for giving is welcomed. This almost always takes place at public occasions, with a chance for carefully arranged displays of food, and long speeches in which a man boasts of his ability as a warrior. These same public occasions are always risky, however, since clans linked by marriage are potentially hostile, as we know, and there is always the danger that fighting will break out.

Those men who have the physical strength and energy to prepare gardens for more than one wife, who have the ability to gain the cooperation of wives, who have acquired reputation as warriors, and who have the understanding of character which enables them to get the most out of other men in exchanges become in their 30s and 40s the village's "big men."

A few men, however, in the early years of their marriages, before they reach their mid-30s, exhibit a form of psychic disturbance: they go "wild." They are usually men unable to fulfill their economic exchange obligations. These men demand insignificant objects, are given them, and then make a great show about how valuable the objects are. They then go off, wandering around for days, and finally return having discarded the objects somewhere.

After such an episode, a man is regarded as marginal to the system of exchanges, and henceforth comparatively little is expected of him (Newman 1964).

Men in their 40s or 50s can become curers. It is not clear from the ethnographies whether "big men" ever do so, or whether the specialty is taken on by ordinary men, or by those who were insignificant in their young adulthood. The personality of curers is rather closed, and they are somewhat taciturn, in direct contrast with the flamboyance characteristic of "big men." It is probably an alternative career in the same way that the career of shaman is among the Eskimo. This career is not open to Gururumba women.

The life of a young married woman is attended by considerable stress. In the transition to betrothal and marriage girls put aside their carefree life and the license to tease men, and they start hard labor under the supervision of their mothers-in-law. Disputes between the two women over work and the distribution of food are frequent. The new wife's contacts with her husband are few, so that if he was originally a stranger to her he is apt to remain so for a long time. Few women in the village are likely to come from her own native locality; opportunities to become friendly with any women are rare since each works her own garden. All this adds up to a rather lonely life for a young woman.

In her own right a woman derives no personal satisfaction from her husband's public exchanges; in fact, she suffers thereby the loss of the pigs which she has so carefully nurtured. Some women look for consolation by taking on lovers. Even if they do not they can be accused by their husbands of fickleness, a common Gururumba charge made by men against women in general. Women are also accused by men of wilfully failing in their two major obligations to a man's patrilineage: procreation and productive horticultural labor. They are accused of unwillingness to bear children, Actually, women sometimes secretly terminate pregnancies by abortions; they sometimes commit infanticide in anger against their husbands. Abortion and infanticide in polygynous marriages sometimes stem from a woman's jealousy of her husband's other wives, who will have exlusive sexual access to the common husband while the postparturient wife is under taboo.

With regard to their other obligation, the women are frequently accused of laziness and of the wilfull neglect of their gardens.

An interesting question is why women do not identify themselves, as do the wives of the leaders of Eskimo whaling crews, with their husband's prestige. If they did so, they might consider it in their own interest to provide children for them, and to work hard to help them by producing food for their exchanges. Why does it not usually seem to their advantage to do so?

I believe that the answer lies in the structure of the Gururumba system, in which it is to the advantage of the men to maintain good relations with their affines, and in which structurally defined occasions frequently occur when affinals are expected to meet for the purpose of maintaining such relations. One effect of this is that wives regularly have access to their own patrilineal kinsmen and do not easily lose their loyalties to them. Nor would their husbands want them to do so. The assistance of a cooperative wife who has maintained close relations with her kin is very valuable.

Women, in turn, want to stay on friendly terms with their brothers and others of their patrilineage. These are their only allies in case of excessive mistreatment by their husbands, and in any case these relatives have responsibilities toward the women's children. All this militates against the wive's whole-hearted identification with her husband's prestige.

To revert to an earlier topic, we are now in a position to see why the form of residence in which a man moves into his wife's village is comparatively rare. Full social approval is withheld from this type of residence because, as a result of it, the man instead of the woman becomes the link between affinals, and he is not as efficient a link.

As a man and co-resident of his wife's male patrilineal kin, he has many occasions for cooperating with them. He uses their patrilineage lands, joins them in making gardens, helps them with labor for their exchanges, inhabits the men's house with them, and is a fellow-host when visitors come.

All this is quite unlike the experience of a woman who goes to live an isolated life in her husband's village. The uxorilocal man becomes almost a *de facto* member of his wife's patrilineage, and his need for his own patrilineage's help and the closeness of his ties with it are lessened. As a worker in his wife's village he is welcomed; as an ambassador to his own lineage he is almost valueless.

The fact that this man's wife continues to reside in her own village lessens her value, too, as a link between patrilineages. She has no connections with or in her husband's clan or village. It is not necessary for a husband's kin to perform services at the life-cycle rituals of a wife's children, transcending village lines, as it is for a wife's kin if she lives in her husband's village.

In view of all this, it is no wonder that the virilocal pattern predominates; only 28 percent of Gururumba marriages are uxorilocal.

The rituals of Gururumba society reiterate, as we should expect, the stresses and strains caused by the incompatability of the elements which women are expected to bring into harmony. Some of the rituals associated with the life-cycle will be useful to us in demonstrating this.

Both boys and girls, in addition to the rites of early childhood, undergo major rites of passage which change their status from that of unmarriageable children to that of marriageable man or woman, ready for procreation. Ceremonies for both sexes involve public rituals; that for girls starts out as a private, domestic rite and is conducted for each girl individually when her first menses appear; that for boys is a group ritual and lasts for weeks or months.

At menarche a girl, as we have come to expect, is believed to be polluting to herself, as well as to men and to pigs. She remains secluded in her mother's house, where she may not touch her body, or even eat with her fingers. Her state is one believed to represent her fertility and procreative powers; she must avoid drinking water so as not to "cool" her sexuality. Her menstrual blood, the most powerfully polluting agent, must be collected and eventually disposed of in such a way that all possible contact with men or pigs will be avoided. Men stay away from her for fear of falling ill.

During her seclusion the girl is given instructions as to how she must behave at all future menstruations: she must not step over food, or straddle a stream, or hand food directly to anyone, including her own sons and daughters after weaning. She is constantly admonished about how dangerous her sexuality is to men and pigs in this period.

A day or two before the end of the menstrual period, her father prepares a special meal of grubs and tree bark to insure her procreativity, and of peppery nuts to revitalize her and make her active.

At the end of the period when she emerges from the house, she walks on varieties of tanket leaves. One type is symbolic of growth and productivity; a second, red in color, symbolizes the procreative rather than the dangerous aspect of menstruation. A third type symbolizes pigs. Among the leaves forming this carpet are those of a plant with a pliable stalk, which is later used to prepare a girl for sexual intercourse by breaking the hymen and enlarging the vaginal opening.

Her emergence from the house is assisted by three men. She walks through a hoop of sugarcane, contact with which is expected to make her sweet and attractive to suitors. This is also explained as symbolizing a butterfly emerging from the chrysalis. She walks to an earth oven, and becomes the center of attention at a public food exchange. The feast celebrates the community's success in rearing her, and is a public statement of her readiness for marriage.

The girl's sexuality, as evidenced by the diverse significance of ritual elements, involves two kinds of opposing power operating at the same time: the benign and necessary power of productivity and procreation, and a malevolent power which causes weakness, illness, and death in men and pigs. This duality replicates the girl's ambiguous structural position.

Men believe that women can control their polluting power and that they some-times deliberately pollute—in effect poison—a man's food and thus do him harm. They also fear careless women. Women, especially young girls, find menstruation shameful and embarrassing, while menstruating older women do, in fact, sometimes step over food in anger.

Men's initiation rites occur only once every four or five years, usually at the time of the pig festival. They begin with the movement of the candidates, who are in their early teens, into the men's house of the village section. There they are teased about their lack of cooperation in working in the past, their lack of physical strength, and their lack of sexual prowess. They are told that they must accept men's responsibilities and prepare themselves physically for them.

After a few days the boys, who have been hearing a strange sound which they believe to be that of a mystical bird, are told that it is made by men playing the sacred flutes. The flutes must never be seen or even known about by women. For several weeks the boys spend time deep in the forest, learning to play the sacred tunes on the flutes. The sounds themselves are thought to represent male vital essence and sexuality; these are aspects of growth and strength. The flutes are used in other rituals and are treated as supernatural beings; food is sometimes offered them, and they are ceremonially decorated.

The second phase of initiation introduces the neophytes to the ways in which they are expected, for the rest of their lives, to purify themselves from contamination by women, and to control their own growth and strength. They believe that they have been contaminated by the dead menstrual blood which they ingested in their mothers' wombs and by the remnants which still remain in their bodies of food given to them by women before they started the initiation process.

The purification procedures are demonstrated by a contingent of initiated men, magnificently dressed and decorated as if for war. These thrust small bundles of sharp-edged grass in and out of their own noses to cause bleeding. This blood is called male menstruation by the Gururumba.

The neophytes are then held by their sponsors, and sharp grass is thrust up their noses to bleed them.

The second method of purification, again first demonstrated, and then forced on the candidates, is the insertion of a piece of bent rattan down the throat; this is then worked up and down until vomiting occurs. The first time this is done to the neophytes, it is believed that the cane breaks a tissue inside the body. This tissue, the Gururumba believe, must be pierced in order for the penis to grow properly and for semen to develop. Striking is the parallel with the use of a similar device by girls to pierce the hymen, making the girl ready for intercourse and childbirth.

At the end of the day on which the second stage of the initiation takes place, the men and the neophytes return from the streams near which the ceremonies were conducted. On the way they are met by a wailing group of women, among whom the mothers of the neophytes are smeared with white clay as a symbol of mourning, and as an expression of their sorrow at the loss of their sons to the men of the society. The women assail the men with stones and pieces of wood, actually injuring some of them. The men try to move through the crowd of women, ignoring their presence. If, however, the women appear to be attacking with serious intent to do harm, the men may start fighting back, at which point the women retreat.

The final phase of initiation consists of an ascetic regimen, some aspects of which last a year, some until the new initiate consummates his marriage, and some throughout the initiate's life, until he is an old man. In general, during this phase the men cannot accept any food from the hand of a woman, any food given by a woman, or any food distributed at ceremonies connected with pregnancy or birth. These new initiates also avoid sexual contact with women, and, as we have seen, are expected to wait until all their age mates are betrothed before they consummate their own marriages. Until they are old men they may not eat lizards, snakes, frogs, or salamanders, because these are believed to feed on menstrual blood. For several months during this phase the boys purify themselves by vomiting in a nearby stream each morning, bathing in cold water, and making their noses bleed frequently. They also rub their bodies with stinging nettles, eat only "male" foods, and practice on the sacred flutes. This is all done in the interests of maintaining health and strength; similar personal purification is carried out by Gururumba men during the rest of their lives before entering upon any major undertaking.

The masculinity of fully initiated men is symbolized by the wearing of carefully tended artificial beards and in recent times by wearing similarly treated wigs as well. During the early years of their marriages, when the men abstain from excessive sexual intercourse in the belief that it is weakening to them, the beards and wigs are carefully dressed and protected. The wigs and false beards represent a controlled sexuality; their eventual neglect by older men suggests the more relaxed attitude toward their own potency which the men have acquired as the years have passed (Glasse 1973).

The final public rite of initiation occurs many weeks after the first purification ceremonies. Women and guests line up to greet the new initiates. These enter the village preceded by the old men, and flanked on both sides by men in the panoply of fully equipped warriors.

The boys are now men; they are fully dressed and painted, and their heads are adorned by huge, heavy bark-cloth ornaments, elaborately decorated. The women rush toward them, pretending not to recognize them in their new guise. Eventually the mothers find their own sons and brothers, whom they anoint with pig's grease.

The rest of the day is spent in dancing and feasting on large numbers of pigs slaughtered for the occasion, and on entertaining visitors who come to dance, eat, and thereby become debtors in the round of exchanges.

In these ceremonies opposition between men and women, overtly expressed by Gururumba statements that sexual intercourse, through the loss of semen and contact with women, involves a loss in male vital energy and strength and health, is clearly restated by several ritual elements: the male monopoly on the knowledge of the sacred flutes, the food taboos, the mock—and sometimes real—battle between men and women. The association of maleness with war is also clearly proclaimed.

But the male dependence on women for their daily food, for their cooperation in raising pigs, for their acceptance of motherhood, and, most importantly, for their position as links to allies in war and to trading partners is, I should like to suggest, symbolically expressed by the forms of purification used by the men. These, in a sense, turn men into women: men impose a symbolic form of menstruation upon themselves, and, with the help of canes, penetrate themselves as if they were women. Both danger and strength come simultaneously from female physiology in this system of symbolism, just as in the material world both enemies and allies come through women.

If we turn now to the rituals accompanying marriage itself, we find that they have what is, by now, familiar symbolic content. Mildly symbolic is one preliminary to the marriage, a series of parades of the bride accompanied on her way into the public arena of the village by carefully and elegantly dressed young girls, led by an older woman, all singing and behaving in sexually provocative ways.

On the day on which the pigs and money which are part of the bride price are actually transferred, the men of the bride's village, returning home from the groom's village with the pigs they have received, are waylaid by women of the bride's clan, who attack the pigs. The accepted limit is for the women to kill only one small pig, but, on occasion, they break out in real fury and kill two or more.

The eve of the girl's departure from her patrilineage to go to her husband's mother's house is spent inside her own house with her kin; singing goes on throughout the night. The bride and her age mates are secluded behind a screen in the house, and from time to time the bride is instructed by her unseen kinswomen on her proper duties as a wife. The next morning the money portion of the bride price is distributed to all those entitled to a share, including those of the bride's clanswomen who live at a distance, but come especially to share in the distribution. Then the entire company feasts on pork and vegetables.

Eventually the bride enters, encircled and hidden by her age mates, who sing as they approach. Then a man of the bride's clan rushes to the group of girls, trying to reach the bride. He is later joined by others in the same atttempt. If the bride has younger brothers, they jump up and stage a mock battle with the men trying to reach her. The mock struggle lasts for several moments, until the men break through the girls' circle and seize the bride. She is then taken in a procession of men and women to her husband's village, where her husband's kinsmen and allies are massed in large numbers. These serve to warn that force will be resorted to in case at the last moment the bride's clan should refuse to turn her over to them.

These ritual events seem to replicate the reluctance of women, both those older than the bride and her age mates, to give up a girl to the men of another community. They also restate the resentment which these women feel against their own men who have made the bride-price decisions. But the rites also demonstrate the ambivalence of the girl's male kinsmen about giving up the girl, for these men must fight each other—some on the girl's side—before the girl is finally surrendered.

We have space for only one other example of the symbolic aspects of Gururumba life. As we have seen, curing is a male prerogative. However, witches are believed to be women, and only women are prosecuted for witchcraft. Witches are believed to be envious and insatiable, and to work for no purpose but their own pleasures. They are said to grow gardens for themselves but not for their kinsmen or for exchanges, to attack the pigs of others, to steal food, to attack by supernatural means warriors who are all decorated for the fray and therefore especially vulnerable to such attacks. It is believed that these hostile acts are directed against the witches' own kinsmen. It is possible for a man to consort with a witch to further his own ends, but not to become one himself.

The Gururumba assign to witches attributes which, in the mind of a Gururumba man, might be the characteristics to be expected of a Gururumba "superwoman"; a witch is strong willed and has never reconciled herself to working for the exchanges which glorify the men of her husband's patrilineage and clan; she rejects her position as a despised though valuable link in the ambivalent relationships between men. It is possible that some women do, in fact, practice witchcraft. If a woman is accused, several developments are possible. She may be killed or commit suicide. Or, if the harm she is believed to have caused is not too severe, she can pay compensation for damages. Finally, she can be rehabilitated through an exorcistic rite that rids her of the witch substance.

The Gururumba are a society in which both men and women suffer from the conflicting requirements of their roles. Men are subject to the control of their elders, and are dependent on them to start their careers, but they must eventually develop new alliances and a degree of independence from the earlier authority, without losing the chance of support when it is needed. Men's relations with women have a similar structure: they are dependent on them to start their careers and to improve their alliances, but men must also attempt to control women's activities so as to bend them to the men's interests.

Women are subject to the control of their elders, dependent on men to enable them to grow food, and to bear and raise children. Their structural position, however, gives them some autonomy in that during the courtship period they have control over their relationship with men, and later can take lovers; they can also control the number of their children through abortion and infanticide. A woman's control is largely negative: she can gain some respect through fear of her noncooperativeness; but there are no avenues of reward which enable women to gain positive satisfactions.

The Gururumba present a situation in which the uncertainties and pressures of competition among men structure the unfavorable attitude which men have toward women and which women have toward themselves.

Men of a subclan and their wives arriving in another village as mourners. Note the men in front and the women in back. (Courtesy of Philip L. Newman)

Gururumba men and women entering a village with gifts for a new bride. Note women are the burden bearers and men of the recipient village are taking the gifts from them. (Courtesy of Philip L. Newman)

Both Men and Women Raise Staple Crops; There Are No Prestige Crops:
The Bemba of Zambia (Richards 1935, 1956) *

The Bemba of Zambia are a matrilineally organized horticultural people with a population of about 115,000. They use slash and burn methods to raise crops.

The grain called finger millet is their staple food plant. Subsidiary crops include edible gourds, and small quantities of maize, nuts, pulses (leguminous plants), sweet potatoes, and cassava.

Millet is pounded into flour, which is then used to make a thick, almost solid porridge. As long as the millet supply lasts, the porridge is made almost daily. Relishes eaten with the porridge consist mostly of wild greens, pulses, and nuts. Meat and fish relishes are highly prized, but the supply of both is scanty, and they do not constitute a significant part of the diet.

A second and equally important use of millet is for brewing beer. In contrast with porridge, beer is a feature of special occasions only.

The poor quality of the soil, the topography and climate of the area, and the methods of cultivation result in relatively low yields. The average household is able to produce enough millet to last only about nine months of the year. The Bemba expect to be perpetually hungry the rest of the year, when they are reduced to living on gourds, maize, wild fungi, and caterpillars.

Millet is therefore a limited resource. A cleared garden can produce for about five years, after which a new garden is started elsewhere. Residential units consist of villages with 30 to 50 huts near the gardens. Consequently, villagers move to new sites and build new huts every four or five years.

Men clear the land. This, in the Bemba environment, requires a hazardous process of tree pruning during which several men are seriously injured or killed each year. Men also fence the gardens against the incursion of wild animals, a job which involves about a month of heavy physical labor. Fences must be rebuilt after two years, because the logs of which they are constructed rot or are eaten by white ants.

After the men have pruned the trees, it is the women's task to collect and pile up the fallen branches to prepare them for burning. This is considered the heaviest work women have to do. From this point on men and women join in the work, burning the branches, sowing the millet, and hoeing the fields as the plants grow.

For the subsidiary crops grown in mound beds around the village, the men first construct the mounds, after which again men and women work together.

But it is only the women who reap both the millet and the subsidiary crops, and who carry the produce to the homestead. Women are also the regular food processors, and they gather firewood and fetch water for all the cooking. The preparation of porridge for each meal involves two or three hours of threshing and pounding grain. Even when there is a supply of stored millet women will not undertake the cooking of porridge unless relishes are also available. The fact that women alone collect the bush foods and reap the subsidiary crops used for side dishes gives them

---

* The description is based on conditions in the 1930s, but the present tense is used.

control over how much food will be prepared for the daily meals. On any day on which a woman is too tired or too busy to collect relishes, she simply does not cook.

Women also brew beer, the item essential for hospitality and special occasions. The preparation of a batch of beer takes between four and seven days of intermittent activity.

Men are responsible for most tasks around the homestead not connected with food. They sew the simple clothing the Bemba wear. They wash them as well, and take considerable pride in their skill as launderers. In former days the men made the bark cloth then used for clothing. Men build the huts and granaries, make fish-traps, furniture, and musical instruments; iron-workers are male specialists. Pottery making is the only craft allocated to women.

In the routine life of the Bemba male and female tasks are fairly strictly segregated, and at no time do women hunt or cut trees. But when tributary labor for chiefs is required, men do women's tasks as well as their own: they pile branches for burning and harvest grain. They also cook for male chiefs when these important personages pass through their village.

The Bemba, unlike many other African groups and unlike the New Guinea highland populations, do not raise either pigs or cattle; nor do they have shells, beads, or similar articles to be used as units of value or exchange (by the 1930s British money had begun to be used). The most important type of material wealth for the Bemba is raw grain stored in granaries.

From the standpoint of productive resources, there is a shortage of labor for cultivating and processing food, rather than of land on which to grow it. Although land use rights must be allocated in some fashion, labor is the strategic resource to be controlled. To understand the allocation of land and labor among the Bemba a brief discussion of their political organization is needed.

Unlike the Gururumba, the Bemba have a centralized political system, headed by a paramount chief. In addition, the Bemba have chieftainships and other offices which are held by men and women who are eligible for them by right of their hereditary positions in the royal matrilineal clan. The degree of control over other human beings exercised by a Bemba chief is far greater than that possible for a Gururumba "big man." Competition for the most important power positions is not open to all, but is confined to a restricted group of men and women in the royal clan.

The paramount chief must be a male member of the royal clan. He is believed to own all the land. The territory of the Bemba is divided into administrative districts, one of which is ruled directly and completely by the paramount chief (140 villages in 1934). Several other large territories are under the paramount chief's particular jurisdiction, but are ruled directly for him by hereditary chiefs who are members of the paramount chief's own matrilineage. The remaining territories are ruled by chiefs belonging to the royal clan. Each of the territorial chiefs appoints royal clan members to serve as subchiefs.

Sisters and maternal nieces of the chiefs and subchiefs are reckoned as being of chiefly rank themselves and as such may rule over villages. The paramount chief's mother has a small territory exclusively under her jurisdiction. She participates in the sessions of the paramount chief's council. The chiefs and subchiefs appoint the heads of villages, of whom roughly half are not of the royal clan but are male commoners.

Apart from this hierarchy of positions based on jurisdiction over localities, there exists a set of 40 or 50 fixed hereditary titles. Many of the officials who hold these titles are also of the royal clan. They function as ritual specialists and as councillors to the paramount chief, although not all of them live in the royal village. Each of the chiefs other than the paramount chief has some of these specialists as part of his official entourage. These specialists can also be appointed to village headships. Only men are eligible for these titled posts.

The paramount chief appoints still another group of male officials whose loyalty is owed only to him. The most important of these are the officers of his army. Traditionally, male members of the royal clan concentrated on warfare; they never learned tree-pruning skills and so were effectively barred from the productive labor force. The male population of commoners is consequently able to concentrate primarily on food production and is only infrequently subject to being called up for army service.

Titles and rank throughout this system are highly prized. Patterns of deferential behavior to superiors, that is, formal indications of respect, are numerous and punctiliously observed.

In the period before British colonial rule when the political apparatus just described was developed, the chiefs' primary interest was in military conquest. Success in warfare enabled a chief to exact tribute in the form of labor and of food from larger and larger populations. The chiefs reckoned their wealth by the number of their subjects, not by the size of their territories.

Though warfare has abated with the coming of colonial rule, the system of extradomestic exchange characteristic of the precolonial period has continued. It is of two types: first, balanced reciprocal exchange in which the chiefs give food and beer in return for labor in their gardens and in construction (and formerly for military service as well); second, a system of redistributive exchange. Chiefs are entitled as a perquisite of rank to receive foodstuffs and beer as tribute from commoners, as well as to exact labor from them. They are thereby able to maintain a surplus of grain for distribution back to the population during lean periods of the year, and at feasts which accompany large-scale ritual ceremonies; in earlier times the chiefs provisioned their armies from these collected stores.

What impels the ordinary Bemba men and women to work for chiefs and to submit to their demands for goods? Before the colonial period a paramount chief's ability to command tribute and labor was based on his absolute power, backed by his army, over the life and death of his subjects. Even lower level chiefs and subchiefs were entitled to kill, enslave, or sell their subjects, and in the case of women to bestow them in marriage.

It is still true that in Bemba ideology the chiefs own the land itself and the labor of its population. No commoner can cut a new garden without first declaring allegiance to the chief of the territory in which it is situated, and to the headman or headwoman of the village in which he lives. Once allegiance is established a man can choose for his garden any uncultivated plot within the territory, subject only to the right of the chiefs and headmen and headwomen to have first choice. Chiefs and commoners alike have rights to the crops from any land on which they have cut trees or built mounds, that is, from any land on which they or men acting in their behalf have expended labor.

The chiefs among the Bemba are thought to have a second source of power in addition to that which they exercise through the control of the army. They are thought to have a mystic relationship with the ancestral spirits, who, in their turn, are believed to have the ultimate influence on the fertility of the land and the welfare of the population. To maintain the goodwill of the ancestors the paramount chief in particular, but the other chiefs as well, are careful to preserve their own physical health, and to perform the personal rituals which the Bemba consider necessary to defuse the power for evil of sexual intercourse (though this is thought to have power for good as well). The chiefs and their entourage also contribute to the welfare of the population, it is believed, by conducting rituals connected with the cultivation cycle.

As we have seen, women in the royal clan can be appointed to chieftainships and to village headships. They perform all the functions of these offices. Feminine heads are not rarities or exceptions: in one chief's territory they constitute 33 percent of all such functionaries belonging to the royal clan.

Bemba women—both members of the royal clan and commoners—are entitled to plead their own cases in the Bemba courts.

The economic functions of village heads include the direction of village wide enterprises, the decision as to when to move the village, and, in consultation with the elders, the choice of a new site. Headmen or headwomen also settle minor disputes between villagers, and represent their people at the chief's court and at the British Colonial Office. They perform ritual functions as well.

In summary, the political organization of the Bemba constitutes a feudal system at a level of technology which prevents major absolute differences in the material standard of living of the population, but which does permit and encourage differentiation in control over people. The acquisition and retention of followers who will perform labor, contribute food, and receive bounty at feasts and rituals is the aim of chiefs, village headmen and headwomen, and heads of households. Eligibility for certain offices and titles is based on hereditary membership in the royal clan, but among those eligible—men and women alike—there is strenuous competition for succession to office. Women's extradomestic, formal political power is confined to those holding offices for which eligibility is based on heredity. But male commoners can hold offices, and the men engage in open competition for them.

From the level of household through that of village, district, and royal compound, the search for people to control is pervasive. In the daily, routine domestic organization of the Bemba as well as on special occasions, the extradomestic distribution of cooked food and beer are a means whereby one person gains control over others. Let us see how.

The ideal pattern of a Bemba household to which all aspire, and which many achieve, is one composed of a woman and her husband, their daughters, sons-in-law, and grandchildren by the daughters. In other words, it is an uxorilocal extended family. Women related through their mothers and grandmothers are the residential core of the group. The men are brought in as husbands, or they are temporarily retained as unmarried sons. The likelihood that the core of the household will be perpetuated down through the generations depends first on the number of daughters born into the unit, and second, upon the success of the father and mother at holding their sons-in-law. A son-in-law is a source of labor as a tree cutter and cultivator. The more sons-in-law a man has the more food he can produce for consumption and distribution. A son-in-law also adds to the number of those having political allegiance to the head of the household. He also fathers the female grand-children who will attract still other husbands to the group in the next generation. A head of house who is seeking high rank or who aspires to start a new village as headman is especially eager to keep his sons-in-law in his household. But Bemba culture affords alternatives to a man who comes to live in his wife's household, so that conditions in his father-in-law's homestead and village have to be favorable to him in order to hold him there.

A man is obligated to stay and work for his parents-in-law (bride service) until his wife has borne two or three children, usually about ten years. After that, he can ask for his father-in-law's permission (customarily granted) to leave and take his wife and children away with him. Where might he want to go? Bemba cultural rules enable a man to move to one of his mother's brother's compounds, or back to that in which his mother and his sisters live. Under Bemba principles of matrilineal inheritance and succession, a man has the right to inherit as a wife his mother's brother's widow, and he can succeed to his mother's brother's name, rank and title. A maternal uncle can always command the labor of his sister's sons. Because, under uxorilocal residence rules, a man at marriage moves into his father-in-law's com-pound, it often occurs that a man's mother's brothers live in a village different from his own. If a man has an opportunity to succeed to titles, or if one of his mother's brothers has a large number of followers, or if his village has a more distinguished headman or headwoman than that in which the man in question is living, he may want to leave his father-in-law. The Bemba also believe that it is reasonable for a man to want to return to his natal village, where his mother and some of his sisters still live: in this case, his allegiance reverts to his mother's father, whose juridiction he left at marriage.

With all these possibilities of withdrawal, a father-in-law is in the best position to keep with him a son-in-law and his daughter's children if he has several grown daughters, each of whom has brought in a husband. These men constitute a basic set of followers, who can in turn attract others. The more adherents a person has, the more he is likely to get. Consequently for a Bemba man (and for a Bemba woman too, for reasons we shall consider later) the birth of daughters is a cause for rejoicing, while the birth of a son presages only the loss of a man from his father's control. The Bemba say "to have sons is 'to throw away the seed' . . ., but to have daughters is to 'set up a local group' " (Richards 1939:113).

As for women, they can shift their residence even without their husbands. In precolonial times, old women could leave their husbands to go to an elder brother's compound, provided that the brother gave the husband one of his daughters as a substitute wife. Under the conditions of the 1930s, when men had begun to leave villages to work in the copper mines, their wives had the option of returning to the protection of the women's elder brothers.

In this setting a Bemba man's labor and allegiance are subject to a twofold call from elders: either (a) from the men and women of his matrilineal kin group, the consanguineals from whom he inherits, or (b) from his affinal elders, his wife's father and mother. The potential conflict can be eliminated and the bonds between men strengthened if a man's father-in-law is also one of his mother's brothers. Such an outcome can be achieved by following a cultural rule which permits and indeed encourages the marriage of men to their mother's brother's daughters (cross cousins), and the Bemba in fact have such a rule. A man can also marry his father's sister's daughter; this second rule is technically called "preferred symmetrical cross-cousin marriage." In one locality, cross-cousin marriages account for about 30 percent of the total.

For most men, however, the conflict exists. The outcome of forces influencing residence among the Bemba is a shifting population for any one village over time. Each village is likely to have, first, a core population of several sets of parents of grown daughters with their husbands and the children of the daughters, and second, a subsidiary population of men of the same matrilineage as the core of women: their unmarried brothers or sons, and their returned brothers or sons with their wives and children. The situation results in common village residence for men of different matrilineal kin groups.

We are now ready to consider the spatial arrangements within a village. The huts of a village fill spaces within a ring of garden plots. When a new village is started elder men construct large, well-built huts, each on a slight rise in the ground, and sons build huts near them. Granaries for millet are built near the huts of householders. At one end of the village unwalled huts function as men's club houses.

Men and women and boys and girls work together in the gardens. In the late afternoon they return to the village. In small groups not limited to the extended family women and girls work outdoors at the preparation of porridge and relishes. The tasks are sufficiently arduous so that one woman alone, isolated from any feminine help, has difficulty in fulfilling her obligations. A woman without grown daughters relies on her mother, her sisters, or other women in the neighborhood for help. The men and boys stay away from the cooking and rest in the men's club houses or near the boys' huts respectively.

When the cooking is completed the drama of the extradomestic cooked food exchange begins. Unlike Gururumba wives, who daily distribute cooked food only to their husbands and children and an occasional visitor, Bemba women regularly distribute porridge outside of their own extended family households and do not necessarily distribute food to all their own children. The Bemba eat in a variety of separate commensal (meal-sharing) groups organized by sex, age, kinship, and friendship. Men and women eat separately, and so do boys and girls. It is considered shameful for the sexes to share meals, because eating is equated with sexual intercourse. Indeed, the only exception to the prohibition against the eating together of persons of the opposite sex is found in the snacks eaten by a husband and wife in the privacy of their own hut, in striking parallelism with the privacy of their marital sexual intercourse. In contrast, a woman who eats with a man in public is assumed to be a prostitute. We shall return in our discussion of symbolic forms both to the spatial and to the commensal segregation of the sexes. Here our primary interest is in the principles of the distribution of cooked food.

In addition to the separation of the sexes, there is a pattern of separation among males: all men and boys of a village do not eat together either. Powerful elders who are kin eat in one group. Young men divide into two eating groups: one for those born in the village; the other for those who have married into it. They form two rings sitting back to back, because it is considered improper for a man to eat with his wife's relatives.

Respected elder male visitors to the village are given separate dishes for themselves; they may eat alone or share their food with the elder eating group. Young boys of nine or ten are in a kind of eating limbo. They are considered too old to eat with the women, but not old enough as yet to eat with men. They must forage for themselves and wait for scraps from the young men's groups.

Women's eating groups are not as fixed as those of the men. Women and girls from two or three closely related households tend to eat together. Girls and women continue to eat with their mothers whenever they eat in the same village.

Where do the commensal groups get their food? From the standpoint of the relations between the sexes, it is significant that the mature older women from whose granaries the millet to prepare the porridge has come are the distributors, and, as we would expect, they gain a measure of control over others by functioning as food donors. Each woman who cooks on a given day divides the porridge and the day's relishes into several portions which are carried by children to their destinations. The female donor has in each of the male eating groups either a husband, a son-in-law, or a visiting maternal nephew (a potential affine), who is the official recipient of the food and is expected to share it with his eating mates.

If eating groups do not correspond to uxorilocal extended families, how is the decision made as to who cooks for whom and whose grain is used for each basket of food? Here we need to consider the nature of the domestic unit that controls cultivation and owns the raw grain. A well-established adult married man lives in a group of huts inhabited by cooperating women: his wife, his daughters, and their daughters. As we have seen, a son-in-law is brought in as a working member of the unit. A marriage is arranged for a girl when she is ten or twelve years old. She has no influence on the choice of husband, but neither does she have to leave her parents' village, and certainly not at once. At the time of her betrothal, her prospective husband builds himself a hut near that of her father (his father-in-law to be), which his small fiancée is allowed to sweep for him. Several months later she is permitted to sleep in his hut and to engage in sex play with him, but full intercourse is not permitted. When her first menstruation is believed to be imminent, she is separated from her betrothed until after having actually menstruated she has undergone, jointly with other girls similarly situated, the public female initiation rite called the Chisungu. Subsequently, there is a marriage ceremony which signals approval for the young people to enter into full sexual relations. All through this period her fiancé has been working for her father and mother.

Marriage does not mean that the young couple immediately gain economic independence from the girl's parents. They do not have a granary of their own. Even after the young husband has made a separate garden to work, he keeps his grain in his father-in-law's granary, and it is taken by his mother-in-law, not by his wife, to be cooked. The young man depends on his mother-in-law for food, which he shares with his eating group. Finally, after two or three children have been born to the couple, the father-in-law permits his daughter's husband to build a granary of his own. In the meantime his young wife has had no fireplace of her own, nor has she had her own hearth equipment on which to place her cooking pots; she has been receiving cooked porridge from her mother. Gradually, as a young bride, she is given some millet to grind and cook for herself or to brew into beer. This is a highly regarded privilege, because it enables her to become a food donor in her own right: to distribute food to her husband, to his kin and to his friends, and also to her own mother and sisters and to her sisters' children. Indeed, even if at a later date she has moved away from her mother and sisters, she continues to send gifts of food back to them. It is not until about the time that her husband gets his own granary that she is considered really skilled enough in the judicious allocation of stored grain to know the rate at which it can safely be used up, and the amount to cook to honor her husband's guests if she chooses to do so.

The young couple have of course been working in the gardens all along, and have been contributing to the food stores of the older couple. The transfer to the young couple of control of the food which they produce is important enough to be marked by a ceremony; it is also the time at which a son-in-law may request permission to move away.

Just as a man's mother's brother is a rival of his father-in-law for his labor and alliegiance, so is a man's sister a potential rival of his wife for the right to the grain in his granary and to the little meat that he may bring back from the hunt. A sister rarely exercises the right, however, unless a man's wife divorces him or dies.

The right and the duty regularly to control the use of stored grain gives a Bemba woman direct power over her own husband's success and over that of her sons-in-law. Stinginess with porridge is a way of insulting and even of getting rid of a lazy or ill-tempered son-in-law. It is also a way in which a woman may ruin her husband's chances of gaining adherents, through his generosity as a host, from among the members of his eating group and his visitors. Conversely, a woman's success as a bountiful donor is a source of respect for her in the community and of her own self-esteem. During lean periods women do without food for themselves and their young children in order to provide porridge for their husbands and sons-in-law; women routinely eat less than men.

Like Gururumba women, Bemba females depend on men for labor to prepare gardens. However, unlike Gururumba men, Bemba males regularly help in cultivating staple foods. A Bemba woman's hard labor in making porridge and beer is reciprocated by the horticultural labor of the men of her household; a lazy or stingy women risks losing that labor. An underfed son-in-law considers himself free to leave his father-in-law.

The interests of opposite-sexed affinals among the Bemba—husbands and wives, mothers-in-law and sons-in-law—are harmonious with each other. Opposite-sexed affinals exchange labor for cooked food; each profits from the generosity of the other.

Moreover, the idea that for a man and woman to eat cooked food in each other's company is equivalent to sexual intercourse is perhaps a replication of the system of distribution of such food. Women cease regularly sending porridge to their own sons when the boys are in what we called the limbo period in regard to eating. Women do not routinely cook for their fathers once they have their own cooking pots, nor do they send food to a brother, even if he lives in the same village. All such males are in the category of consanguineals and are of course not potential spouses. Women can and do, however, send food to their maternal and paternal grandfathers, who according to Bemba rules are in a category of men they are entitled to marry. When the women were little girls these elders jokingly referred to these grandchildren as their "wives."

The exchange of labor for cooked food characterizes large-scale enterprises as well, and operates on the model of domestic exchanges. Those who do tributary labor for a chief, frequently in regions distant from the home villages of the workers, are fed in return. The men's food is cooked by the chief's wives, but women workers are given raw flour to cook for themselves. It is as if the chiefs were in the role of a father whose men workers are his sons-in-law for whom his wife provides food; the women workers are like his daughters and sisters, entitled to raw grain from his granaries. The chief's obligation to give cooked food to male tributary laborers makes the chief's acquisition of several wives to augment his labor force a practical necessity. Commoners, by contrast, are usually monogamous.

What is the structural position of men and women among the Bemba under the conditions of division of labor between the sexes which we have just described? We begin with the women.

The women of a matrilineage—a mother, her sisters, and their daughters—are likely to be living in the same village and in adjacent huts. They work, live, eat, and rear children in the same area and in cooperation with one another. They can mobilize into a solidary pressure group if a situation warrants this. For example, if a woman in her judgment has been unjustly beaten by her husband, she and her female relatives acting together throw her cooking pots out of her hut; the injured wife refuses to cook for a time.

These women do not compete for rights to land. Nor do they strive, the one with the other, for the acquisition of an energetic son-in-law: such a man represents strength for the entire matrilineage, regardless of which of these women acquires him as a husband for her daughter. When sisters are newly married they and their children share the grain which all of their husbands have contributed, as well as that which they and their father and mother have themselves garnered. Co-wives in polgynous households do, to be sure, compete with one another in food distribution, but most Bemba commoners are not polygynous.

We have already discussed the amiable relations possible between affinals of the opposite sex, that is, those between a woman and her husband and her son-in-law. The matrilineages or matriclans from which each partner comes are not enemies, and indeed, if they have been exchanging their children in marriage, they have an opportunity thereby to diminish whatever tensions may exist. For examples of such tensions, a wife has some concern lest her husband's sister make claims on his granary, and a husband that his wife's brother will entice his sons-in-law away. Another point of tension between husband and wife, especially prevalent since men have started working in the copper mines, can be the time at which a man wishes to leave his wife's father's household. Women in this case sometimes refuse to accompany their husbands and divorce them instead. But all these and similar tensions are mitigated, as we have said, by the lack of hostility between the natal matrilineal groups of husband and wife, and possibly still further by friendly relations engendered by successive marital exchange. The absence of a bride price or other elaborate property exchange at marriage eliminates problems common in societies which have them. Moreover, a woman, by her own direct distribution of food, shares directly in her husband's success in attracting followers.

What about the relations between a woman and her daughters and sons? As we have seen, a woman and her daughters work together and stay in communication all their lives. A woman's relationship with her son is warm: women may send their sons gifts of food all their lives if they wish. But after a son is married, a woman does not expect to depend on him for support, and certainly not during the first decade of his married life. Women look elsewhere for male labor in the main; to their husbands and sons-in-law on the one hand, and to their brothers and maternal uncles, the males of their natal matrilineal group, on the other. A woman does not feel displaced by her son's wife either as his food donor or as his hut mate; the son had left his mother's hut as a young child, and had stopped regularly receiving food from her since he was nine years old.

The obligations of a son to his mother are similar to those of all the men in her matrilineal line to all the women in that line. All these men will accept her in their village, especially if she still has unmarried daughters who accompany her. The mothers of headmen gain prestige from the success of their sons, but so do the sisters and nieces of well-known headmen. In the royal clan both the mother and the sisters of the chiefs hold political office, as we have seen. In other words, a mother is an elder in the matrilineal line of her son, and the two owe each other the obligations which go with that relationship. The relationship between mother and son thus is not special and distinct. Among the Bemba it is rather the brother-sister relationship which appears to have a special quality of affectionate regard and mutual helpfulness.

For Bemba women training of children and control over them takes its place among other sources of satisfaction, instead of being the be-all and end-all of her life. After marriage a woman gradually increases her autonomy in relation to her matrilineal extended household, although she can always count on cooperation from its women. She has a degree of direct influence on her husband's career, as we have noted more than once, by her distribution of food for hospitality. If she is of the royal clan, she supports her brothers and mother's brothers by giving them sons for their daughters to marry, by persuading her husband to join their entrourages, and by working to gain chiefly positions herself.

Although women commoners cannot hold official ritual titles, a few of them may achieve public recognition as ritual specialists conducting the Chisungu, the girls' puberty rite. In her old age a Bemba woman, if she is vigorous, can continue to direct the work of her household and receive its support. After the menopause she is also entitled to join the elder men during beer drinking bouts.

Bemba men are more vulnerable and more sensitive than Bemba women. In the course of his life a man ordinarily shifts residence more often than a woman does. At each shift he must establish relationships with new sets of men and women. When he is a young boy his food supply is uncertain, and obtaining it requires him to cajole or beg from men slightly older than he. It is true that in the absence of male initiation rites and bride-price payments he does not need the material assistance of his elders for these purposes. Yet, once betrothed, a Bemba man is in a difficult position. The majority of such men move to another village and start work for their fathers-in-law. Such a bridegroom, like all young married men among the Bemba, is considered to be an object of ridicule and pity. He works under his father-in-law's control and direction, depends on his mother-in-law for food, and acquires sexual access to his child wife only gradually. The position is reminiscent of that of a young bride who in a patrilineal, virilocal system works under her mother-in-law's eye. A Bemba man's only recourse in the first decade of his marriage is the threat that he will divorce his wife if he is too badly treated; balancing this is the fact that according to Bemba custom he can be sent away by his father-in-law if he is lazy at his tasks.

We have already discussed the improvement of a man's situation after he has fulfilled his procreative service to his wife's matrilineal group by fathering two or three children. If a woman does not conceive, the Bemba believe that it is her husband's fault, and she can divorce him if she wishes. As we know, a husband has the option of leaving his father-in-law, which requires his wife's consent unless he is prepared to have her divorce him.

Once a man has acquired social maturity by coming into control of his own granaries, he is expected to compete for followers. He cannot even succeed to his own mother's brother's titles unless the deceased relative's followers pledge to stay on with the nephew; he must compete with his own brothers and other eligible men for these retainers' support. In the royal clan competition of offices and titles sometimes results in civil war.

The total situation creates among men role relationships which are fragile and uncertain. A man's exact rank in relationship to other men is a shifting thing, and is continually tested by the degree of deference which others, including women, are willing to pay him. Symbols of deference to those older or of higher rank than oneself consist of behavior so obvious that people can judge their own and others' relative positions by means of them. On ceremonial occasions inferiors sing songs of praise to superiors, approach them on their knees, and even roll on the ground before them. Traditionally, women were supposed to offer such deference to their husbands, but apparently by the 1930s were doing so less and less frequently. High ranking women are approached deferentially by lower ranking men.

Bemba men are, as we have said, touchy and sensitive about their prerogatives, and are preoccupied by questions of status, rank, and position. As adolescents and young men, they try to prove themselves by feats of physical valor; men of the royal clan by prowess as warriors, male commoners by risking their lives to show bravery at tree cutting and pruning—quite literally by going out on a limb. Such hunting as is done is also conducted so as to display physical skill and valor.

In summary, power, privilege, and opportunities for autonomy and self-esteem are more balanced as between Bemba men and women than they are for the Gururumba. A man's subjugation to his father-in-law and to his wife's mother in the early years of his marriage is probably a greater and more intensely felt deprivation of autonomy than anything a Bemba woman has to undergo except for the degradation period in her puberty ritual. Otherwise, men but not women are subject to call for military service; however, women can be bestowed as wives by higher ranking chiefs, while men are not so given as husbands. Men and women can both institute divorce proceedings and can plead their cases in court. In sex relations men are expected to take the initiative, and women are expected to comply, but sexual intercourse is admittedly enjoyed by both men and women. Indeed, the prerogative of princesses of the royal clan is to have many consorts to give them sexual pleasure as well as to produce children for the chiefly clan. We may also note that the Bemba are a people on whom there are no population pressures on land, and no inhibition of sexuality which sometimes accompanies such pressures.

Women are more severely punished than men for adultery, however. We shall return to this subject later.

Witchcraft is not strongly feared by the Bemba; to whatever extent it is believed to exist, it is attributed to both men and women.

Men hold and have access to more political positions than women do; in Bemba ideology they are thought to rank above women. In this sense men have an edge in power over women, but it is not overwhelming. Indeed, Bemba women are known among neighboring tribes for their "fierceness."

The economic basis for this relative degree of balance between men and women lies in the woman's labor contribution to cultivation and in her distribution of cooked food outside her household. The political basis, valid only for women of the royal clan, lies in their hereditary rights to hold office.

Tension between men and women among the Bemba does not, as it does among the Gururumba, spring from a combination of overwhelming male dominance and an ambiguity of the loyalties of women to their affines. For the Bemba, the tension lies in the uncertainty of a man's social position. A man has to display physical strength as a successful worker, and sexual prowess and potency as a producer of children: all this in a situation of subordination to his affines and spatial separation from his matrilineal kin. His control over the marriages of his children is subject to the wishes of his wife's brothers and of her mother's brothers, who have prior rights to arrange their betrothals. A man's loyalty fluctuates between his allegiance to his father-in-law and that to his mother's brother, between that to his wife and that to his sister. To a man his wife is a donor of food and children. However, his control over her is limited by her alternative means of support for which she can call upon the men and women of her own matrilineage, especially if she has daughters.

This ambivalence in a man's attitude toward his wife, together with the crucial significance of the conjugal relationship as a basis for the exchange of labor and food, are in combination replicated, I suggest, in the Bemba idea that there is a mystic power in sexual relationships between spouses. Sex relations between husband and wife are thought to have both beneficial and harmful aspects. On the good side, the sex act is a producer of children and a source of sensuous pleasure to husband and wife alike. On the bad side, such intercourse is a dangerous polluting force which can harm children and others in a vulnerable position if purificatory rites calculated mystically to control its effects are not performed.

The importance attached to the enjoyment of sex is shown by the fact that coitus interruptus during a mother's period of lactation, rather than full postpartum taboo, is used for the spacing of children.

The mystic power of sexual intercourse between husband and wife is believed to be strong enough to make it necessary to maintain absolute privacy when it is going on or likely to go on, to the point of excluding children past the weaning period from the sleeping hut of sexually active people.

A married couple sleep in a hut together only with their as yet unweaned infant.

When the child is two or three years old and is thought to be ready to cease nursing, he or she is sent to sleep in the hut of an elderly grandparent nearby or in another village. The expedient of sending children to sleep with grandparents is used only for very young children. As a girl grows older, she moves for sleeping to the hut of a young married woman whose husband is away or to that of a widow. Boys in similar cases club together in groups of two or three and construct sleeping huts of their own. Sexual intercourse in the bush is forbidden. Therefore these living arrangements are needed to insure privacy for marital coitus. Such privacy is a Bemba requirement for circumscribing a variety of mystic powers when they are in operation; for example, it is in complete privacy that chiefs and other functionaries pray to the ancestral spirits.

The importance attached by the Bemba to transactions between affinals involving cooked food is replicated by their idea that cooked food is one medium through which the baleful power of sex can be transmitted. It is also the medium by which its harmful effects can be eliminated. The Bemba believe that men and women not purified after sexual intercourse can transfer the harmful mystical effects either by touching someone directly, or by touching a hearthstone, deliberately or accidentally: after this, anyone who eats food cooked in a fire on that hearth may fall ill or even die.

Purification from the contamination of coitus can be accomplished by performing a rite involving the hearth-fire and food cooked upon a re-kindled flame. But this purification is subject to limitations which we shall soon discuss.

Sexual intercourse is, in Bemba thought, only one of a category of activities which spark what they consider dangerous "hot" power in its participants. The killing of a human being or a lion are others. In a separate category, menstruating women and menstrual blood itself are believed to have dangerous power which is communicable by direct contact or through food. This mystic force is classified by the Bemba as "cold," along with that emanating from blood of all kinds and from corpses.

That menstrual blood is classified as a kind of death substance makes sense from the standpoint of the Bemba understanding of conception. They believe that semen, through the power of intercourse, activates the wife's matrilineal guardian spirits, whose activation is necessary for the joining of the blood of both the husband and the wife to form a child. The menstrual flow indicates that such a life-giving event has not taken place; it symbolizes death. It represents the failure of the conjugal bond to perform one of its functions, that of procreation.

Let us return to the power of sexual intercourse. Not everyone is equally vulnerable to its harmful effects. In a general way, it is thought that the mystic power of unpurified sex is especially dangerous to those who are on the threshold of acquiring a new status. Those in this position are, for instance, a new-born infant, a girl at the end of the Chisungu rite, a couple who have just consummated their marriage for the first time, and a new chief about to assume his office.

The Bemba also believe that unpurified individuals who are in a particular social relationship to each other can cause each other harm, and this is the aspect of Bemba beliefs that is most interesting in regard to sex roles.

The first sexual intercourse of a newly married couple endangers the health of both partners, the Bemba believe, unless they purify each other immediately after the act. Subsequent intercourse, not decontaminated by the appropriate rite, endangers the life of the couple's children. Purification is a private rite in which the wife pours heated water over her husband. The water is poured from a miniature pot given to the bride by her father's sister at the time of the marriage and subsequently kept in a secret place. Both husband and wife hold the rim of the pot while the water is heating; the fire is then extinguished. A new fire is made and used for cooking, and some of the food thus cooked is eaten.

The important point is that only husband and wife can purify each other after sex relations. The secrecy of the process means that no one can be sure that purification has taken place. Unpurified men and women are a danger to all hearths and fires, and therefore to all children. As a result, mothers with young children do not attend beer-drinking parties for fear that some polluted man or woman may accidentally touch the fire or hearth in the place where the party is held.

Within this framework adultery creates a particularly dangerous situation in the Bemba view. Adulterers cannot be purified from the contamination of the sex act, because only spouses can perform this service for each other. An adulterous man is believed to endanger the life of his children. An adulterous woman is regarded as even more irresponsible, because she is believed to endanger the health not only of her children but of her husband and her own life as well. It is thought that she is particularly likely to die in childbirth. Adultery puts at mystical risk the maintenance of the Bemba population in a way that parallels the risks in the material world. Let us see how.

Men as husbands provide procreative powers and labor, but a husband's attachment to his wife is subject first to the strain of his obligation to his sister. A man's sister can endanger the nutrition of his children by her rights to his grain; the Bemba also believe that a man's sister can curse her brother's children so that they will die. In Bemba symbolic terms her power is brought under control by her presentation of the purificatory marriage pot to the new bride. Second, a husband's interest in other women can strain the marriage and become a preliminary to a divorce. If divorce occurs, his children lose the benefit of their father's labor services to their mother. Consequently, they lose food; mystically, it is believed that his adultery can kill them. His wife loses his sexual services and thus her chance to perpetuate her matrilineal group; symbolically, she is dead to her matrilineage.

On the other side, when a wife commits adultery she destroys the basis upon which her husband has agreed to marry her and to furnish labor for her and her children, that is, the exclusive right to her sexual services and the right to be the genitor of her children. The proper employment of his virility is at risk; in a sense, his life is at stake. In traditional times chiefs physically punished and sometimes killed adulterous wives.

The point of view that mystic rites symbolize characteristics of relationships in the real world receives some support from a consideration of a change in Bemba behavior since men have been leaving to work in the mines. The labor service of men to their fathers-in-law is gradually giving way to cash payments, and the men are not under the direct supervision and control of their wives and the elders of their wives' villages. Their responsibilities to their wives are no longer those of personal service; they are compounded and mediated by money, a general commercial medium of value. Concurrently, the anxiety of women about the pollution of fires is decreasing, and the purification rituals are performed less carefully. In their place, women in order to protect their children have begun to use charms, which might be called generalized mystical mediums of value (Richards 1935).

The importance of the conjugal relationship for Bemba society as the means of organizing labor and distributing food is further expressed symbolically by the Chisungu initiation rite for girls: both by the fact that the rite exists and by its content.

The Chisungu, and not the physical menarche, is the marker, the rite of passage, which signalizes the boundary between a girl entitled to consummate a marriage and thereby to have children—to "found a house," as the Bemba put it, and a girl without these privileges. As with all rituals, it is not only a marker; it is also believed to provide the mystic powers which help the girl fulfill her new role. The physical menarche itself is noted only in a private household ceremony. The Chisungu is public and collective; it is held at intervals for all girls in a district who have had their first menstruation since the last Chisungu.

Most girls for whom the Chisungu is "danced," as the Bemba phrase it, are already betrothed. Their fiancés, in whose huts they have been sleeping (with intercourse forbidden), participate in the ceremony and contribute to the cost of hiring the woman who is the ritual specialist for the rite. The provision of beer and food is undertaken by the parents of the girls, assisted by the parents of the bridegroom.

The woman asked to conduct the Chisungu is usually elderly, and has achieved some fame as a midwife. She is also one who is believed to have the knowledge, organizational and managerial skill, and personality to enable her to manage a ceremony which lasts at least a month (traditionally six months or more) and which involves scores of helpers. The ritual specialist should also be well known enough to attract to the rites women from the surrounding area.

Frequently a woman with all these qualifications is a member of the royal clan, and has had a mother or a father's sister who had the requisite knowledge. Whatever her hereditary advantages, each woman has to achieve the status of a Chisungu ritual specialist in her own right. In earlier times her success was signalized by her right to wear the kind of headdress worn by chiefs and hereditary counsellors. The ritual specialist at a girl's Chisungu stands in a special relationship to the girl throughout the rest of her life, and is usually called upon to deliver her first child.

The Chisungu is one of the Bembas' favorite rituals. The participating women sing and do solo dances meant to depict certain events or to imitate certain animals. Dancing among the Bemba is a way of showing respect: by commoners to a chief, by a younger man to an elder, by a senior man to a senior affinal woman. The dancer moves and sings directly in front of the person honored. The Chisungu dancing therefore clearly honors the girls for whom it is performed.

In addition to songs and dances, there are serious mimes depicting domestic and agricultural activities. Sacred emblems with secret meanings are brought into play at various times. These include wall designs, bundles of items like food and red dye, and pottery models of objects familiar to the Bemba, sometimes made of unfired clay and destroyed later in the same day.

Some parts of the ceremonial take place in the village in an initiation hut, in front of which a dancing place has been cleared; other sequences are conducted some distance away in the bush.

The Chisungu that Richards describes lasted almost a month. There is insufficient space here to present either a summary description of the rite or all of Richards' own analysis and interpretation, or to attempt a treatment that would do justice to the quality of her work. The following discussion is limited to a few special points which are relevant to the other material we have presented on the Bemba.

The structure of the Chisungu ritual fits that which we expect in rites of passage:

(1) *Separation*: The girls at the beginning of the rite and throughout much of the ceremony are kept hidden under blankets in the initiation hut, and sleep in still another hut in strict seclusion. They are never seen unless they are actively participating in the rite. The hiding in the darkness may symbolize a return to the womb.

(2) *Transitional or Liminal Period: Degradation*: Typically in rites of passage symbols of former statuses are removed or defiled: the old role is symbolically killed, and the candidates submit utterly to the authority of those conducting the ritual. In relation to each other the initiates are equal in misery, lack social position, and are even sexless. As we have seen, pain is sometimes inflicted on initiates. In the Chisungu these aspects of the rite include the requirement that initiates wear old and shabby clothes, arranged so as to bare their breasts (ordinary clothes of Bemba women cover the breasts). They are not allowed to shave their heads (the usual practice among Bemba women). They may not wash; they go dirty and often hungry, and are prodded and pushed from one action to another. Modest and subdued behavior is expected of them throughout the ritual, despite the fact that they are teased and tormented at one point of the ceremony by the tying of tight bands around their heads, and similar painful practices. They are tested by making them catch darting water insects with their mouths.

(3) *Reintegration in a New and Superior Role*: Bemba girls, at the completion of the ceremony, are given food cooked on a new fire, bathed, and dressed in clean and proper clothes. Thus attired, they are brought out to face the community in their new guise. The new and better Bemba girl after the ceremony is different from her former self in several ways:

(a) She is protected from the ill effects of menstruation (in the course of the ceremony her body has been coated with whitewash, which is believed to have this effect).

(b) She is ready to marry and to have children. Fertility and the sex act are represented by a variety of symbols: for one, her fiancé participates by shooting an arrow into a wall behind the girl.

(c) She has acquired a new set of relationships with women, especially with the ritual specialist. She is expected to help this woman in future Chisungu rites which she conducts. The older woman is entitled to give the girl sexual instruction, in contrast with the girl's mother who does not. As we have seen, the specialist will act as midwife for the girl's first childbirth. This puts her in a position to reveal or conceal difficulties in childbirth which might lead to accusations that the young mother has been guilty of adultery. In a sense the ritual specialist becomes the sexual guardian of the girl and of her child. In addition, the girl has learned her own place in the rank order of the women of the area. This comes about through the fact

Tribute labor. Carrying in the Paramount Chief's crop of ground nuts. (Photograph from Land, Labour, and Diet in Northern Rhodesia, *by Audrey Richards, 1969. By permission of the author.*

Women pounding millet. (Courtesy of Audrey Richards)

that certain ceremonies in the ritual are conducted in the strict order of the women participants' ranks. The song which expresses the Bemba notion of rank order, "The Armpit Is Not Higher than the Shoulder," is sung again and again during these rank-ordered ceremonies.

(d) Under severe personal tension the girl initiate has been exposed to a restatement in concentrated form of the role requirements of women. At one point in the rites all the women, including the initiates, sing songs and handle objects representing domestic duties, cultivational tasks, the mutual obligations of husbands and wives, and various aspects of motherhood.

The Chisungu signalizes a change not only in the roles of the initiates but in their outward behavior. Before the Chisungu a girl may, and frequently does, behave lazily and is lackadaisical about her work without incurring criticism thereby. After initiation girls work with enthusiasm. They are severely reprimanded for any negligent or improper behavior. The girls now begin sexual intercourse with their husbands in the hope of becoming pregnant.

It is highly significant that the Chisungu does not include any symbol of antagonism between the sexes, such as mock battles between men and women, that we have seen in other cultures. Bemba male-female tensions lie in the nature of the conjugal bond, rather than in any opposition between masculine interests on the one hand and feminine on the other. The participation of men as fathers and bridegrooms in parts of the rite (though the Chisungu is carried on largely away from men's eyes) marks this lack of antagonism.

In sum, the ritual and symbolic activities of the Bemba which we have described duplicate the relative balance between masculine and feminine power, with what appears to be only a mild degree of conflict of interest between men and women sexually accessible to each other. The lines of hostility for the Bemba are between those with and without rank and offices, and between the older and the younger, rather than between the sexes.

Epilogue

We are now ready to summarize some of our findings about sex roles among hunters and gatherers and horticulturalists in order to see what perspectives we may have gained for the understanding of sex roles in industrial society. A thorough treatment of the parallels we shall present is far beyond the scope of this book; our purpose here is merely to suggest approaches for further thought and study.

DIVISION OF LABOR AND EXCHANGE

We have shown that among hunters and gatherers and horticulturalists men have greater control than women over the extradomestic distribution and exchange of valued goods and services. The basis for this greater control by men is, among hunters and gatherers, the male monopoly on hunting large game; among horticulturalists, the monopoly on the clearing of land and its allocation.

Among foragers men rather than women hunt big game not primarily because of their greater physical strength, but as a consequence of a complex set of circumstances centered upon the difficulties of carrying burdens, food or children, in the course of a search for large animals. Among horticulturalists men rather than women clear land for cultivation because new lands are frequently on the border of the territories of other peoples, with whom warfare is a potential threat. Why is warfare primarily a male responsibility? We have suggested that the physical protection of human societies is largely in the hands of men because a population can survive the loss of men more easily than that of women. Men, by their control of warfare and land allocation, are more deeply involved than women in economic and political alliances which are extradomestic and which require for their maintenance the distribution and exchange of goods and services.

Among hunters and gatherers and horticulturalists the relative power of women is increased if women *both* contribute to subsistence *and also* have opportunities for extradomestic distribution and exchange of valued goods and services. In situations in which women either do not contribute to the food supply at all, or, while working hard and long at subsistence tasks, are not themselves, in their own right, responsible for extradomestic distribution, their own personal autonomy and control over others is likely to be most limited. Moreover, the relative degree of difference between men's and women's opportunities is the point at issue. Where men's chances for giving away goods and services are not markedly better than women's, there are fewer differences between the sexes in power and autonomy.

We have already compared the plight of the Eskimo woman who contributes negligible amounts to the food supply and depends on men for the basic resources of meat and skins to that of the nonworking housewife in the United States. Here, the traditional preoccupation of high school and college girls with dating, clothes, and interpersonal relations in general, and the social class segregation in high schools are clearly adaptive to the very serious business in which the girls are engaged: the search for a proper mate. Their traditional expectation is that their livelihood and that of their children will depend on their ability to attract the right husband. Their own economic and social position for the rest of their lives will depend on those of the men they marry. High school counselors report that they have difficulty convincing girls of the hazardousness of relying on marriage and wifehood as a permanent way of earning a living. The statistical probabilities of losing husbands or their earning power through divorce, widowhood, illness, or unemployment are very real but hard to demonstrate to adolescent girls. Nor can they easily be led to understand how such a mischance may result in the economic helplessness of occupationally untrained women, and in an abrupt lowering of the standard of living even for middle-class women, to say nothing of the resulting sense of personal inadequacy with its serious psychological consequences for themselves and their children.

But what of the working wife? If our analysis of foragers and horticulturalists is applicable, such a woman, if her income is used primarily for consumption within the household, may gain some degree of parity in domestic affairs, but this is limited to the confines of the family and does nothing for her prestige and power outside it. Unless her occupation is at a managerial or professional level high enough to enable her to distribute goods and services to persons outside the home, or her income is great enough to be maneuvered or manipulated or exchanged in business, political, or community contexts, her public power and autonomy are not significantly changed by the mere fact of her outside employment (in this, incidentally, she does not differ from her husband). The women's movement which stresses equality of opportunity for women in managerial and administrative positions is profoundly right from the standpoint of equalizing the public power of the sexes.

What about the woman who has substantial wealth derived through inheritance or gift? She also does not differ from a man in a like situation. To the extent that the funds are given over for management to professional brokers or bankers, and not actually managed by her personally for investments which bring with them the control of business enterprises, she gains no public power from her wealth. To be sure, inherited and accumulated wealth, however managed, may be a source of power and autonomy for a woman within the domestic circle, and may free her from dependence not only on her husband, but on the employment market as well. Moreover, a woman with such resources can exercise dominance over her children and other kin who are potential inheritors of her legacies.

POLITICAL ROLES

We have shown that among horticulturalists political power is much more likely to be available to women in societies where eligibility for political office is inherited than in those in which it is not. Certainly this pattern is consistent with the history of the political power wielded by queens and empresses in the royal families of Europe and Asia.

In the modern industrial world women who have acquired the highest positions of political power in nonmonarchical societies have also in most cases done so through kin connections. Indira Gandhi was preceded by her father as Prime Minister of India; Sirimavo Bandaranaike was preceded by her husband as Prime Minister of Sri Lanka (Ceylon), and, when Juan Peron died in Argentina, his wife succeeded him as head of state.

In the United States widows of men who have held political office have often succeeded their husbands. In 1974 Corinne Boggs of Louisiana and Cardiss Collins of Illinois were both elected to the House of Representatives after the death of their husbands, who had held the same Congressional posts.

The point is not that in the modern industrial world this form of quasi-inheritance is the only way for women to gain political office, but rather that in societies such as the United States, where political power is routinely achieved by men in competition with other men, a woman closely connected with a prominent man may upon his death inherit his male prerogative for office, and may in a sense be freed from the political curse of her femininity.

CHILD-REARING

We have shown that among foragers and horticulturalists the spacing of children and the allocation of responsibility for the care of the young are dependent on the subsistence tasks assigned to women in a society and not *vice versa*.

The biological female functions of conception, pregnancy, childbirth, and lactation are obviously related to the universality with which the main responsibility for infant care lies with women, and for the close bond in human cultural categories of "women and children." But how many children a woman bears, how they are spaced, who spends time and energy in supervising their activities, where the children are kept, and until what age supervision is considered necessary for them, all these questions and their answers are systematically related to the total social and cultural system of a society and not exclusively to the biological potentiality of women for motherhood.

In industrial societies, for example, the number and spacing of children bears a close relation to the occupation of the mother: women who work outside the home have fewer children than those who do not. What about motherhood as an impediment to outside employment? In the United States in 1970 over 40 percent of white women in the child-bearing years between 16 and 45 and 50 to 60 percent of minority women in those ages were working outside the home. More than a third of the working women had children under 6, and over half had children between 6 and 17 years old (Gager 1974:440–442).

In spite of economic discrimination and a cultural ideology that discourages the employment of women, more compelling forces operative since the World War II have resulted in an increase in the proportion of women, especially of married middle-class women, who have gone out to work. The location of schools in residential rather than in business or industrial areas, the ineffective public transportation systems, and a social organization based on the nuclear family are all geared in the United States to the expectation that women will stay home with young children. Even with these severe handicaps the millions of working women with children in the United States have managed somehow to cope with the situation. They have found varieties of ingenious ways to take care of their children while they work. Our point is that economic and social conditions in the United States which resulted in the employment of women in factories during World War II, the expansion of the proportion of white-collar jobs in the economy (jobs which had been thought suitable for middle-class women as early as the late nineteenth century), the rise in both costs and in standard of living which increased the difficulty of supporting a family on one person's income, and the desire of many women to do work which they considered more satisfying that that of the housewife, all these factors impelled women, married and single, with or without children, into offices, factories, schools, and hospitals to earn money (see Chafe 1972). The women's movement is in part a response to these events; the trends were manifest at least a decade before the movement surfaced. It remains to be seen whether American women will be content to limp along with the present makeshift adaptations, or whether they will insist upon the development of new methods of child care which will systematically provide an alternative to the home-bound woman.

STRUCTURAL POSITION OF THE SEXES

We have maintained that the position of men and women in the social structure among foragers and horticulturalists has consequences for the quality of the relationships between the sexes, and for cultural beliefs about maleness and femaleness and sexuality. The reader will remember, for example, the analysis of Gururumba society as a system in which husbands and wives are representatives of antagonistic kin groups that nevertheless depend on each other in crisis situations; consequently, loyalties of women are mixed, and relationships between men and women sexually available to each other are strained. Here, sexual intercourse itself is viewed as dangerous to men. Again, our discussion of typical lines of cooperation and strain between the sexes in patrilineal-virilocal and matrilineal-uxorilocal societies gave similar indications. We have also suggested that cultural rules with respect to premarital sex relations are related to property exchanges at marriage.

What of contemporary industrial society? Some of the lines along which the comparable analysis would go for the United States include the conflicts in loyalties that a married woman has between the needs of her husband and those of her children, and of a husband between his responsibilities to his wife and children on the one hand and to his personal career and recreational interests on the other. Since the social position of a wife has traditionally been dependent on that of her husband and since that position is made visible through conspicuous consumption of goods and services that are status symbols, wives have traditionally pushed their husbands toward greater efforts in the competition for higher incomes. Men, in their turn, have been burdened by their responsibilities as the sole economic providers for their families. They have assumed that giving material goods to their wives and children therefore properly fulfills their responsibilities, and have considered other calls upon their time and energies by their families as an imposition.

The tensions created by these circumstances have helped to bring about the ambiguousness of attitudes toward sex in the United States. Women without access to external sources of power have been forced to behave in contradictory ways. At one and the same time, they behave toward sexually available men as passive, docile, supportive, and decorative mates, and as demanding, insatiable, and critical taskmistresses. Men sexually available to women are forced in their relations with women into wariness, selfishness, and dominance on the one hand, and indifference and contempt on the other. The attitudes toward sexual relations have been bedeviled by these ambiguities.

To what extent very recent trends in relationships between the sexes in the United States depart from this pattern it is too early to say. However, if deep and lasting changes in these relationships are to be brought about, basic alterations in the structural framework within which men and women operate will be necessary.

RELIGIOUS SPECIALTIES, RITUALS, AND SYMBOLS

Among the peoples we have discussed virtually the only access for women to a religious specialty involving supernatural beings of importance to the community as a whole has been acquired in horticultural societies as a concomitant to an inherited position of political power. There does not seem to be any parallel to this situation in contemporary industrial society.

There is, however, one aspect of supernatural specialization among foragers and horticulturalists with which a parallel in Western European culture can be drawn. Women in the societies which we have discussed may acquire a shamanistic specialty through mystic possession. Among the horticulturalists, we have suggested, this situation, in which women are thought to be subject to minor and foreign deities outside the mainstream of the community's devotion to the supernatural, symbolically restates women's lack of domestic or political power.

In Western civilization women have been prominently associated with possession and possession cults. We need consider only the witchcraft trials in Europe and in the American colonies, and the case of Joan of Arc, accused by the British of being possessed by the devil (though the French sanctified her), to see that this is so. The spectacularly successful film of the early 1970s, "The Exorcist," is about a twelve-year-old girl possessed by the devil.

In Western thought possession or mystic experience for women has sometimes taken on a benign aspect, as we see from the French view of Joan of Arc and the mysterious voices she is thought to have heard. Women are prominent in the United States in Pentacostal churches, in which they are believed to be visited by the Holy Spirit, who endows them with the power to "speak in tongues" to promote healing. Mary Baker Eddy founded the Church of Christ Scientist after having had a mystic experience, and remained pastor of the Mother Church in Boston for the rest of her life.

But women have nowhere achieved leadership in the main established religions of Europe and the United States, and efforts to bring them into the priesthood, the pastorate, and the rabbinate just began to gain momentum in the early 1970s.

In our discussions of ritual and symbols connected with masculinity and femininity, we have interpreted them as restating relationships between the sexes. We have given illustrations primarily from life-cycle rites for boys and girls among foragers and horticulturalists.

In the contemporary industrial world the symbolic systems associated with maleness and femaleness are heavily involved with the body and its decorations, in hair styles and clothing and jewelry. The initial emotional reactions of older men to the wearing of long hair and beards by boys and young men in the 1960s attested to the symbolic significance of these traits. The short crew-cut stood not only for masculinity in contrast to femininity, but also for a commitment to sexual and other restraints and discipline; the new style conveyed the message that the young wanted to abandon these "virtues." The abandonment by women of long skirts in the 1920s and their donning of trousers in the 1930s initially signaled a stride toward greater public freedom of movement for middle-class women, and the initial success of the post-World-War-I feminist movement. By wearing some parts of men's clothing and by cutting their long hair, women signalled their admission to activities previously restricted to men.

The "unisex" movement of the 1960s and 1970s is an opposite phenomenon, a pattern in which men are decorating themselves in some ways that used to be restricted to women. They wear bright colors and some jewelry, symbolizing their greater participation in tasks such as domestic chores and some types of white-collar jobs that had been restricted to women. But the changes have not led to any real "unisex," of course. As men's hair grew longer so did their beards, but women did not take to wearing beard wigs to obliterate the difference. Men do not ordinarily paint their faces with cosmetics, nor do men and boys in the United States ever wear skirts. It is indeed an indication of the lower social status of women that male skirts have not even been suggested. (Complete male and female transvesticism, the attempt of men deliberately to impersonate women and women men is another phenomenon altogether, and is outside the scope of our discussion.)

In so far as clothing symbolizes relationships between the sexes, it still holds true that women have attempted to take on male clothing more assiduously than men have accepted female. Moreover, class differences in female clothing are particularly noticeable. Working-class and lower middle-class women are thought by the upper middle classes to like gaudier and more blatantly sexual clothes and hair styles than those of the more favored classes. In a significant study of a high school sorority initiation, it is shown that in the degradation phase of the ritual the pledges must deck themselves out in outlandish clothing, be smeared with lipstick, and pomaded with hair lotions, all of which the investigators interpret as symbolizing the sloppiness and sexuality of the lower class girls from whom, as sorority sisters, the initiates will wish to distinguish themselves (Schwartz and Merten 1968).

ECOLOGY AND SEX ROLES

In discussing the determinants of variability in sex roles, we have listed as possibly crucial the relationship of population size and distribution to (1) the availability and spacing of food and water sources, and (2) the nearness and numbers of neighboring human populations. Among the Amazon jungle peoples warfare over women, it has been suggested, had the consequence of spacing human populations sufficiently widely to insure an adequate supply of wild game for all. In our discussion of the highland New Guinea populations, we mentioned the possibility that the hostile attitude toward sex relations was correlated with population pressures on land, and had the consequence of inhibiting human population growth.

In the present state of anthropological scholarship, these hypotheses are highly tentative, and still more tentative must be any attempt to apply them to present industrial culture. We shall therefore conclude merely with a question:

What relationship, if any, is there between the drop in birth rate in the United States in the early 1970s, the discussions here of childlessness as an acceptable pattern of life or, to put it another way, the de-emphasis on motherhood, and the world population explosion and a deepening concern over the continuing availability of adequate energy for human needs?

Glossary

Affinals: Relatives by marriage; "in-laws."

Bilaterality: Reckoning descent and succession through both males and females.

Bride Price (sometimes called Bride Wealth): Transfer of valuables from a groom's kin to the bride's kin as a necessay condition of marriage.

Bride Service: The work performed by a man for a woman's kin so that he can acquire the right to her as a wife.

Clan: A group of people who claim descent from a common ancestor, usually distant; the descent is calculated by whatever cultural rule for descent reckoning is used in the society. Clan members cannot demonstrate exactly how they are related to one another; they do not necessarily act together. The clan is often subdivided into lineages (see Lineage).

Consanguineals: Relatives by blood descent, not or not solely by marriage.

Corporate Kin Group: Lineages or clans holding property rights in common (see Lineage; Clan).

Cross Cousins: Term applied to the relationship to each other of children of opposite sexed siblings. "My cross cousins are the children of my mother's brothers and of my father's sisters." (see Parallel Cousins).

Domestic: Taking place within, or pertaining to, the home or household. Where "domestic" is used with reference to a particular society, the household meant is that defined in the discussion of that society in the text (see Extradomestic).

Egalitarian Political Systems: Those in which formal or informal leadership and power are achieved by individual effort; competition is open to all men or all women or both. These systems are often accompanied by egalitarian redistribution (see Redistribution).

Emics: Distinctions in thought and action that are meaningful (although not necessarily consciously so) to the participants in a culture (see Etics).

Etics: Distinctions in thought and action that need not be meaningful, consciously or unconsciously, to participants in a culture (see Emics).

Extradomestic: Taking place outside the home or household. Where "extradomestic" is used with reference to a particular society, the household meant is that defined in the discussion of that society in the text (see Domestic).

Ideology: The beliefs, ideas, and values overtly expressed by participants in a culture.

Lineage: A group of people who claim descent from a known and relatively recent common ancestor, by whatever cultural rule is used for reckoning descent in a society. Members of a lineage can demonstrate their relationship to one another and are likely to act together. The lineage is frequently a subdivision of a clan (see Clan).

Matrilineality: Reckoning descent and succession exclusively through females.

Menarche: First occurrence of menstruation.

Money, General Purpose: Objects with a standardized value, which can be exchanged for almost all commodities, including labor (see Money, Special Purpose).

Money, Special Purpose: Objects with a standardized value which can be exchanged for only a limited number of types of different objects, e.g., cattle for wives but not for food (see Money, General Purpose).

Nonegalitarian Political Systems: Those in which eligibility for formal leadership and power is limited to people in certain kin groups; the positions are institutionalized, often hereditary, offices. These systems are frequently accompanied by nonegalitarian redistribution (see Redistribution).

Nuclear Family: A domestic group consisting of a married pair and their children.

Parallel Cousins: Term applied to the relationship to each other of children of same sexed siblings. "My parallel cousins are the children of my mother's sisters and of my father's brothers." (*see* Cross Cousins).

Patrilineality: Reckoning descent and succession exclusively through males.

Polyandry: The marriage of one woman to more than one man.

Polygyny: The marriage of one man to more than one woman.

Reciprocity, Balanced: Exchange with overt calculation of value, limit on time for completing the transaction, and overt expectation that the transaction will result in an even exchange (*see* Reciprocity, Generalized; Redistribution).

Reciprocity, Generalized: Exchange without overt calculation of values, or stated term for completing the transaction, or overt expectation that a balance is ever required (*see* Reciprocity, Balanced; Redistribution).

Redistribution (egalitarian and nonegalitarian):   Collection of valuables for later sharing out. Egalitarian if amount disbursed is approximately equivalent to amount collected; nonegalitarian if those who collect are left with larger share than those who receive. Forms of generalized reciprocity: *see* Reciprocity, Generalized. *See also* Egalitarian and Nonegalitarian Political Systems.

Virilocal: The residence after marriage of a husband and wife or wives in or near the husband's premarital household.

Uxorilocal: The residence after marriage of a husband and wife or wives in or near the wife's or wives' premarital household.

References Cited[*]

[*]Ardener, Edwin, 1972, "Belief and the Problem of Women," in J. S. La Fontaine, ed., *The Interpretation of Ritual: Essays in Honour of A. I. Richards.* London: Tavistock, pp. 135–158.

Bascom, William, 1969, *The Yoruba of Southwestern Nigeria.* New York: Holt, Rinehart and Winston, Inc.

Bicchieri, M. G. ed., 1972, *Hunters and Gatherers Today.* New York: Holt, Rinehart and Winston, Inc.

Bohannan, Paul, 1965, "The Tiv of Nigeria," in J. L. Gibbs, Jr., ed. *Peoples of Africa.* New York: Holt, Rinehart and Winston, Inc., pp. 513–546.

[*]Brown, J. K., 1963, "A Cross-Cultural Study of Female Initiation Rites," *American Anthropologist* 65:837–853.

[*]———, 1970a, "Economic Organization and the Position of Women among the Iroquois," *Ethnohistory* 17:151–167.

[*]———, 1970b, "A Note on the Division of Labor by Sex," *American Anthropologist* 72: 1073–1078.

Burch, E. S., Jr., and T. C. Correll, 1972, "Alliance and Conflict: Interregional Relations in North Alaska," in Lee Guemple, ed., *Alliance in Eskimo Society.* Seattle: University of Washington Press, pp. 17–39.

[*]Chafe, W. H., 1972, *The American Woman: Her Changing Social, Economic, and Political Roles, 1920–1970.* London: Oxford.

Chagnon, N. A., 1968, *Yąnomamö: The Fierce People.* New York: Holt, Rinehart and Winston, Inc.

Chance, N. A., 1966, *The Eskimo of North Alaska.* New York: Holt, Rinehart and Winston, Inc.

[*]Chodorow, Nancy, 1974, "Family Structure and Feminine Personality," in Rosaldo and Lamphere, 1974, pp. 43–66.

Clastres, Pierre, 1972, "The Guayaki," in M. G. Bicchieri, ed., *Hunters and Gatherers Today.* New York: Holt, Rinehart and Winston, Inc., pp. 138–174.

[*]Collier, J. F., 1974, "Women in Politics," in Rosaldo and Lamphere, 1974, pp. 89–96.

[*] Items of general interest are starred.

*Douglas, Mary, 1966, *Purity and Danger*. London: Routledge.
*————, 1970, *Natural Symbols: Explorations in Cosmology*. London: Barrie and Rockliff.
Downs, J. F., 1966, *The Two Worlds of the Washo: An Indian Tribe of California and Nevada*. New York: Holt, Rinehart and Winston, Inc.
*Ember, Melvin, and C. R. Ember, 1971, "The Conditions Favoring Matrilocal versus Patrilocal Residence," *American Anthropologist* 73:571–594.
Firth, Raymond, 1957, *We, the Tikopia: A Sociological Study of Kinship in Primitive Polynesia*. London: G. Allen.
Gager, Nancy, ed., 1974, *Women's Rights Almanac 1974*. Bethesda, Md.: Elizabeth Cady Stanton Publishing Co.
Gardner, P. M., 1972, "The Paliyans," in Bicchieri, 1972, pp. 404–447.
Glasse, Robert, 1973, "Male Symbols in Two New Guinea Societies." Paper presented at the Sarah Lawrence Conference on Structuralism.
*Goodale, J. C., 1971, *Tiwi Wives: A Study of the Women of Melville Island, N. Australia*. Seattle: University of Washington Press.
Hart, C. W. M. and A. Pilling, 1960, *The Tiwi of Northern Australia*. New York: Holt, Rinehart and Winston, Inc.
*Henderson, H. K., 1969, *Ritual Roles of Women in Onitsha Ibo Society*. Ann Arbor, Mich.: University Microfilms.
*Hoffer, C. P., 1974, "Madam Yoko: Ruler of the Kpa Mende Confederacy," in Rosaldo and Lamphere, 1974, pp. 173–188.
Hogbin, Ian, 1964, *A Guadalcanal Society: The Kaoka Speakers*. New York: Holt, Rinehart and Winston, Inc.
*Krige, E. J., and J. D. Krige, 1943, *The Realm of a Rain-Queen*. London: Oxford.
Langness, L. L., 1965, "Hysterical Psychosis in the New Guinea Highlands: A Bena Bena Example," *Psychiatry* 28:258–277.
*Leacock, E. B., 1972, "Introduction to Frederick Engels," in E. B. Leacock, ed., *The Origin of the Family, Private Property and the State*. New York: International Publishers, pp. 7–67.
Lee, R. B., 1968, "What Hunters Do for a Living, or How to Make Out on Scarce Resources," in Lee and DeVore, 1968, pp. 30–48.
————, 1972a, "The !Kung Bushmen of Botswana," in M. G. Bichhieri, ed., *Hunters and Gatherers Today*. New York: Holt, Rinehart and Winston, Inc., pp. 326–368.
————, 1972b, "Population Growth and the Beginnings of Sedentary Life among the !Kung Bushmen," in Brian Spooner, ed., *Population Growth: Anthropological Implications*. Cambridge, Mass.: Massachusetts Institute of Technology Press, pp. 329–342.
*Lee, R. B., 1968, and Irven DeVore, eds., *Man the Hunter*. Chicago: Aldine.
*LeVine, R. A., 1962, "Witchcraft and Co-Wife Proximity in Southwestern Kenya," *Ethnology* 1:39–45.
*————, 1966, "Sex Roles and Economic Change in Africa," *Ethnology* 5:186–193.
*Lewis, I. M., 1971, *Ecstatic Religion: An Anthropological Study of Spirit Possession and Shamanism*. Baltimore: Penguin Books.
*Lindenbaum, Shirley, 1972, "Sorcerers, Ghosts, and Polluting Women: An Analysis of Religious Belief and Population Control," *Ethnology* 11:241–253.
Marshall, Lorna, 1965, "The !Kung Bushmen of the Kalahari Desert," in J. L. Gibbs, ed., *Peoples of Africa*, New York: Holt, Rinehart and Winston, Inc., pp. 241–278.
Marwick, Max, 1970, "Witchcraft as a Social Strain-Guage," in Max Marwick, ed., *Witchcraft and Sorcery*. Baltimore: Penguin Books, pp. 280–295.
*Mead, Margaret, 1953, *Male and Female*. New York: Morrow.
*Meggitt, M. J., 1964, "Male-Female Relationships in the Highlands of Australian New Guinea," *American Anthropologist* 66 (No. 4, Part 2):204–224.
————, 1972, "Understanding Australian Aboriginal Society: Kinship Systems or Cultural Categories" in Priscilla Reining, ed., *Kinship Studies in the Morgan Centennial Year*. Washington, D.C.: The Anthropological Society of Washington, pp. 64–87.
*Mintz, S. W., 1971, "Men, Women, and Trade," *Comparative Studies in Society and History* 13:247–269.
Murphy, R. F., 1959, "Social Structure and Sex Antagonism," *Southwestern Journal of Anthropology* 15:89–98.
————, 1960, *Headhunters' Heritage: Social and Economic Change among the Mundurucu Indians*. Berkeley: University of California Press.
*Nadel, S. F., 1952, "Witchcraft in Four African Societies: An Essay in Comparison," *American Anthropologist* 54:18–29.

Nerlove, S. B., 1974, "Women's Workload and Infant Feeding Practices: A Relationship with Demographic Implications," *Ethnology* 13:207–214.

Newman, P. L., 1964, " 'Wild Man' Behavior in a New Guinea Highland Community," *American Anthropologist* 66:1–19.

———, 1965, *Knowing the Gururumba*. New York: Holt, Rinehart and Winston, Inc.

*Oakley, Ann, 1972, *Sex Gender and Society*. London: Temple Smith.

*Ortner, S. B., 1974, "Is Female to Male as Nature Is to Culture?" In Rosaldo and Lamphere, 1974, pp. 67–88.

Pospisil, Leopold, 1963, *The Kapauku Papuans of West New Guinea*. New York: Holt, Rinehart and Winston, Inc.

Rappaport, R. A., 1971, "Ritual, Sanctity, and Cybernetics," *American Anthropologist* 73: 59–76.

Read, K. E., 1965, *The High Valley*. New York: Scribners.

Richards, Audrey, 1935, "A Modern Movement of Witch-Finders," *Africa* 8:448–461.

———, 1939, *Land, Labour and Diet in Northern Rhodesia: An Economic Study of the Bemba Tribe*. London: Oxford.

*———, 1956, *Chisungu*. London: Faber.

*Rosaldo, M. Z., 1974, "Woman, Culture, and Society," in Rosaldo and Lamphere, 1974, pp. 17–42.

*Rosaldo, M. Z., and Louise Lamphere, eds., 1974, *Women, Culture, and Society*. Stanford, Calif.: Stanford University Press.

*Sacks, Karen, 1974, "Engels Revisited: Women, the Organization of Production, and Private Property," in Rosaldo and Lamphere, 1974, pp. 207–222.

Sanday, P. R., 1973, "Toward a Theory of the Status of Women," *American Anthropologist* 75:1682–1700.

*———, 1974, "Female Status in the Public Domain," in Rosaldo and Lamphere, 1974, pp. 189–206.

Sangree, W. H., 1965, "The Bantu Tiriki of Western Kenya," in J. L. Gibbs, ed., *Peoples of Africa*. New York: Holt, Rinehart and Winston, Inc., pp. 41–80.

*Saucier, Jean-François, 1972, "Correlates of the Long Post-Partum Taboo: A Cross-Cultural Study," *Current Anthropology* 13:238–249.

*Schlegel, Alice, 1972, *Male Dominance and Female Autonomy: Domestic Authority in Matrilineal Societies*. New Haven, Conn.: Human Relations Area Files.

*Schwartz, Gary, and D. Merten, 1968, "Social Identity and Expessive Symbols: The Meaning of an Initiation Ritual," *American Anthropologist* 70:1117–1131.

*Siskind, Janet, 1973, "Tropical Forest Hunters and the Economy of Sex," in D. R. Gross, ed., *Peoples and Cultures of Native South America*. New York: Doubleday, pp. 226–240.

Spencer, R. F., 1959, *The North Alaskan Eskimo: A Study in Ecology and Society*. Washington, D.C.: Smithsonian Institution Press.

———, 1972, "The Social Composition of the North Alaskan Whaling Crew," in Lee Guemple, ed., *Alliance in Eskimo Society*. Seattle: University of Washington Press, pp. 110–120.

*Strathern, Marilyn, 1972, *Women in Between: Female Roles in a Male World: Mount Hagen, New Guinea*. London: Seminar Press.

*Sussman, R. J., 1972, "Child Transport, Family Size, and Increase in Human Population during the Neolithic," *Current Anthropology* 13:258–259.

Tiger, Lionel, and Robin Fox, 1971, *The Imperial Animal*. New York: Holt, Rinehart and Winston, Inc.

Uchendu, V. C., 1964, "Kola Hospitality and Igbo Lineage Structure," *Man* 53:47–50.

———, 1965, *The Igbo of Southeast Nigeria*. New York: Holt, Rinehart and Winston, Inc.

*Van Gennep, Arnold, 1960, *The Rites of Passage*. Chicago: University of Chicago Press.

*Wallace, A. F. C., 1958, "Dreams and Wishes of the Soul: A Type of Psychoanalytic Theory among the 17th Century Iroquois," *American Anthropologist* 60:234–248.

*Webster, Paula, and Esther Newton, 1972, "Matriarchy: Puzzle and Paradigm." Paper presented at the 71st Annual meeting of the American Anthropological Association, Toronto.

*Whiting, John, 1964, "Effects of Climate on Certain Cultural Practices," in Ward Goodenough, ed., *Explorations in Cultural Anthropology*. New York: McGraw Hill, pp. 511–544.

Wilson, Monica, 1960, "Nyakyusa Age-Villages," in Simon and Phoebe Ottenberg, eds., *Cultures and Societies of Africa.* New York: Random House, pp. 227–236.

Woodburn, James, 1968, "An Introduction to Hadza Ecology," in Lee and DeVore, 1968, pp. 49–55.

Young, F. W., 1965, *Initiation Ceremonies*, New York: Bobbs-Merrill.

Case Study Interactions

The problems suggested below are intended to serve as examples of ways in which ethnographic materials may be used by students for further exploration of sex roles.

1. Compare and contrast the relationship between men and women among the Eskimo (Chance 1966) and the Washo (Downs 1966). What aspects of the culture are shared? What basic differences existed in the attitude toward women in the two cultures?
2. Compare the status of Gururumba women (Newman 1965 and text pp. 101–115) with that of women in another horticultural society such as the Hano Tewa (Dozier 1967) by designating what avenues a woman has open to her for gaining positive satisfactions.
3. Using any two cases listed in the suggested reading, describe how symbols and rituals reflect the attitudes toward sex and the actual social relations which exist between men and women held by the members of the society. (See discussion of ritual in Part I/8.)
4. Describe and explain how youth and old age act as modifiers of sex roles, using any two or three of the studies in the suggested reading list (e.g. Chance 1966; Chagnon 1968).
5. Whereas men usually hold most of the important public roles in a society, how do women often gain informal prestige and power? (Use examples from cases such as Chiñas 1973; Pospisil 1963; Holmes 1974).
6. Compare the role of a new husband in a matrilineal, uxorilocal residence group (e.g., Dozier 1967) to that of a new husband in a patrilineal group with virilocal residence (e.g., Tiwi [Hart and Pilling 1965].)
7. Compare the roles of a working mother to those of a nonworking mother in suburban American culture by interviewing a sample of each. Describe what effects a monetary contribution to the maintenance of the household has upon the mother's role (i.e., (a) in making important family decisions [the buying of items such as a car, boat; where the family will spend vacations, what the children will do after high school graduation: (b) in the amount of status accorded her [respect for her ideas, attention paid her when she speaks, etc.]).

Relevant Case Studies*

The Case Studies listed and annotated below all contain material on sex roles. Other relevant literature is listed under References Cited.

Basso, Ellen, 1973, *The Kalapalo Indians of Central Brazil.* This is a case study of a lowland South American people with a culture relatively unaffected by the outside world. Marriages are arranged by parents. Often the request for a girl is made by a kinsman and cannot be denied. Dr. Basso devotes a section to "The Opposition of Men and Women," dealing with spatial distinctions, sexual contact and pollution, childbirth ritual, female

---

* Edited by George and Louise Spindler, and published by Holt, Rinehart and Winston, Inc., as Case Studies in Cultural Anthropology. The author of the present volume expresses appreciation to the editors for preparing the Case Study Interactions and the Relevant Case Studies for this book.

puberty rituals. Boys and girls are expected to be different from an early age, and both are secluded at puberty for periods of several years.

Chagnon, Napoleon A., 1968, *Yanomamö: The Fierce People*. This is a study of people whose men engage in chronic warfare and use hallucinogenic drugs almost daily. Their violence is barely held in check by a system of exchanges and alliances. In this patrilineal society women are frequently beaten and are viewed as valued commodities to be traded with political allies. Only older women can gain some measure of respect.

Chance, Norman A., 1966, *The Eskimo of North Alaska*. This study is of the modern Eskimo who still retain some of the material and symbolic aspects of the old Eskimo ways. They are both modern and traditional in behavior, attitudes, and thinking. It is a group where men's hunting provides almost all food and women do the processing of all food and skins. The book depicts the complementarity of the husband-wife relationship. A wife's sexual services were traditionally viewed as a desired commodity and used for establishing alliances with other men. This has changed today, however. Sexual aggression against women was common in the past also but no longer exists.

Chiñas, Beverly L., 1973, *The Isthmus Zapotecs: Women's Roles in Cultural Context*. This book deals with sex roles in the context of a wide-ranging descriptive analysis of salient features of Isthmus Zapotec culture. The author distinguishes between formalized roles, most frequently held by the men, and nonformalized roles played by the women. These latter roles are often unexplicated but are of great importance to the functioning of the family. Dr. Chiñas describes the complementarity of the sex roles and the essentially egalitarian partnership existing between males and females.

Dentan, Robert Knox, 1968, *The Semai: A Nonviolent People of Malaya*. The Semai are a good example of semisedentary horticulturalists in forested areas. Robert Dentan stresses the nonviolent orientation of the Semai and describes how interpersonal and marital relationships, sex, and aggression are influenced by the nonviolent image the Semai hold of themselves. Great attention is paid to women during pregnancy, childbirth, and menstruation, as these are considered dangerous situations.

Downs, James F., 1966, *The Two Worlds of the Washo*. The author does an excellent job of reconstructing Washo traditional life and the adaptations made to the coming of the White man. Men and women worked together as a team. They were not segregated from each other in most daily activities, and either men or women could make decisions concerning band movements. Shamanism was open to both men and women. Women had a special menarche rite performed for them. They had a substantial basis for self-esteem.

Dozier, Edward P., 1966, *Hano: A Tewa Indian Community in Arizona*. The author gives the reader an understanding of the historical forces which shaped the pueblo communities and an analysis of the adjustive interrelationships of Whites, Tewa Indians, and Hopi Indians. Females are initiated into the Kachina Cult, have a special puberty rite, and inherit the land. Men have no right to ownership or inheritance of land, which they work, however. The males do hold the important public statuses.

Hart, C. W. M., and Arnold R. Pilling, 1960, *The Tiwi of North Australia*. The Tiwi system of influence and power is based upon the exchange of women, who represent a form of currency. All females are valued, as the prestige of a male depends upon the number of women a man controls. The authors discuss the far-reaching effects of the missions upon this system.

Holmes, Lowell D., 1974, *Samoan Village*. This study presents the reader with a working knowledge of the basic elements of traditional Samoan culture as it is lived out today. Though comparatively stable, the culture is changing. The most radical changes came with the acceptance of Christianity, when such practices as polygamy, divorce, political marriages, adultery, premarital sex, gift exchanges at marriages, public tests of virginity, prostitution, and nudity were abolished. Men and women share in horticultural work. One of the few cultures with men as the chief food-preparers. If a woman's husband becomes a headman at middle age, her status is also elevated in the women's committee and in the household. Otherwise, a wife's most important role is that of child-bearer.

Lessa, William A., 1966, *Ulithi: A Micronesian Design for Living*. Dr. Lessa describes the total design for living, including the entire life cycle. Importance is placed on ancestor worship and sexual behavior. In sexual behavior, both license and restrictions and attitudes of modesty are discussed; these areas are related to family life. The nuclear family does not have much importance in performing the basic services of feeding, sheltering, and training for the young.

Newman, Philip L., 1965, *Knowing the Gururumba*. The author describes how he found the patterns in Gururumba behavior and the arrangement in social groups and roles. He also clearly describes the values and themes running through Gururumba life. In a section, "Men and Women," Newman describes the different roles played by men and women. In this culture it is dangerous to cohabit with a woman over an extended period. Men play a wider variety of roles than do women, who have no avenues open for prestige. In fact, there is very little property over which a woman can exercise final control except her own personal belongings. The two sexes are, however, considered symbolically to be complementary, as represented in male and female initiation rites.

Pospisil, Leopold, 1963, *The Kapauku Papuans of West New Guinea*. This society, unlike most preliterate societies, is characterized by a form of "primitive capitalism," with well-developed trade, money, and legal systems. Men and women cooperate in horticultural activities, which are geared to providing food for the pigs. Successful pig breeding enhances male status. Kapauku men must work hard preparing the soil in order to keep women busy. A wife represents a large investment in bride price and is important economically. A mother can gain considerable status by loaning money to her sons for the bride price.

Turner, Paul R., 1972, *The Highland Chontal*. Dr. Turner provides a clear, simple and direct understanding of the way of life in this Mexican Indian village. Focus is on the kinship system as related to behavior. There is a good account of the socialization process as related to the familial and community dimensions. Both men and women in this horticultural society share many tasks (planting, weeding, harvesting).

Williams, Thomas Rhys, 1965, *The Dusun, a North Borneo Society*. The Dusun culture has retained its character. Thomas Williams describes the many rituals, concepts of life and death, health and disease, patterns of subsistence, kinship and social organization and authority and justice in a compelling manner. Women often become ritual specialists but their status is inferior to that of the male specialist as they are unable to appeal directly to important spirits. This is believed to be due to an inherent female inability to maintain emotional stability in the face of such contacts. In the nuclear household, a man's authority should be, ideally speaking, unquestioned.